T0304920

Trelawny's
Cornwall

Trelawny's Cornwall

A Journey Through Western Lands

PETROC TRELAWNY

WEIDENFELD & NICOLSON

First published in Great Britain in 2024 by Weidenfeld & Nicolson
an imprint of The Orion Publishing Group Ltd
Carmelite House, 50 Victoria Embankment
London EC4Y 0DZ

An Hachette UK Company

The authorised representative in the EEA is Hachette Ireland,
8 Castlecourt Centre, Dublin 15, D15 XTP3, Ireland (email: info@hbgi.ie)

9 10

Copyright © Petroc Trelawny 2024
Map by Michael A. Hill

A CIP catalogue record for this book is
available from the British Library.

ISBN (Hardback) 978 1 4746 2509 8
ISBN (eBook) 978 1 4746 2511 1
ISBN (Audio) 978 1 4746 2512 8

Typeset at The Spartan Press Ltd,
Lymington, Hants

Printed in Great Britain by Clays Ltd,
Elcograf S.p.A.

MIX
Paper | Supporting
responsible forestry
FSC® C104740

www.weidenfeldandnicolson.co.uk
www.orionbooks.co.uk

For my parents, Richard and Jennifer,
and my beloved late brother, William.

CONTENTS

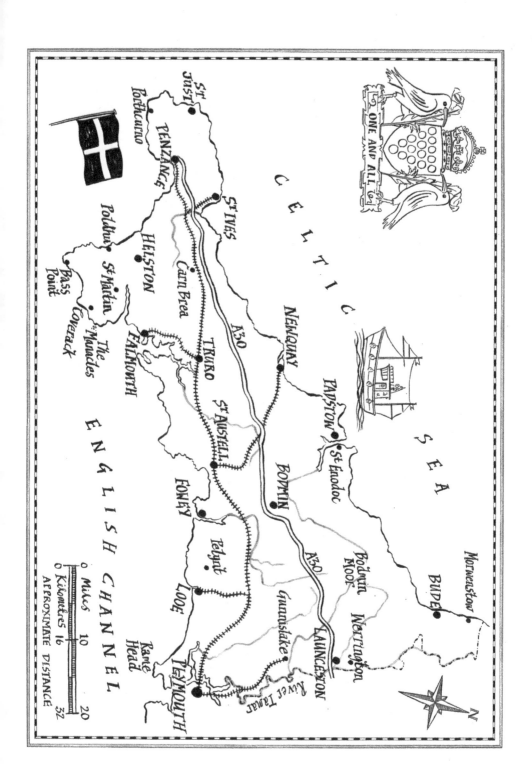

And Shall Trelawny Live

Trelawny Day is celebrated in Pelynt on 30 June each year. I am unaware of this fact as I drive into the village, which sits on the road that leads towards the port town of Looe. The sign board makes me feel immediately at home – 'Welcome to Trelawny's parish'. A second or two later the 14th-century tower of St Nun Church comes into view, just off to the right. A visit to Pelynt church has long been on my to-do list, but an earlier check of its website informed me that it closes at four. I lingered too long over lunch in Fowey, and now it is well after five. The sun is shining, so I decide to stop and look at the building's exterior and churchyard. As I pull off the road, I see that the church door is wide open. A middle-aged woman is coming out. We smile at each other and she waves me over. 'Come in and have a look around.'

The church's interior is something of a Trelawny museum. Gently rounded, carved letters on a marble memorial stone celebrate a Trelawny baronet who served his country in Parliament for twenty-one years. Another stone remembers Colonel Edward Trelawny, Governor of Jamaica for fourteen years from 1738. The monument to an earlier Trelawny of the same name is inscribed: 'Here lies an honest lawyer, wot ye what. A thing for all the world to wonder at.' A brass plaque indicates the place of the family vault, where 'rests the mortal remains of Jonathan Trelawny, Bart, Lord Bishop of Winchester'. His bishop's chair and crook stand nearby. In a frame, a red-edged piece of needlepoint sets out Robert Stephen Hawker's words to 'The Song of the Western Men'. Some loyal parishioner once spent their winter nights sewing into canvas the words of the song better known as 'Trelawny', still today sung lustily at any Cornish gathering, and considered the de facto national anthem:

With a good sword and a trusty hand
A merry heart and true,
King James's men shall understand
What Cornish men can do.
And have they fixed the where and when?
And shall Trelawny die?
Here's twenty thousand Cornish men
Will know the reason why.

My reverie is interrupted by the friendly-faced warden. 'Can I ask you what your interest in the Trelawny family is?'

'Well,' I reply, my heart beating a little faster, 'I am one of them.'

She seems delighted. 'We have a service this evening, it's Trelawny Day. You must stay.'

The event isn't starting for an hour, but I promise to come back. To kill time, I return to the car, and drive for another five minutes to Trelawne, a manor house listed in the Domesday Book that was the Trelawny family home for over three hundred years.

A three-storey tower stands over an impressive entrance range and the chapel built by Bishop Trelawny immediately catches the eye. No member of the family lives here now; today its residents are transient visitors. 'Staycations start @ Trelawne Manor'

2

proclaim signs dotted around the site. The family sold it in the 1920s; three decades later it became a home for retired vicars, and then a holiday camp. Surviving topiary from the well-established gardens half hides the house from hundreds of static caravans set out in neat rows, pot plants placed on their stoops to add a flash of colour. Under the old tower, umbrellas shade holidaymakers downing pints in plastic glasses as they wait for fast-food orders to be delivered. A neat prefab houses a Mace convenience store, signs point to swimming pools, tennis courts and a laundrette. It is a safe, reasonably affordable holiday location, and it feels a happy place.

By the time I get back to the church, fifty or sixty villagers are gathered and the star guests have arrived – the brother of the late Trelawny baronet, and his wife. The vicar introduces us, but the pair are not immediately friendly. She looks me up and down, waiting a second before delivering her *coup de grâce*, ponderous at first: 'Yes... I have heard of you.' She pauses again and looks me directly in the eye. 'You... you are the fake Trelawny.'

There is no chance to reply as the vicar comes over to tell us he is ready to begin. The service should have been magical, the sun setting behind the lichen-encrusted tower of an old Cornish church, the blue-blazered members of the local male-voice choir standing around the Celtic Cross in the graveyard, singing 'Trelawny', 'Cornwall My Home' and 'Lamorna'. But I feel like I have been punched in the stomach. A bit of me just wants to run to the car and drive at speed to the Travelodge in Plymouth, where I am due to spend the night.

Afterwards I chat with a man who turns out to be a Radio 3 listener. But eventually our conversation reaches its natural end and I decide I have to seek out the baronet's brother's wife. I ask her what she had meant earlier. 'You are on the radio,' she starts off, 'so I assumed you adopted Trelawny as a nom de plume, a romantic pseudonym to make you sound more Cornish.' I smile and explain that the name is on my birth certificate. 'I'm real,' I say. The ice broken, we laugh together, she offers me a drink, and we swap details, promising to be in touch to further celebrate our familial connections. But as I drive off into the half-light of a Cornish summer evening, I'm still shaken. Her line about me being a fake has rattled me. She may be right.

* * *

It is late evening at Paddington Station. The halogen lamps cast a cold, uncompromising light over the concourse. Pret a Manger and Caffè Nero have closed, their doorways now blockaded by metal shutters. Even Burger King is locked up. Little in the way of greasy, starchy sustenance is available to the straggle of evening drinkers boarding the 2248 to Neath, the 2250 to Worcestershire Parkway, the 2332 to Bristol Temple Meads.

A red warning light flashes from the machine polishing the shiny concrete floor, its operator slaloming between the concessions which earlier had offered cookies, cupcakes and souvenir soft toys. Two men in high-vis waistcoats inspect a damaged crowd-control barrier. The ash-blonde woman in green uniform sitting behind the help-desk yawns. The daily drama that fills Isambard Kingdom Brunel's theatrically triple-arched train shed is slowing down for another day; the actors – revenue officials, security inspectors, short-order chefs, customer information agents, passengers – are leaving the stage.

As each last service departs, the column of glowing orange text that lists its calling points disappears from the information board. Soon just one express train will remain – the Night Riviera to Penzance. Its rake of dark-green carriages rests at Platform 1, a gentle put-put sound coming from *Pendennis Castle*, the locomotive that will power tonight's journey west.

Attendants wait by the carriage doors, holding clipboards bearing lists of passengers' names and details of their accommodations. The cheapest tickets provide an upright seat and little else, regular budget travellers remembering to pack an inflatable pillow, and eye-shades to block out the never-dimmed ceiling lights.

Those who have paid for a berth have the comfort of a bed to look forward to, and access to the first-class lounge, once the royal waiting room. Brunel, the all-powerful begetter of the Great Western Railway, knew Queen Victoria would be his most eminent passenger. In Paddington he gave the first monarch of the railway age a station of breathtaking elegance. Platform 1, its grandest departure point, was the obvious location for the memorial to GWR staff killed in the First World War – a larger-than-life bronze sculpture of an infantryman reading a letter from home.

Nearby stands the three-faced station clock, its black hands slowly brushing past Roman numerals, an unstoppable count-down to the sleeper's 2345 departure time. Some have already been on board for the best part of an hour, first-timers making a night-train adventure the memorable start of their Cornish holiday. Others cut it finer, passengers whose names are known to the crew: a businessman coming straight from a dinner pitching to clients; a Cornish MP contemplating the problems that will emerge during tomorrow's packed schedule of constituency sur-geries; an investment banker who fits her London commitments into three days a week.

Finally it is time for departure. The doors are slammed shut, the attendants hang their clipboards on the wall of their tiny end-of-carriage cubbyholes. The no-shows are on their own now; they will have to make their own way to Cornwall. The train dispatcher, himself eager to get home, blows his shrill whistle. An introductory jolt, a lurch back, a more confident thrust, and slowly the *Night Riviera* pulls out of Paddington Station.

* * *

St Martin, my home village on the Lizard Peninsula, was not the best place for a train-loving boy to grow up. The nearest railway station was fifteen miles away. The branch line to Helston, our local town, had been shut down nearly a decade before I was born. By the early 1980s the national railway system seemed gravely ill. The car had triumphed; infrequent main-line services meant trainspotting in Cornwall was a lonely, drawn-out experi-ence. Not that I was particularly interested in engine numbers or rolling stock anyway – it was the idea of the journey that excited me.

If any member of my family was making a trip, I would beg to be allowed to call the British Rail inquiry line at Truro Station to clarify train times. It was a place I dreamt of working. It seemed a heady prospect – sitting, telephone headset on, surrounded by every timetable book and official railway document available, providing essential information to the travelling public. Some of the operators answered the phone with a sigh and had to be pushed into giving more than the most basic details. But one anonymous man in Truro treated every question with glee and enthusiasm. No query was too much as he thoughtfully considered and answered my (often spurious) demands to know about connections in the Midlands, dining cars to Norwich, and through train–ferry tickets to the Isle of Wight. I created an imaginary life for him – the shelves of his sitting room were filled with Continental timetables, his spare time spent planning trips to Communist Poland or a journey from Istanbul to Baghdad, making the best use of the discounts offered by his International Railwayman's Concessionary Travel Pass.

It was the idea of the night train that thrilled me most – an express pressing ever onwards through the small hours, passengers at rest while the lamp on its locomotive lit up a seemingly infinite ribbon of cold steel track. And remarkably, Cornwall had its own sleeper service.

Occasionally my father would use it if he had cause to visit the capital. As he set off, I'd whisper my request that he bring me souvenirs of the trip. The small cake of medicated soap issued to passengers would become an object of minor veneration, never actually used to wash, as that would destroy the double arrows of the British Rail logo stamped into the surface of the bar. A branded bottle of water was equally treasured, so too the disposable shoeshine cloth. This piece of flimsy, waxy paper had added value, as beside the logo were the words 'Inter-City Sleeper', printed in BR's distinctive Rail Alphabet typeface.

Dad used the sleeper for the last time on a Sunday night in 1983, returning from Paddington to tell me the news that my mother had died the day before. A booking mix-up meant that he had to share his berth with a jolly younger man who kept joking and chatting until the early hours. Not wanting to face an awkward situation, my father refrained from telling him our terrible news.

The next morning at Helston School, the metalwork class had just started when I was called out, and told to report to the headmaster's office, where I found my father waiting. I'd last seen my mother three weeks earlier at Camborne Station, where we had put her on the sleeper that took her to London and the army hospital where her breast cancer was being treated. I was twelve. We held hands as the train started to move. Soon she had to let me go, but I continued to run alongside, waving and smiling. The service picked up speed and the final carriage overtook me, its red warning light getting fainter and fainter before finally disappearing from view.

* * *

As part of my preparations for a journey on the sleeper I will have cadged half a zopiclone from an insomniac friend. I hang my coat, lay out fresh clothes for the morning, and tuck my shoes in the space under the narrow bed, before swallowing the bitter-tasting tablet. At home I sleep well unaided; in this moving bedroom the click-clacking of the tracks, the ship-like roll caused by a sharp curve and the intermittent screech and hiss of the brakes make the chemical assistance welcome.

The Night Riviera will pass the racecourse at Newbury and cross the Kennet and Avon Canal. At around three it will climb the Wellington Bank, where in 1904 a London-bound service drawn by the locomotive *City of Truro* made claim to be the first 100mph train. At four-thirty it will run down the west side of the River Exe, meeting the sea at Dawlish. Here, every few years, winter storms and waves conspire to flush out the ballast from under the track, cutting the far west's link to the rest of the Kingdom. On clear summer days, the sun reflects on the water to support the illusion that the railway carriage has become the salon of an ocean liner. Did the moon illuminate these scenes this night? I don't know. I was lost to dreams, sleeping my way through the outer London suburbs, through Royal Berkshire, Wiltshire, Somerset and most of Devon.

I am woken at five-thirty by the incessant electronic bleep of my phone alarm. We have reached Plymouth. The drab, utilitarian concrete of the 1960s station reminds me of Eastern European termini where I have waited to cross borders: Brest in Belarus, Bratislava in Slovakia. This too is a frontier – the last major station before the Tamar is crossed and the ancient land of Cornwall reached. The sleeper waits here for half an hour or more, as if it needs time to conserve its energy for the last push, the sector of this journey that will finally deliver me home.

The sun is rising as we start moving again. We are on time – I will be on Cornish soil by six. We creep through city halts at Devonport, Dockyard and Keyham, before a branch line loops off for Calstock and Gunnislake, communities higher up the Tamar. St Budeaux Ferry Road is the last Devon station, before the two lines of track join as one to cross the Royal Albert Bridge. Soft shadows made by the structure's iron frame are cast onto the walls of my berth, the thick rivets that bond it together pass by just a few inches beyond the window. The bridge was Brunel's last masterpiece – Prince Albert opened it in the spring of 1859; by that autumn its engineer was dead.

Where does Cornwall start? Saltash Station, at the western end of the edifice, is the actual entry point, but that leaves the bridge itself as some sort of geographical no-man's-land. I take the central pillar, buried deep into the river bed, as the marker for the beginning of Cornish territory. As we pass it I smile to myself, and mutter the Cornish mottos, *Onen Hag Oll* (One and All) and *Kernow Bys Vyken* (Cornwall Forever).

* * *

Six weeks after my eighteenth birthday I crossed Brunel's bridge in the other direction. I was an adult, had finished school and yearned for the bright lights. Cornwall felt dull, remote and stifling. I was aware that I had had a privileged, idyllic childhood, and had been blessed with a father and brothers who loved me and friends who understood me. But that wasn't enough. I wanted out, and I didn't see myself coming back.

I remember a sense of giddy anticipation as my eastbound train made its steady way across the Tamar. I was bound for Exeter, where I had got a job as a trainee broadcaster at BBC Radio Devon. Though the cathedral city's illuminations were far from dazzling, the place offered me the freedom that I craved.

A week later I was back in St Martin, desperately homesick. My father met me off the train, hugged me, cooked me dinner, washed and ironed my laundry, and the next day drove me back to the station. With our eyes fixed on the road ahead, he told me he didn't want to see me again for at least six weeks. His tough love worked – I made friends, found a groove for myself, and came to relish my independence. My career took me to Hong Kong and then London. For the next few decades my return visits were desultory, the odd weekend two or three times a year, mainly to see my father.

I suppose I considered myself an adopted Londoner, relishing my life in the heart of the city – but I remained proud of my Cornish roots. They were challenged by the coming of Wikipedia. At first I kept trying to edit my entry, but it always defaulted to the black-and-white facts – the truly Cornish Petroc was actually my third name, preceded by the defiantly English James and Edward. And, the website suggested, I was a West Midlander, having been born in Worcester. To those who saw this as reason to challenge my Cornishness, I would point out that my birth location was merely the result of where the Army had posted my father, adding an unoriginal line about Christ being born in a stable, but not turning out to be a horse. The truth was that I was relaxed about where I came from – prepared to make the case for my true place of origin, but not concerned enough to get into a fight about it.

One day, around 2010, I was in a studio at Broadcasting House presenting Radio 3's afternoon concert. I had just introduced a performance of Tchaikovsky's Fifth Symphony – so there were three quarters of an hour before I needed to speak again. I made tea for myself and the engineer, and then decided to attack the overflowing inbox of my BBC email account. The first few messages were from people asking for details of recordings I had played, or wondering if I might mention a performance of Mendelssohn's *Elijah* or Bach's B Minor Mass by their local choral society. Then I clicked on a note from Vesta Darnell. She introduced herself as an amateur genealogist, who was working on an up-to-date Trelawny family tree and had a few questions to ask. Family history was of little interest to me then, but I knew my father would be happy to engage, so I put the two of them in touch.

Email and the internet never featured in Dad's life, and for his last years he didn't have a phone either, so updates on his and Vesta Darnell's communications came just occasionally, either when I saw him in Cornwall, or when he wrote me a letter. At first all seemed okay. 'She's got entirely the wrong end of the stick, but I'm going to make sure she gets it right,' my father announced. The next feedback was not so positive: 'She is trying to redraw the family tree – without us.' When I saw my father a few months later I sought another update. 'We are no longer in contact,' he informed me, his look making it quite clear that the matter was closed.

The Trelawny name was established in Cornwall by the 11th century, when an Eduni de Treloen was recorded as holding estates at Altarnun on the north-east edge of Bodmin Moor. By the 15th century branches of the family were to be found at Menheniot and Coldrenick near Liskeard. In 1600 Sir Jonathan Trelawny paid the ageing Queen Elizabeth £2,840 to purchase Trelawne, an estate that already bore his name, even though it had no connection to the family.

Sir Jonathan's son, John, served time in the Tower of London, held there following a dispute with Charles I over the election of local Members of Parliament. He was released after four days and created the first Trelawny baronet. His grandson, another Jonathan (the name is never far away on the family tree), was also imprisoned in the Tower.

Educated at Christ Church College, Oxford and ordained in 1676, the Revd Sir Jonathan Trelawny was rector of South Hill and St Ive churches in east Cornwall. He was a Royalist who showed his loyalty to James II by helping raise a Cornish Militia to counter the Duke of Monmouth's threatened West Country rebellion of 1685. His reward was a bishopric – not rich Exeter, as he had hoped, but instead poor Bristol. Three years later he was one of the seven prelates charged with seditious libel by James II. The King wanted the Church to give Catholics greater freedom to worship, and insisted that Sir Jonathan and his colleagues should join the list of bishops who had already pledged their support. The declaration would have suspended the laws that enforced conformity to the Church of England – a major step towards increased religious freedom. The bishops' refusal infuriated the King, who saw the recalcitrant churchmen as rebels who had to be punished. They were sent to trial, and as they refused to pay bail, they were imprisoned in the Tower. Their court appearance, at Westminster Hall on 29 June 1688, lasted ten hours. The next day they were called back for the verdict – not guilty. The bishops were freed and the King's control of his realm started to look uncertain. Bells rang out at Pelynt, and Bishop Jonathan's career progressed apace – he got the Exeter job he so wanted, and later was appointed Bishop of Winchester. He died in Chelsea in 1721, at the age of seventy-one. It was probably his experience of imprisonment that inspired a popular Cornish ballad, which the Revd R. S. Hawker used as the basis of his anthem 'Trelawny'.

Subsequent Trelawnys were colonial governors, army generals and Members of Parliament. One was the adventurer Edward John, friend and biographer of Lord Byron and Percy Bysshe Shelley, and organiser of the latter's cremation on a beach near Viareggio in Italy. As a child as yet untroubled by the concepts of imperial oppression or class privilege, I was thrilled by the tales my father proudly told of the adventures and experiences of our ancestors. The stories reached the 20th century. My paternal grandfather Clarence died six years before I was born, but seemed to live on thanks to his military exploits – the heroic commander of HMS *Spitfire* at the Battle of Jutland in 1916, he was considered so useful that in the Second World War he was recalled to naval service and promoted to the rank of captain, despite being nearly sixty. Two of his siblings had had successful careers in the Egyptian civil service.*

---

*My great-grandmother, Rosalie, died in Egypt. Fifteen years ago, while visiting Alexandria, I took the tram to Shatby, the seaside suburb that was once home to the city's expatriate English community. Now worshippers at the parish church are largely Sudanese Christian refugees, but the British consul general remains ex-officio church warden, and holds a set of keys. David Roberts, then holder of the office, took me for an early-evening visit. No sooner through the door, the first memorial I spotted was a plaque marking Rosalie's death in 1906.

Dad had a framed photograph of his father and uncles hanging above his desk. At the front of the formal sepia portrait proudly surrounded by his sons, backed up by his sons, sits Edward Trelawny. He was the main person of interest in Vesta Darnell's inquiries – she referred to him as Edward Green – not a scion of a grand Cornish family, but a man born in Eastbourne, with roots in Hull.

Dad never denied that his grandfather had been born with Green as his surname. Edward enjoyed a distinguished career in shipping, working for the Peninsula and Oriental Steam Navigation Company in Australia, India and Egypt. In retirement he wrote a private autobiography, in which he claimed his father, John Harry Green, was a true Trelawny, a blood relation of a Harry Trelawny, born in 1818. Vesta argued that this Harry had died at the age of eight, leaving him no time to produce any heirs.

Clear proof, she said, that there was not a familial connection between the Greens and the Trelawnys.

My father countered with a dramatic story that explained the name change. He typed it up for Vesta Darnell, who kindly sent me a copy after his death. John Harry Green, he argued, had been born a Trelawny. As a young army officer he had fought a duel with a fellow soldier over a young woman called Sophia. The other officer was killed, and as duelling had become illegal, John Harry had to flee to France in disgrace, assuming the name Green. After the scandal blew over, he returned and married Sophia, but the Trelawny family wanted nothing more to do with him. Broke, and in poor health, John Harry died in his late forties. His son Edward was determined to right a wrong: 'Grandpa was determined to resume his correct name of Trelawny before he married,' my father wrote. 'He became a proper Trelawny again in October 1871, in time for his wedding the following August.'

I wanted to believe my father, but he provided no sources for his tale other than 'family legend' and a frustrating reference to 'a full account' he had read 'in a book which I can no longer trace'. Furthermore, several of the dates and locations he referenced were different to the documentary evidence produced by Vesta Darnell. A glimmer of hope came from a letter between Edward and an Edgar Trelawny – the latter referring to them as 'Two Trelawnys' and signing off, 'your affectionate cousin'. Could this offer some proof of a link – or were they just friends, Edgar complicit in encouraging Edward to swap Green for a rather more exotic-sounding identity? It seems he had good reasons to rename himself. His father lived a rackety life – a jobbing wine trader and broker, he was several times a bankrupt. His two daughters ended up in children's homes, before emigrating to the US and New Zealand and breaking off contact with their family.

Though he didn't want to talk about it, I knew Dad was upset by this questioning of his lineage – and I hoped something might emerge to challenge Vesta Darnell's case notes, some thin bloodline that would make a link between my immediate ancestors and the ancient Trelawnys of old. I felt his anguish – even out of context, the accusation that I was a 'fake Trelawny' hurt. Perhaps I am a 'new' Trelawny, but given that the name has been used across a century and a half by my father, my grandfather and, for most of his adult life, my great-grandfather, I have no doubts about my right to claim it. The whole affair has led me to think more about my Cornish identity, and my place here. How Cornish am I? My father's death prompted me to try and find out. Without him around I could have the place on my own terms, spend time here as myself, not my father's son. A few months after his funeral I booked two weeks in a cottage in Coverack. As I unpacked, I realised this was the longest period I had been back since my teenage departure. The trip fired something in me – a desire to revisit the Cornwall I grew up in, to reclaim my Cornishness, to fill in the gaps in my historical and geographical knowledge, and to get to know and understand the social and economic divisions playing out in the place that I consider home.

* * *

The sleeper passes through Saltash and skirts along the Hamoaze, the rich, ancient-sounding name given to the estuarine River Tamar. I look back up the river and am rewarded with a fine view of the moored frigates and supply ships and the great submarine sheds of Devonport Naval Base.

Majestic granite viaducts carry us over the Lynher and Tiddy rivers, both tributaries of the Tamar. The Cornish railway Brunel laid out relies on these soaring bridges – originally made of wood, then rebuilt in stone; structural reminders of the challenge he faced establishing his route through rolling hills and deep valleys.

I dress and then open the door of my berth so I can look out on each side. Several carriages from an earlier railway age rest beside St German's Station – now converted into holiday accommodation. At Liskeard another viaduct carries us high above the line to Looe; its single-coach train waits at a dislocated platform a sharp right-angle from where the sleeper makes its stop.

Glimpsed road signs suggest a sense of Cornish otherness – Doublebois, Dobwalls, Herodsfoot, Two Waters Foot, the Taphouses, East and West. I sing the jingle of an old local radio advertisement to myself – 'Trago Mills Got a Great Deal Happening' – as we pass high above the Glyn Valley and the Cornish discount chain's warehouse below.

Bodmin Parkway, once Bodmin Road – with a branch to Padstow on the Atlantic, one of the routes the poet John Betjeman would take as he made his way to his Cornish bolthole at Trebetherick. Next Lostwithiel, which once had a passenger connection to Fowey, a port on the English Channel. Even far inland the sea is never distant – nowhere in Cornwall is more than twenty miles from the coast.

Par, change for Newquay. 'Jesus for Your Life's Journey' reads a banner on the side of the Methodist Chapel. Most of these nonconformist places of prayer have shut now – the faith introduced by John Wesley in the 1740s remained dominant in Cornwall until it suffered an abrupt demise at the close of the 20th century. Beside the building a marker-sign reports there are still fifty-eight miles to run to Penzance. Par Docks are covered with the fine dust of china clay. Inland several centuries of workings have left a landscape lined with vast redundant pits and adjacent white-tipped mountains of spoil, nicknamed the Cornish Alps.

Brief glimpses of the sea across the golf links, and then St Austell, the eye drawn to the pale blue and white of the twelve-storey Park House, Cornwall's one and only experiment with high-density social housing. Twenty minutes later at Truro, the triple spires of John Loughborough Pearson's Gothic-revival cathedral seem to touch the clouds. Some of the disembarking passengers wait for a connecting train to the towns of Penryn and Falmouth, the first a medieval centre of Cornish learning that is now home to our modern university, the second a spectacular natural harbour from where an empire's mails were once sent and received.

Between Camborne and Redruth is a landscape studded with the relics of old mines that produced copper and tin, and made the surrounding land among the richest in the world. There is a Station Road still at Gwinear Road but no actual station, little evidence of where the tracks for Helston once broke away from the main line. A stop at Hayle, then St Erth for St Ives. It was the new railway that encouraged an international colony of artist-settlers here. They lived alongside the fishermen and took to wearing their smocks and ganseys. But now the fishermen have left their cottages and the tightly packed terraces have become holiday lets and second homes, sitting dark for half the year.

I gather my luggage in the narrow corridor as we pass St Michael's Mount. The tide is on the way in, but there is perhaps half an hour more before the causeway that links Marazion to the island-castle becomes impassable.

Finally Penzance. As we draw near my eye scans the shore-line: *Scillonian III*, the ferry to the Scilly Isles, and the art-deco saltwater lido gleam in the morning sun. Beyond is Newlyn, Cornwall's main fishing port, and at the far end of the bay, the village of Mousehole. The light darkens as the carriages pass under the shadow of the train shed and gently creak to a halt. I step down onto the platform and hungrily gulp in the cool, salty air. I feel a sense of purpose; I am ready to start a journey through my Cornish hinterland.

CHAPTER I

Home

London to Penzance counts as long haul – the sleeper train takes the same time to reach its final destination as a jet aircraft does to cross the Atlantic. But after a shower, breakfast and brief nap, I am refreshed and ready for the next part of my Cornish journey. It will cover just a few miles. I could draw you a sketch map of St Martin-in-Meneage on a single sheet of A4, with space for a nod to every house, farm, lane, hill and bend in the road.

I have never seen St Martin in one of those coffee-table books about beautiful Cornwall; the village is unlikely to provide a backdrop for the television travels of Rick Stein or Fern Britton. The cluster of cottages around the parish green are sturdy rather than pretty; while it is close to both river and sea, there is no beach, cottage-lined waterfront or 18th-century harbour to catch the eye. For much of the year the local lanes are caked with mud and silage from the farms that form a circle around the village centre. It is neither shabby nor unprosperous, but there is no sense of great wealth either. Most visitors pass straight through on their way to the more obvious charms of Helford, Manaccan and St Anthony, barely giving a second thought to this community of houses snaking out along either side of the road. But St Martin is my village. The place of my childhood.

I wasn't born here. My father Richard spent his life in the army. One of my brothers was born in West Germany, another in Singapore. When I arrived, Dad was stationed at Norton Barracks in Worcester. Soon after, he transferred to the Ministry of Defence in London; my early childhood was spent in the suburbs, living in a red-brick military quarter in West Byfleet in Surrey. When I was five he retired from the Royal Signals and brought the family back to Cornwall, moving into the house that had been the home of my late grandparents; the place where he had been born.

It never had a name or a number – 'the last house on the right if you are heading towards Mawgan' was the clearest way to identify it. It was a large cottage built of stone topped with cob, the traditional Cornish building material: four parts subsoil, three parts straw and one part water.

A row of outhouses stretched along one side. My father turned one of them into a workshop where he would repair things and make me toys – a barn for my model farm, an engine shed for my Hornby railway. Repurposed Lyons coffee tins lined the walls, neatly written labels revealing their contents – silver screws 1½ inch; assorted hinges; rawl plugs, small. At the edge of the yard stood a long wooden shed with a tin roof, an old army hut used between the wars as the rehearsal space for St Martin Silver Band. It became my playroom. Dad built me a stage at one end, with a plasterboard proscenium arch and a pair of moth-eaten curtains that had once hung in my grandmother's sitting room.

The sheds, and the mature hedges that surrounded the garden meant that little of the house could be seen from the road. It had an entrance hall, a dining room and two sitting rooms. Once the home of the village parson, my grandfather moved in after the First World War, renting it from Sir Courtenay Vyvyan, 10th Baronet and scion of the local landed family, the Vyvyans of Trelowarren.

Perhaps relieved at the opportunity to divest himself of an expensive liability, Sir John, the 12th Baronet, happily sold the place to my father. Dad spent his army retirement bounty replacing the roof, rewiring the electrics and installing a new bathroom and kitchen. He laid slabs of reclaimed local slate in the hall, built bookcases and hung green Thai-silk curtains made by my mother. Later he set out a substantial vegetable garden and strung up mesh fencing to create a safe run for a brood of Rhode Island Red hens.

After a lifetime of packing and unpacking in married quarters around the world, my mother Jennifer could finally set to work on the garden she had dreamt of. Her bedside table was crammed with books on the subject, dry-looking guides to hardy perennials and shrubs suitable for Cornish soil, alongside richly illustrated compendiums of the designs of Capability Brown and Gertrude Jekyll. She coaxed elderly rhododendron bushes back to health and created a rockery filled with heathers, cyclamen and gentian. Her proudest achievement was her knot garden, framed by pastel-coloured roses that she trained on wire frames. Immaculately trimmed box hedges and stone paths no more than a foot wide marked out the inner and outer borders, the beds within planted with marjoram, thyme, rosemary and camomile. An arch of yew would provide an entrance, its shape echoing the lintel over the front door. But she did not survive long enough to see the garden mature. The breast cancer that had grown within her for eight years killed her before the yew trees matured and fused together. The garden that she had created became a living memorial.

* * *

The route my family called 'The Circuit' has always been first on the list of things to do upon arrival back in St Martin. I first walked it with Mum and our Irish terrier Tessa. Later, as a teenager, I would set out alone, using it as a space where I could attempt to process the anxious dilemmas of adolescence – questions about identity, sexuality and my place in the world, worries around fitting in, daydreams about the slightly scary potential of the big city, and the thrilling possibility of escaping the mundanity of remote rural life.

Today my sister-in-law Alison's spaniels Rocky and Belle accompany me. Their energy and mindless joy never fail to lift my mood, helping me revel in the thought that I have got out of the city again and made it back to this familiar, deeply comforting place, where every gate, tree and corner seems freighted with memories. The route along tarmacked lanes takes just over an hour to walk. Each new first circuit of The Circuit feels like a stamp in the passport, a mark of return to be completed in any weather.

Cornwall is a different place to what it was when my mother first led me along this path nearly half a century ago. But apart from a handful of new houses, The Circuit is unchanged. It is richly satisfying on a close summer's day, or in autumn when the accumulation of golden-brown leaf mulch makes the lanes slippery underfoot. It is equally pleasing on a crisp November night as the frost prepares to make its entrance and the stars shine bright through the trees, untrammelled by any urban electric glare. Or on a January afternoon when the wet sea-wind blowing directly across this outcrop of land tugs my hair and tests the seams of my well-worn waxed coat.

It starts with the road north out of the village. Past Primrose and Miranda Cottages the land immediately becomes agricultural; the lane bordered by Cornish hedges, six feet high, six feet broad at their base. These ancient constructions are solid, impregnable, and cast long shadows, creating the illusion that the road is some sort of cutting, deeper than the fields on either side. For much of the year they are rich with plant life – red campion, the star-shaped white flowers of greater stitchwort, cow parsley standing erect after a night of rain, delicate buttery-yellow primroses, the poisonous purple foxglove. The hedge breaks at Sworne Farm where the nearest field is planted with summer cabbages, set out in perfectly ordered rows like the graves in a military cemetery.

At the crossroads there is a bricked-up post-box which once served the farms that lie in all directions, to the right Withan, Carnbarges and Landrivick, straight ahead Mudgeon and Treveador. I turn left, towards Tremayne, Chynale and Mudgeon Vean. A pheasant is startled by my unexpected appearance, running erratically backwards and forwards across the road, furiously squawking and flapping its wings before eventually gaining enough unwieldy lift to carry itself over the hedge. In the silence that follows I climb onto a stone and look over the fields across the Helford River valley to the church tower at Constantine, two miles away as the crow flies, six miles by road.

When I was growing up, Tremayne was farmed by the Phillips family. Evidence of their time as dairy producers remains in the old stone milk stand, now almost covered by wild foliage. Here tin churns of fresh milk would be left out to be collected by lorry, a process that continued until the summer of 1979, when the old system was replaced with bulk tankers collecting milk kept fresh in refrigerated vats. The efficiencies of the system were clear, but the need for expensive new milking parlours forced many small farmers out of the dairy trade, their churns finding new uses as planters and props in domestic gardens. Their land, often just eighty or a hundred acres, was purchased by richer neighbours who wanted to create super-farms better suited to modern agribusiness. Their well-built farmhouses became desirable residences, homes where dirty boots and muddy trousers were no longer welcome in gleaming new kitchens.

The road drops down and narrows – a lane to shock the unwary driver faithfully obeying the instructions of their satnav. Delivery lorries and broad tractors have polished smooth the mud at the base of the hedges; reversing cars have left bald gashes in the vegetation. By a stream at the bottom of the hill half a dozen vehicles are parked, their owners walking the woods that run along the south side of the Helford River.

Until they gave these woods to the National Trust in 1978, they were the private pleasure grounds of the Vyvyans, who for centuries tended the established sessile oaks, and added sycamore, limes, elms, holly and giant firs. Sir Ferrers Vyvyan, the current master of Trelowarren House, is the 13th Baronet, the latest inheritor of a title created in 1645 – although the family had been here for several hundred years before that.

Immaculately hewn stone steps lead down to an almost hidden boathouse, just a glimpse of its sharply pitched roof visible from the path. Gaps in the thick canopy of vegetation allow unexpected glimpses of the tidal river, its creeks once valleys, flooded as the seas rose after the last Ice Age. It is low tide, and I look out over a mass of oozing milk-chocolate coloured mud; a home to tube and peacock worms, cockles, razor clams and sea slugs. A narrow, winding channel of water remains, traversed by a trio of swans, their white feathers in sharp contrast to the smelly brown sludge around them. Twice a day seawater floods in, refloating boats and washing keels clean, and creating a mirrored surface that reflects the trees that reach down to the highwater line.

I stand right on the edge of Tremayne Quay and lean out as far as I dare to get a glimpse of the 1930s wooden bungalow that sits on the edge of Frenchman's Creek. Further downriver, two dozen boats are moored off Helford. Opposite, tight-set, naked winter oaks shimmer silver; from beyond I can hear a party out shooting, their shouts and the sounds of their guns discharging amplified by the wide river.

The National Trust take good care of this quay, repointing the stones, cutting the grass and providing fire pits for the wild campers who started to come here in Covid times. Opposite, upriver, the stones of Merthen Quay sit askew like unkempt teeth, but Tremayne Quay looks as smart as it did when its slabs of Cornish granite were laid in preparation for a visit by Queen Victoria in the late 1840s. Under the direction of Sir Richard Vyvyan, 8th Baronet and MP for Helston, a well-surfaced road was laid out to transport the monarch from the river to Trelowarren. Alas, bad weather at Falmouth prevented the Royal Yacht from setting sail and the Queen's visit was abandoned. The quay had to wait for royal patronage until 1921, when the Prince of Wales landed. He was said to be much impressed by his passage through the woods; elaborate arches were built over the road in St Martin to welcome the future Edward VIII.

In the school summer holidays my mother and I would make expeditions here with the Lawrences, who farmed Mudgeon Vean. Susan Lawrence was my best friend; we would walk ahead playing complicated, fantastical games, diving in and out between the trees, our mothers following behind, one holding a thermos, the other a bag of sandwiches filled with Shippam's meat paste or home-made raspberry jam. When we arrived at Point Field, Susan and I would leap down the tangle of tree roots that formed a natural set of steps, and play on the shingle beach as our mothers set out tea.

Now my bones are stiffer, I am more cautious as I clamber down to the water. The faded yellow hull of an abandoned cabin cruiser lies on its side. Low-hanging branches brush the wreck, seaweed reaches across coloured cables and bilge pipes, plants grow inside the cabin. The boat has been rotting here for at least a decade. It must have a good backstory. Perhaps it was involved in modern-day smuggling, used for a while to run parcels of drugs ashore in these remote, unwatched creeks, and then abandoned. Or maybe it was the toy of a wealthy incomer, someone who dreamt of making a new life here, creating a fantasy that did not play out as hoped.

I dream about these woods – sometimes at night but more often in the day when my mind wanders and I fixate on the comforting, cool cover the trees provide. In places they loom out towards the walker at oddly threatening angles; elsewhere eight-storey-high trunks evoke the pillars found in the lofty naves of great cathedrals. Sometimes the sun shines in, often the light is weakened by the thick cover. The water ebbs and flows, animals scuttle around the undergrowth of the woodland floor, the bodies of long-fallen trees slowly rot. Rich colour comes when the sunlight is reflected off shower-sodden bark, or when the odd narcissus blooms in January and February; or as April turns into May and the ground is set thick with a blurry, hazy spread of bluebells.

It's a steep climb up the winding lane out of the valley, the hedges lined with moss and ferns in myriad shades of green. On top sit gnarled trees, their branches twisted into shapes that look like oriental parasols, or the elaborately arranged hair of a teenage boy. At the top of the hill is another junction – I turn right, temporarily breaking off the 'official' Circuit route and follow the road down to Gear Bridge.

This is where armed conflict once came to St Martin, the location of a brief incursion between Parliamentarians and rebels still loyal to the Crown in the Second English Civil War. A Royalist force under the command of a Major Bogans of St Keverne had established a position on the hill above the bridge, planning to defend what was a strategically important route. When Parliamentarian soldiers drew near it was immediately obvious to the rebels that they were outnumbered. The men deserted their post and, according to the early 19th-century historian Richard Polwhele, Bogans 'fled to Hilters Clift in St Keverne and concealed himself in a cave in the rocks'. The Gear Rout, as it became known, was the end of a short-lived pro-Royalist rising that had broken out in the west of Cornwall in May 1648. At school in Helston we covered the basics of battles at Bosworth Field, Flodden and Stamford Bridge; how much more alive history might have seemed with a school trip to the site of this skirmish, but a few miles from our classroom.

Two hundred years ago a new bridge was built over Gear Creek, designed for the horses and carts that were then the primary traffic. The bloated cars of today have to creep across; there is little give on either side. I listen out for traffic, and hearing none, walk out into the middle. The only sound is the gentle dripping of water and the plashing of two more swans slowly passing between the stone quays. I imagine the scene four centuries ago – the distant noise of the approaching caravan of soldiers, the shouts of commanders, the clash of steel swords and the last cries of the seven or eight rebels who met their ends here.

Back on The Circuit, I stop to catch my breath by the pair of granite gate piers that sit in front of Caervallack Lodge, guarding what was once one of the many entrances into the Trelowarren demesne. It is a cottage I have long coveted, its architecture touchingly delicate – neatly symmetrical outer windows framing an arched doorway, with a tiny arched window above. So many lodge houses, originally built on country tracks, now sit hard against busy roads; this one is pleasingly set back, and surrounded by a mature garden. In the field opposite a pair of rare-breed pigs slurp through their feed.

I walked this way one summer night in 1987. I was sixteen and worried about my exam results. In my first year at secondary school I had been a model student. Most subjects were streamed, and I was in all the top groups. Then my mother died. I lost interest in studying, stopped reading, became disruptive in class, and gently slid down the academic slope. My father and my teachers were frustrated but I didn't really care, reckoning, with the confidence of youth, that formal education was overrated, and that I could pursue the journalistic career I wanted without it.

It wasn't that I lacked ambition. I bombarded the local newspaper, the *West Briton*, with requests to do work experience, and spent time at its offices in Helston and Truro. I wrote again and again to Television South West, the local ITV broadcaster, until they allowed me to come to Plymouth and shadow the evening news. I made my first tentative broadcasts for the hospital radio station in Penzance. When my father expressed concern I cockily dismissed his worries with tales of famous reporters who had started out as teenage copy boys, or writers who had picked up their education as they travelled the world. But again and again in newsrooms and studios I kept meeting kind adults who told me the world had changed, that I really did need some qualifications. Finally, a matter of months before my exams, reality hit. I studied as hard as I could, but I knew I would be lucky if I scraped through with the grades required to stay on for sixth form.

On that warm night, with just hours to go before the postwoman was due to deliver an envelope containing my results, and unable to sleep, I put my boots on and set off for a solitary walk. It was perfectly clear, with a fine view of the constellations of Cassiopeia and the Plough. Transfixed, I stared upwards, and suddenly a star fled across the skies. Seconds later there was another, and then two more shot by. That was the end of the brief display, specific enough that I took it as a hopeful omen. The next day's letter brought confirmation that I had passed 'O' Levels in English, English literature, history and drama. By the narrowest of margins I had avoided the ignominy of being thrown out of school. Dad was much relieved, taking me for a celebratory pub lunch.

My father had a short temper, which as a teenager I seemed to pick up. We would have arguments that blew up from nothing, and quickly became loud and expletive-ridden. The rows would subside as quickly as they had started, both of us left looking at each other sheepishly, not quite sure what had just happened. Sometimes anger would linger longer in the air; on one occasion when I was thirteen I decided I was going to leave home. I packed a bag, and set off to seek sanctuary with my Aunt Anne, who was then living in the village. Anne was my father's sister, but the two of them had not spoken for decades, the exact cause of their disconnect lost to history. Anne was an interior designer, author and craftswoman. Her creative outlook and relaxed attitude to life made me think of her as a comrade-in-arms. Though I knew my father did not like me seeing her, he never tried to stop our friendship. It took me forty-five minutes to walk to her house. When I arrived I saw light peeping out from around tightly drawn curtains, and the smoke of a fire rising from the chimney. I knew that Anne would take me in, feed me, give me a bed, reassure me. But I also knew how humiliated my father would be at the thought that I had run to her at a time of trouble. I stood outside her front door for a moment or two before turning round and returning home. My father could be unpredictable, difficult, even alarming at times, but he was my sole-surviving parent, and I loved him more than anyone else.

One of his great qualities was the ability to appear utterly unconcerned about what I was up to. Much of my St Martin life played out in other people's houses. Electricity had not troubled Grove Cott where Mrs Cliff lived. The corrugated-iron roof of her house, on the main road, was red with rust. The kitchen smelt of the paraffin that she used to fuel her lights. A range in the main room provided heat; a damp, dark shed across from the front door offered a cool space for milk, butter and cheese even on the hottest days.

On a Saturday afternoon we would look at television together. Mrs Cliff's small black-and-white portable set was powered by a 12-volt car battery. Wrestling on ITV was the principal attraction, the honeyed voice of commentator Kent Walton welcoming 'grapple fans' to set-piece bouts between fat men with nicknames like Big Daddy and Giant Haystacks. During the commercial breaks Mrs Cliff would delve into some shadowy corner of her kitchen cupboard to find me a chocolate digestive or a packet of crisps, before pouring us tea from a pot warming on the edge of her Cornish range, an all-purpose stove that hungrily consumed its fuel – coal, wood, household rubbish – by the bucketload. I remember Mrs Cliff as a tiny, kind, elderly figure, a benevolent character from a folk tale. But she was well capable of leaping into action when the TV battery went flat, dismissing the sparks and crackles as she nimbly switched the crocodile clips from one set of terminals to another.

One of the vast parabolic dishes of Goonhilly Satellite Station, from where information was fed around the world, was in St Martin. The runway at RNAS Culdrose, then the largest helicopter base in Western Europe, was barely two miles away. Each day the sonic boom of Concorde rattled our roof tiles as the flight to New York passed over the Cornish coast. I would imagine David Frost or Joan Collins taking a first glass of champagne and making themselves comfortable. But below, in St Martin, there were still people living without electricity.

Bathrooms were not guaranteed either. When my parents were elsewhere Beatrice Mitchell would keep an eye on me after school. I would do my homework sitting at the kitchen table, all the time urging Mrs Mitchell to switch on their big box of a colour television. This ran off mains electricity, to which the Mitchells were connected, but their sanitary arrangements were as old-fashioned as their 18th-century cottage. A tin bathtub hung from a hook on the kitchen ceiling and was used for both bathing and doing the laundry, the water heated up on the well-scrubbed range that was lit every morning. Use of the lavatory entailed a trip to the bottom of the immaculately kept garden, where a shed accommodated a privy, its shiny wooden seat crowning a hole in the ground. A carton of Izal Medicated Lavatory Paper sat on an adjacent shelf, above a bucket filled with ash, a forkful of which would be hurled on top of freshly discharged excrement in an attempt to mute its smell.

Mrs Mitchell and Mrs Cliff's televisions were of particular interest to me because Dad refused to have one in our house. 'It's a fast route to an atrophied mind,' he proclaimed. Instead we got our news and entertainment from the radio, and I found myself ploughing through books at a rate that seems inconceivable today. At times I was embarrassed by the situation, telling visiting schoolfriends that the set was away for repair, and reading newspaper reviews to ensure I was fully briefed to discuss shows I had never actually seen. Ida Lanyon, one of my babysitters, considered my father's decision unfathomable, and when my parents had a night out, she would bring her portable set with her. We'd eat the plate of chicken sandwiches that Mum had made earlier, and then watch a *Carry On* film as Ida smoked her way through a tin of Café Crème cigarillos. Sometimes she would tell me about the village of old, when Wheelwright's Cottage was still home to a wheelwright; when James Carlyon Cooke was the village carpenter, making washboards, wagons and barrows, and the blacksmith's shop opposite employed six men.

Those businesses had long gone but St Martin still had the necessary accoutrements of a fully functioning village. Mrs Cardwell was the first shopkeeper I remember. As sub-postmistress she helped me to open a National Savings Account with £15 of accrued birthday money. Next to the postal counter, from where she sold stamps and paid pensions, were tightly packed shelves of groceries and a chiller cabinet where she kept the hams and blocks of cheese that would be cut to order. The lights came on early in her sitting room so the mail could be sorted before postwoman Brenda Steer set out on her daily round, first delivering to the village, and later heading down rough lanes to isolated cottages and farmhouses.

St Martin was generally a quiet place, but three or four days a week the distinctive roar of Wessex and Sea King helicopters from RNAS Culdrose would cut through the silence. Several naval pilots lived in the village, where they were treated as local heroes, always on standby to rescue stricken sailors, whatever the weather, or transport the pregnant, sick or injured from the Isles of Scilly to hospital in Truro. In the cold winter of 1978/79, when St Martin was cut off by snow for nearly a week, the Navy sent a helicopter to deliver bread and milk. But Culdrose's real purpose was the defence of the United Kingdom. It was a major Cold War military base. Just as thought of the climate emergency disturbs and frightens teenagers today, in the 1980s we worried about the seemingly very real prospect of nuclear obliteration. It was a time of edgy paranoia. Leafing through a kitchen drawer one day, in among recipes clipped by my mother and warranty booklets for toasters and kettles, I found our copy of *Protect and Survive*, the sobering booklet issued by the Home Office in 1980. In startled silence I worked my way through its stark text and bleak illustrations. How families should use a sturdy table surrounded by heavy furniture filled with sand, earth, books or clothing as a basic fallout shelter. How bottles, containers and buckets should be filled with a fortnight's worth of water. How each family should have a portable radio and spare batteries. 'Your radio will be your only link with the outside world.'

Our four-minute warning would come from St Martin's shop. By now Mrs Cardwell had retired and the Meyricks had taken over. Their son Simon had become a schoolfriend, and I was a regular visitor to the house. In the passage between shop and sitting room, two grey plastic units were mounted on the wall. One was an anonymous flat-fronted cabinet, the other a loudspeaker with its volume-control switch turned to maximum. Cables came out of the bottom and ran into a brown telephone junction box, branded with the initials 'G.P.O.' Simon's dad was at first evasive when I asked him what it was, but eventually my questioning wore him down. He opened the cupboard underneath and showed me what looked look a fan, operated by a wooden handle. He turned it a few inches and for a second or two the unmistakable drone of an air-raid siren rang out.

St Martin post office was at the end of a national system which would issue the warning in the event of imminent nuclear attack. After receiving reports of incoming missiles from one of its radar stations, RAF Strike Command at High Wycombe would trigger remote sirens in towns and cities, and alert 250 major police stations. Simultaneously an automatic signal would be issued to 20,000 rural warning points – equipment installed in the homes of vicars, magistrates, council officials and other so-called responsible people, and in village post offices. On hearing the alarm, Mr Meyrick was to run outside and wind his siren to notify us of the imminent Armageddon. The code name for the system was Handel, an allusion to his oratorio *Judas Maccabaeus*, with its famous air, 'Sound the Alarm'.

The shop has closed now – and so has the school I went to until I was eleven. Motorists are still warned of its presence by signs on each side of the road, red circles around a silhouette of two children holding hands. 'All visitors report to reception' says the notice on the back gate. But weeds grow over a set of mini goalposts, the pitch between covered in a thick layer of buttercups. The modern classrooms, barely a quarter of a century old, have had their doors and windows boarded up.

The handsome Victorian schoolhouse behind is now a dwelling, with two cars parked outside. The shiny silver pipe of a solid-fuel burner pierces through the roof. In my time as a pupil here in the late 1970s and early 1980s a black enamel coke-burning stove belched loudly and scattered its glowing embers as Mr Teague, the headmaster, added more fuel.

There were just two teachers. Mrs Pascoe supervised those aged between five and eight, Mr Teague taught the remaining three years. The whole school, around thirty pupils in my time, would gather in the main room for assembly, and then regroup at noon for lunch. Food for primary schools across the area was cooked centrally in Mullion and then dispatched in insulated metal boxes. The main course would be lukewarm by the time we got to eat it: pies, pasta bakes, sausage and mash with stringy green vegetables or dry salad. Tepid steamed puddings and fruit pies followed, often accompanied by custard lightly coloured pink or green in an effort to make it more exciting.

A large radio sat on one of the windowsills; each Monday morning we would gather in front of it to join in with the BBC Schools programme *Singing Together*. The television was in the room next door, which was also the library and Mr Teague's office. There we'd patiently watch a digital clock tick down to the start of a documentary about life in India or America, or a studio-based dramatisation of a novel that was on the curriculum.

I was there when the school celebrated its centenary. A commemorative book was published, including a class photograph – I am in the second row, wearing shorts and a hand-knitted jumper, boasting a fine pudding-basin haircut. A couple of years later the school was threatened with closure and my father helped lead the fight to keep it open. I have a cassette recording of a heated meeting that he chaired; parishioners sending the man from the council home with a flea in his ear. The school survived.

A decade later it had more than fifty pupils, but by 2017 numbers were barely in double figures. The academy trust that had taken control argued for closure, pointing out that it could not field a sports team and warning that there might only be one pupil in the infant class the following year. And so its fate was sealed.

With only 370 residents, St Martin is never going to produce a stable number of schoolchildren to suit a statistician's demands. But there are still young families here, who in five years or ten will have children needing schooling, children who will now have to leave the village to start their education.

My friend Tatiana has lovingly converted the school into a house, working hard to preserve the architectural integrity of the old building. We have drunk wine together in the room where, nearly half a century ago, I recited multiplication tables and learnt about the Norman Conquest. She grew up in the village; she understands when I tell her of the sense of melancholy I feel at the sight of her new house sign – elegant white letters carved into dark-grey slate – 'The Old School'.

* * *

Nikolaus Pevsner passed through St Martin in 1948, his wife Lola at the wheel of the unreliable pre-war Austin 10 that his publisher had lent them. The architectural historian identified only one structure here that was worthy of a write-up in the Cornwall volume of his series *The Buildings of England* – the parish church. He had little to say about its nave, an undistinguished box built after the original had burnt down in 1830, but was more enthusiastic about the 15th-century tower, which somehow survived the blaze. Its two stages are topped out with battlements and pinnacles, with simple gargoyles, their features decayed by centuries of wind and rain, what remains of their lips, foreheads and other features now disguised by thick coats of silver lichen.

Around the church are the gravestones of the dead of the 17th and 18th centuries. They stand at jaunty angles, as if raising their hats to the 21st-century visitor. Lugg, Cooke, Hendy, Wills, Pascoe and Tripconey are among the recurring names, families still present in the St Martin of my childhood.

The churchyard is noisy today. Songbirds perform on all sides, distant rooks barking out a bass line. A buzzing bee shoots in front of me and there is a gentle dripping sound as the last residue of the night's rain falls down the drainpipe into the water butt that sits under the eave of the church roof. For a second my nostrils catch the sickly smell of rotting vegetation – the remains of bunches of pink carnations and white roses hurled over the hedge, having served their mourning duty.

Part of my family tree is here, written out on slate and granite. The graves of my brother, my parents, my grandparents, two uncles and an aunt. My father's grave is equidistant to that of his younger brother William, who died aged fifteen in 1945, and his older, longer-lived siblings, Aunt Anne and Uncle Robin.

All around stand stones marking others who held this community together as I grew up. Hannibal Nicholls who ran the garage; the farming brothers William and Trevor Bryant and Wesley and Rex Hosking; Mrs Cardwell of the shop; George Witherwick, who laid out gardens tumbling down to the Helford River at Trelean; Eileen Stephens, who cleaned my widowed father's house and took me on childhood outings to Plymouth; Michael Kaye, the village builder and undertaker, responsible himself for half a century of St Martin funerals.

Mickey lived in the house next to the graveyard. A shed in his garden, grandly described as the Chapel of Rest, was the place where late parishioners would spend the days between removal and burial. Those who engaged him as a builder accepted that he might be called away from work on a new bungalow or bathroom extension to remove and lay out a body. His hearse was battered, the leather on its seats split, the bodywork gently rusting. Mickey's feet hurt, so he had swapped polished leather shoes for more comfortable black trainers. His striped trousers were too long, his tailcoat was held closed by a piece of black string, the silk of his top hat had rubbed thin around the brim. But there was no better funeral director, no one more determined than him to give the parishioners of St Martin a decent, respectful burial.

The last Trelawny funeral he conducted was that of my brother William, who had died of cancer in a London hospital. A smart city firm collected him from the place of his death; its staff were efficient, well dressed, smooth in their manner, a little obsequious. In a moment of welcome black comedy, Mickey reported that they would not transport him all the way to Cornwall. William would be exchanged from one hearse to another in the car-park of a service station on the M5 near Bristol. There was a great sense of relief when he called to say my brother was safely in his hands. William was the third generation of Trelawnys that Mickey had buried; he himself was part of a long rural tradition of village builder-undertakers, which ended in St Martin with his own funeral a few years later.

* * *

On a February morning there are seven of us in the congregation for matins. A plaque commemorating my grandfather's thirty-five years of duty as church warden is mounted on the wall behind the harmonium. In the 1980s my mother and Mrs Cardwell used to share organist duties; today there is no one here who can play. The hymn singing is accompanied by recordings from a machine operated by Annabel Phillips, one of the church wardens.

There has not been a full-time vicar for more than a decade, the congregation served by a rota of retired priests and volunteers. Often Annabel has to read the service herself. A few times each year the church is busier – at Christmas or for a wedding or funeral. But most of the time the number of worshippers remains in single figures. It is increasingly hard for the congregation to meet the target set for its contributions to the diocese, and to raise the funds needed to heat, light and maintain the building. But at least it is still here, a community asset that has survived, unlike the school, the shop, the filling station and the Methodist chapel.

CHAPTER 2

Chapel

The Cornwall of my childhood seemed a God-fearing place. Every other village owed its name to a saint, cinemas were closed on Sundays, pubs had restricted hours, and the landscape was dotted with places of worship, ancient churches heavily outnumbered by 19th-century chapels. Methodism was the dominant denomination. Of my thirty or so fellow pupils at St Martin School, nearly half would attend a Sunday service, everyone except me going to chapel.

Mum always seemed to be on the rota for vestry duty at the church, so we would arrive half an hour or so before the service to give her time to unlock the Edwardian safe, set out the communion wine, polish the chalice and light the candles. Today the smell of melting beeswax immediately evokes a memory of sitting in a pew propped up against a pile of embroidered kneelers, reading my book as I waited for the service to start. Dad had no time for organised religion, so if Mum was playing the harmonium, I'd be on my own for the whole hour. She was one of the younger members of the congregation and unless it was Christmas, Mothering Sunday, Easter or Harvest Festival, I would be the only child.

Going to church felt boring, and, more importantly, it marked me out as being different to my Methodist schoolfriends. They reported livelier goings-on at chapel – the worshippers were younger, the hymns had better tunes; a Sunday school with paints, paper and Christian pop was altogether more exciting than the whispered sermon delivered by the Revd Owen Blatchley, the well-meaning Anglican vicar. Not long after my tenth birthday I started lobbying my parents for permission to swap churches.

At chapel the preachers were drawn from a rota of lay ministers, their movements set out in the quarterly circuit plan. Many of them had confident, commanding personalities, and were able to bring a sense of awe and entertainment to the weekly gathering. A few were charismatic men and women whose sermons, delivered without notes or amplification, had accorded them a form of celebrity status. As he gave his parish notices, the chapel steward Michael Boaden would be extra enthusiastic if he had the chance to announce the return of a popular preacher, someone who radiated passion and magnetism from the moment they took their place on the dais. It was faith as theatre – a stirring sermon and lusty delivery of popular hymns, accompanied by a proper pipe organ played by Michael's wife, Doris. No wonder the congregation would turn out in Sunday best, bright floral dresses and three-piece suits, the faces of farmers' sons scrubbed and glowing.

During the week Guild meetings and Junior Club would keep us busy; there were choirs to join, plays were staged, and we were all expected to take part in the annual Helston Methodist Circuit Festival. Aged eleven, I won first prize for a rather wobbly treble performance of the New Seekers' hit 'I Want to Teach the World to Sing'. My success was not long lasting; I was quickly eliminated in the next round at Centenary Chapel in Camborne, where half a dozen west Cornwall circuits went head-to-head against each other. These festivals were our version of the Welsh *Eisteddfod* – highly competitive gatherings where we sang, played an instrument, or were tested as public speakers, with adjudicators offering critical feedback and certificates provided to the winners. In Cornwall these contests were very much chapel property.

The annual tea-treat was our reward for showing commitment and diligence over the previous year. The idea, replicated by every chapel in the county, was straightforward – take your faithful youth out for the day, feed them, and return them home filled with the joy of the Lord. The catering arrangements were set in stone – a Cornish pasty followed by a buttered saffron bun. Faded black-and-white pictures of Victorian and Edwardian tea-treats show adult supervisors in starched aprons and hats dispensing food and drink to rows of excited children dressed up for the day.

Trippers were once carried by horse-drawn farmer's cart or open-topped charabanc. We took the train to Newquay one year; the next time St Ives was the destination, to be reached from the park-and-ride station at Lelant. On arrival we were in a state of high excitement. One of the teachers had a made a plan that involved visiting artists' studios and the Barbara Hepworth Museum. But we were more interested in spending our pocket money, eagerly pouring into Woolworths on the quay, finding cheap souvenirs, and fighting the gulls away as we sat on the sea wall eating overfilled 99s from Hart's Ice Cream Parlour.

When we got back to Lelant a corner of the car-park had been commandeered. Two trestle tables were heavy with pasties in paper bags and bright-yellow buns wrapped in cling film. A portable farm generator clanked away in the background, powering the silver urn; next to it were a pair of enormous brown earthenware teapots that came out at every chapel gathering. We sang a hymn or two, and then lined up to collect our prizes, the reward for a year of good work. I was given a children's version of John Bunyan's *Pilgrim's Progress*. More hymn singing followed, but I missed it. Ice cream, pasty, saffron bun and the train journey had been too much; I was being sick behind the station platform, my retching drowned out by the mass voices.

Methodism seemed an unstoppable force. In 1983 a storm blew the roof off St Martin Chapel, a gust of wind lifting the great frame of wood and slate into the air before it smashed down against the building's east wall. The insurance did not cover the full repair bill, so an endless round of fetes, community suppers, coffee mornings and jumble sales followed to raise the thousands of pounds needed.

A year later the building reopened with great ceremony. One of the speakers gave thanks, suggesting that what had happened should not be seen as a disaster but a positive event that would strengthen the position of Methodism in the village. In 1990 St Martin marked the 175th anniversary of its first chapel with a four-day celebration, including three services, visiting organists, a flower festival and *The Spirit*, a musical staged by young people of the Helston Circuit. Little more than a decade later the church had closed. In the language of Methodism, its cause had failed. The people of St Martin had lost interest in their chapel. Today it has been converted into two houses. The 1970s hall next door, where we would gorge on orange squash and chocolate biscuits at the end of Sunday school, has been knocked down, a cottage built over its foundations.

* * *

In 1940 Cornwall had 634 functioning Methodist churches. Between them they had 146,653 seats. Not far short of half the population could have sat down and worshipped at the same time.

Chapel buildings are commonplace in Cornwall, as ubiquitous as the remains of mine-engine chimneys. More than a thousand were built; some towns had half a dozen or more; a tiny village might have had a couple; they were built on the edge of farmsteads and placed by remote crossroads.

Until the middle of the 20th century Methodism was a vital element of Cornish culture; its decline has been steep. Today just a small percentage of chapels are still used for prayer; most have become houses or business units. But the surviving buildings, with their immediately recognisable granite-faced walls, high windows, porches and dedication stones, provide lasting proof of the omnipotent power the church once had.

* * *

When Joseph Turner, a Bristol sea captain, visited St Ives in 1743 he was introduced to members of a small religious society that was challenging the Church of England's status quo in the town. He reported this to his friends, the brothers John and Charles Wesley, suggesting that the place might be open to the ideas of their nascent evangelical movement. The men responded quickly;

Charles arriving in mid July, his elder brother following six weeks later. John's passage was not straightforward – after crossing the Tamar he got lost on the 'pathless' Goss Moor, only finding his bearings when he heard the Bodmin curfew bell tolling in the distance. But the troubles of the journey were quickly forgotten; he got a warm reception in St Ives, and decided that 'little by little' he would introduce Methodism to Cornwall.

The flame was soon burning strongly. Within a few years, thirty Methodist societies had been formed in the west, with other branches in Port Isaac, Camelford, Trewint and Launceston. John Wesley came to Cornwall every year between 1743 and 1750, visiting a total of thirty-two times before his death in 1791. He became a celebrity – people sat on rooftops to catch a glimpse of him in Redruth; in Falmouth the streets were lined with crowds 'gaping and staring as if the King was going by'. He even made it to the Isles of Scilly, where in St Mary's he found an eager audience among the soldiers, sailors and labourers who had been sent there to fortify the island against the threat of French invasion.

Wesley claimed Methodism was not a threat to the Church of England, but something that complemented it. He would go to an Anglican service each Sunday, worshipping at Week St Mary, St Ives, Zennor and St Endellion. He told his followers that their classes and meetings should not be seen as a replacement for their weekly attendance at church. He castigated lazy St Agnes Methodists, telling them he was 'surprised and grieved' that they had forsaken communion and making them promise that they would no more 'give place to the devil'.

Perhaps this was why Cornwall's Anglican clergy under-estimated the impact Methodism was having. Local magistrates were more concerned, the threat of the French on their minds. Might a population no longer entirely loyal to the national church also be less loyal to the Crown? One magistrate, the geologist and priest William Borlase, issued an arrest warrant for Wesley with the plan of press-ganging him into military service abroad. The Revd Borlase was to quickly change his mind when he met the preacher, and realised he was an articulate, impressive, highly educated man.

The force of the new faith seemed unstoppable. In 1827 Joseph Entwisle, one of the church's most senior figures, noted that in Camborne and Hayle there was 'no household without a Methodist'.

If Anglicanism was built on the calm reassurance of unchanging weekly ritual, Methodism thrived on drama. Whole communities would find themselves gripped by outbreaks of intense religious fervour. In 1782 membership in St Just increased from 181 to 300; in 1814 Camborne produced 5,000 new Methodists. These 'Great Revivals', as they were known, were often triggered by news of a thrilling conversion.

The *Wesleyan Methodist Magazine* savoured such tales, reporting several in the 1820s. Richard Trewavas was a sailor from Mousehole who was pacing the deck of his ship in the midst of a violent storm when he came to realise that 'without an interest in the Redeemer's merits I must be eternally undone'. Solomon Burall 'wandered for days around the mine workings at Tuckingmill in spiritual distress'. His cries were so loud that they 'brought a crowd of miners running to his assistance who thought he was in physical pain'. Both men joined Methodist societies, their stories encouraging hundreds to sign up to the cause.

Temperance, education and moral improvement were the key tenets of Chapel life. Members were supposed to renounce the 'pleasures of the world', which as well as alcohol also included sport, theatre, singing secular songs, smoking, card playing and dancing. If a man didn't drink, smoke or gamble he could better look after this family, went the message. Women were encouraged to dress soberly and modestly – an 1834 correspondent cautioning that a 'love of dress was increasing among the Truro congregation'. A few years later female worshippers at St Keverne Chapel were issued with a pamphlet by the American missionary Adoniram Judson that warned the faithful to beware of a suggestion 'made by weak and erring souls who will tell you that there is more danger of being proud of plain dress, and other modes of self-denial, than of fashionable attire and self-indulgence. Be not ensnared by this last, most finished, insidious device of the great enemy'.

The hellfire and damnation message seemed to make an impact. In 1861 James William Gilbart, a prominent London banker and advocate of the moral and religious responsibilities of business, praised the impact of Cornish Methodism. Its effect, he wrote, 'in making the drunkard sober, the idle industrious, the profligate moral and in inducing men to provide decently and comfortably for their families, and give suitable education to their children can be attested by thousands of witnesses'.

* * *

At first Methodists did the bulk of their evangelical work outdoors, and met in private houses to study together. John Wesley described the few early chapels that existed in the 1760s as 'miserable . . . they have neither light nor air sufficient and they are far, far too low and small'.

Chapel building began in earnest at the start of the nineteenth century. Sometimes an individual would take the lead. John Courtice from St Wenn, a 'profligate' who had been converted, prayed at two plots of land, hoping for guidance. 'On the second plot he felt "the holy fire" and rising from his knees went to buy the land, afterwards taking the lead in the erection of the chapel'. The local gentry might gift a space to the community, though Captain Fortescue of Boconnoc near Lostwithiel decided enough was enough when he was asked to give space for a seventh chapel on his land. Subscription was another popular method of fundraising: £300 came from the issue of £3 shares to build Carleen's chapel.

In poorer areas the buildings often opened for services before they were finished. Worshippers would stand on a dirt floor at first; boards, pews and galleries only added when resources allowed. Wealthier towns aspired to emulate Wesley's own chapel, opened in Islington in London in 1778, and soon recognised as the 'mother church' of Methodism. 'City Road Style', as it became known, inspired chapels built in Penzance, St Just and Camborne.

But often the new buildings were far too big, ambitious committee chairmen failing to take into account the likelihood that many of the revival converts would quickly lose their initial zeal. In 1851 Truro's main chapel had 1,600 seats but its largest congregation was 1,000. When the District Redundancy Committee was considering the fate of Carharrack in 1966 it noted that there were 200 more chapel seats than there were people living in the village.

The rush to build was in part thanks to the non-hierarchical structure of the Church. Its power resided in local committees, so there was no body to caution against over-expansion. Until the 1930s Methodism was not a single Church but a series of different sects. While many of those who worshipped each Sunday were casual attendees, it was the signed-up members who ran things. In Cornwall in 1851 the Wesleyans, the most powerful branch, had 73,000 members. Nearly 22,000 followed the Bible Christians, 11,000 were in the Wesleyan Methodist Association and there were 6,000 Primitive Methodists. The smallest groups, the Methodist New Connexion and Wesleyan Reform, each had under a thousand members.

While each group agreed on the big ideas, they were split on a variety of smaller issues, including the use of the liturgy, how communion should be administered and the layout of chapels. Later came fierce arguments about whether authority lay locally, or with the Methodist Conference, the national governing body. Reforming preachers who favoured central control found chapels locked shut when they arrived to preach; at Treligga near Port Isaac, the trustees nailed a legal notice to the door, banning one minister from entering. The move towards union was slow. It started in the late 1850s, but it was not until 1932 that Methodism's recalcitrant siblings made peace, falling numbers and an urgent need for new preachers and Sunday school teachers finally forcing unification.

* * *

In St Martin a public footpath runs directly between church and chapel. Today it crosses the middle of an open field left for pasture; once it would have run alongside a hedge, long since removed in the interests of agricultural efficiency. A stream runs out of sight at the bottom, the billowy fields that rise up behind glow green in the sharp winter sun. I put up a sleepy woodcock as I clamber over the stile in the corner of the church graveyard. From the top step there is a clear view of the chapel's sharply pitched roof, the lines of slate now interrupted by domestic skylights. The earlier chapel, a simpler, square building, also now a house, stands across the road. In my childhood the chapel regularly had fifty or sixty worshippers on a Sunday; the church was lucky to attract more than a dozen.

Why did Cornwall take to nonconformism with such enthusiasm? Though the official story starts in the mid-18th century with the arrival of the brothers Wesley at St Ives, the ground was laid two centuries earlier. The 1549 Act of Uniformity imposed the Book of Common Prayer, and insisted that English, rather than Latin, be used as the ecclesiastical mother tongue. But English was not spoken universally in Cornwall; in the west, in particular, there were still places where Cornish was the only known language. Even if not fully understood, the old Latin words had at least been familiar, and many priests would say the Creed and other key elements of their services in Cornish. As the distinguished historian Philip Payton writes: 'it was the epitome of Tudor intrusion ... there was to be no "special case" dispensation for the Cornish, no separate or sensitive treatment'.

This was simply not acceptable. Protests broke out and the Prayer Book Rebels, as they became known, petitioned the King with their demand that Cornwall be exempt from the new rules. Edward VI responded by sending forces to defeat the uprising. The rebel leaders were hanged, drawn and quartered at Tyburn in London – several of them priests, including the vicars of Gulval, Poundstock and St Veep and St Neot. The Cornish had been defeated but the reputation of the established church had been badly damaged, the Prayer Book Rebellion leaving a sore that has never quite healed.*

The Cornish were eager for an alternative to the established Church, which Methodism would eventually provide. John Wesley's early instruction that his followers should continue to take Anglican communion was soon forgotten. Instead chapel members started to exploit their position as disruptors. Most

---

* In 2007 the Bishop of Truro, Bill Ind, apologised for the actions of the English government, saying it had acted 'brutally and stupidly and killed many Cornish people'. He described the events of 1549 as 'an enormous mistake'.

existing churches were hundreds of years old, and were often not in the places where communities had subsequently developed, found instead in 'churchtowns', hamlets distant from village centres. Chapel went to where the people were, founders ensuring that their buildings were as close as possible to the locations where fishermen, farmers and miners lived and worked.

The preachers were local men who shared the same background as their flocks and often had broad Cornish accents. Until well into the 20th century most vicars saw themselves as members of the gentry class, living in substantial houses with staff to look after them. Bernard Walke, Anglo-Catholic Vicar of St Hilary, did much to help the poor of his parish, but expected a certain level of comfort for himself. When he hosted the Bishop of Truro in 1913, he planned a dinner that started with oysters and a fine Moselle from Pooles, the Penzance wine merchant. The meal continued with lobster mayonnaise and trifle. Travelling Methodist preachers tucked into simpler fare prepared by their congregation: 'meat pies, bacon and egg pies, cold chicken, saffron cake, dough cake, splits and cream, home baked bread and goodness knows what else', washed down with pots of hot tea.

The sense of 'them and us' continued into the service itself; at chapel the semi-formal nature of worship meant the experience was shared rather than didactic. Richard Jones, a former president of the Methodist Conference, described congregations who made no secret of their 'contempt' for the clergy, considering them 'snobs' hidebound by ritual – 'Ken't even say a prayer w'out readin' 'un from a book.' Anglican worship was seen as being bland; chapel offered a combination of faith and entertainment, what has been described as a *Volkskirche*, or people's church, where members were encouraged to take the lead as organisers and preachers. In his *History of Cornish Methodism*, Thomas Shaw talks about the Church having much 'in common with the old Catholicism at its best . . . an intensity of religious experience, a passion for holiness and an awareness of the Communion of Saints'. But it also provided a community based on equality, a place where the young could meet a potential husband or wife, and a source of much-needed entertainment.

* * *

The popularity of Methodism had been helped by the Church of England's neglect of its distant western parishes. For more than 800 years Cornish churchgoers had had to look to Exeter for their leadership – a 50-mile journey from Bude, 100 miles from Penzance. Once upon a time Cornwall had had its own spiritual leader – but the office of Bishop of Cornwall had been abolished in 1050 when the diocese merged with Devon. Bishop Leofric was the last man to do the job, before his office fell victim of an early example of Church rationalisation.

By the middle of the 19th century the Church of England had realised that neglect of its Cornish parishes had allowed Methodism to flourish and challenge its primacy. The 1851 census listed 113,510 Methodists to 47,555 Anglicans. The church responded by creating a new Cornish diocese. The first Bishop of Truro, Edward White Benson, was consecrated in April 1877. The son of an evangelical Yorkshireman whose mother had been raised in a Birmingham Unitarian family, he had a clear understanding of the pull of Methodism, which he immediately praised, saying it had kept faith alive in Cornwall at a time when the Church 'had almost lost the sacred flame'.

His frustration was made clear after a visit to Redruth where he saw 'two enormous, overcrowded chapels and two moderate empty churches'. He may have missed the procession through Camborne in 1880 to celebrate the centenary of Methodist

Sunday schools, but he must have read accounts of it – 8,000 children marched to Pendarves Park, the parade-column taking forty-five minutes to pass.

Bishop Benson went on to speak about how the Anglicans might embrace the best elements of Methodism – something that didn't please many Methodists. One, Henry Smart, saw it as an attempt to 'paralyse' Methodism, proclaiming that its members would 'rally round [their] beloved plot and protect it from this ecclesiastical invader'. The invasion failed – even with an impressive new cathedral in Truro, the Anglicans failed to see off the Methodists.

* * *

At the Royal Institution of Cornwall's Courtney Library in Truro, I am handed two boxes that contain one hundred years of quarterly plans for the Helston Methodist Circuit. These are the railway timetables of Chapel life – a grid of the names of lay preachers lined up against the places requiring their services. There is something of the military operation about it, with transport arrangements listed and reminders to hosts as to the level of catering expected.

Read chronologically, the leaflets chart the decline of Cornish Methodism, getting thinner and flimsier as one chapel after another closes. In 1975 St Martin has fifty-two members, making it the third biggest chapel in the circuit, after Helston and Mullion. A decade later it has fallen to fifth place (thirty-six members). By 1995 it has lost its Sunday evening service and is seventh in the circuit, with twenty-two members. Soon after it closes for good.

St Keverne Parish once had eleven chapels. Tregidden shut its doors in 1901, Tregowris in 1924, Porthoustock in 1963 and Rosuick in 1971. All are now houses. Coverack was still open at the time of my chapel phase; I took myself there on a summer

Sunday while staying with my grandparents. The morning sun felt like it was burning my eyes as it reflected off the stuccoed walls of the 1861 building. A steward encouraged me to sit downstairs but I was determined to be in the gallery, where I was left alone to enjoy the view out over the sea – a view now enjoyed from what is someone's bedroom. Zoar closed in 1992, five years before Coverack. A clause in its deeds meant it had to be demolished once it was surplus to requirements. Dense foliage fills the spot where there were seats for a hundred, the granite posts and rusting metalwork of its arched gates still just evident. St Keverne chapel itself survived until 2017, but it has now been turned into apartments, with the rump of the congregation worshipping in the Sunday school hall.

I say the names of villages and communities on the circuit plan out loud, and feel a sense of that same nostalgia that comes from the list of dead railway stations featured in the Flanders and Swann song, 'The Slow Train'. Crelly, Releath, Manhay, Manaccan, Gweek Bethel, Ruan Ebenezer, Ashton Zion; a sad list of places where people once gathered to seek succour in prayer, but can find it no more.

* * *

On the way home from the library I pass though former tin-mining country, driving ten miles or so between four chapels that help chart the history of Cornish Methodism. Kerley Downs in Baldhu is my first stop, where a church built by the evangelist Billy Bray still stands and still welcomes the faithful.

Nicknamed 'Three Eyes' after its three sash windows, it is a squat, low building that seems to hug the ground, as if hiding from the passing road. The exterior is straightforward and rough-hewn like the man who built it; the interior is softer, but still austere and unadorned, a glass bowl of yellow flowers on a table in front of a white-painted, raised preacher's platform, a portrait of Bray above.

He was born at Twelveheads near Truro in 1794. Aged seventeen he crossed the Tamar and found work as a miner in Devon, where he quickly fell into bad company: 'I became the companion of drunkards, and during that time I was very near hell.' In 1821 he returned home, but continued to drink, neglecting his new wife and children, until two years later he rose in the middle of the night to pray, and never stopped. His brand of worship was muscular and exuberant, with voices raised in joy and energetic dancing; his sermons were filled with fiery attacks on drinkers, smokers and those who failed to respect the Sabbath. 'Old Smuttyface' was his nickname for the Devil; he once told his followers: 'if they were to put me in a barrel, I would shout glory out through the bunghole.'

On next to one of John Wesley's favourite preaching places – the amphitheatre at Gwennap Pit. I drop down the hill into the large village of Chacewater, where the Wheal Busy mine started producing tin as early as the 16th century. High Street leads back out of the valley, the landscape to either side dotted with the old workings of Poldice, Consolidated and United mines. Gwennap was considered the 'richest square mile in the old world' for much of the 18th century, but conditions for miners were appalling, the place described as a 'bleak desert, rendered still more doleful by the unhealthy appearance of its inhabitants'. The area offered rich pickings for Wesley's Church.

In 1762 Wesley was making his fourteenth visit to Cornwall and was due to preach outdoors at Carharrack, but the wind was too strong, so he was brought to Gwennap where a hole caused by a collapsed mine shaft had left a natural amphitheatre. He was to return seventeen times, making the bold claim that on one occasion 22,000 turned out to hear him. Wesley delighted in the way the shape of the pit amplified his voice: 'I believe God enabled me to speak that even those who stood farthest off could hear distinctly', he recalled.

I climb down the grass steps, the leather soles of my boots providing minimal adhesion. At the bottom I address an imaginary crowd, finding I only need to raise my voice slightly for it to echo around. A few miners' cottages abut the edges of the pit, like the workers' terraces touching the football stands in the art of L. S. Lowry. In 1806 the pit was made into a permanent place of worship capable of seating 1,500 around thirteen tiers of grass seating. This may be a church without a roof, but it has the same sense of quiet dignity often found in more conventional Cornish chapels. Now an annual Whit weekend service attempts to recreate the heady days of Wesleyan evangelism.

It's a fifteen-minute drive to Quenchwell, where a common-or-garden chapel sits on a crossroads. The arch above the door is inscribed with the date 1906 – this was a product of the last wave of energetic chapel building. The foundation stones include one honouring Billy Bray. Services stopped at Quenchwell in the 1990s, but it is still a place of worship, Cornish Methodists replaced by Cornish Muslims.

I'm still looking at the old dedications when Tipu Sultan Choudhury, General Secretary of the Cornwall Islamic Community Centre, drives in through the gates. Inside he apologises for the cold, and fiddles with the heating system before we take seats in the middle of the main prayer hall. Born in Bangladesh and raised in Tooting Bec in south London, as a young man he decided he wanted to be a restaurateur, but couldn't raise the funding to open in the capital. He had never heard of Cornwall when a friend told him the county was eager for more outlets offering food from the Indian subcontinent. The Taj Mahal in Penzance was his first venture in 1986; another branch followed in St Austell two years later.

At first he had to drive to Exeter to take part in Eid celebrations. In the early 1990s he and a few friends tried to book a room in the Truro Boys' Club for Friday prayers. When their application was refused, the story made the local press. 'It brought the Muslim community together,' Tipu recalls. 'Lots of people got in contact and we realised in between the catering industry, the medical profession and education, there were probably 300 of us here.'

In 1999 they raised the money to buy a house in Truro, but the quest for a suitable property was stymied by a rise in anti-Islamic sentiment after the 9/11 attacks on New York. Every time the group thought it had found suitable premises, it became a news story and the purchase fell through. Prayers continued in a room lent by Truro College, in the village hall at Tresillian and at the Truro Quaker Meeting House until finally, in 2008, the community bought the chapel at Quenchwell. Soon after the purchase someone broke in and daubed the building's interior walls with racist graffiti; in one sickening attack a pig's head, attached to a cross, was nailed to the front door. 'That seems a long time ago,' says Tipu. 'This is our thirteenth year here. Dare I say, I leave the gates open almost every week and we've not had any worries or problems.'

A floor divides what would have once been a single worship space into two levels. Above is the room where Quranic studies, children's activities and engagement and wedding parties take place – around the edge visitors must duck their heads to avoid the heavy beams. Downstairs the old wooden boards have been covered with a dark-green and gold carpet, its pattern thirty degrees off kilter, so that those praying directly face Mecca.

Tipu points out the minbar, from where the imam delivers his sermon, explaining it is made from the carved wooden steps that the Methodist preacher would once have climbed to deliver their weekly address. He estimates that there are now around 2,000 Muslims in Cornwall. Last year Eid prayers had to be held twice at Quenchwell and still not everyone could fit in. So far Cornish Muslims have mainly come from the Bangladeshi and Pakistani diaspora, but that is beginning to change. 'Now we have Turkish boys in the kebab houses – they are coming forward and showing interest and sincerity. And since Brexit Muslims from central Europe have come here to do seasonal work on the farms . . . quite a group came to pray here during the summer.'

Some heat is finally coming from the radiators, but it is time for me to leave Tipu to his work. I first met him here ten years ago – will he still be improving life for Cornish Muslims at the end of this decade? 'After thirty years I feel ready to hand leadership on to the next generation,' he says. 'Upcountry people fight and lobby over these positions – yet here I am, trying to give up responsibility and no one wants to take over!' We laugh as I pull my boots back on and say farewell to this optimistic man who has done so much to fight discrimination and managed to create a home for one of Cornwall's least visible faiths.

My last destination is Ponsanooth, home to one of the architectural masterworks of Methodism. The main road takes me along the top of Restronguet Creek, with a view over to Devoran. Today it is a prosperous village favoured by commuters working in Truro or Falmouth. In the middle of the 19th century it was the busiest mineral port in Cornwall, its quayside lined with railway sidings from where copper ore was loaded onto waiting ships. The docks and the land around were owned by the Ager-Robartes family of Lanhydrock, who realised their already profitable asset would only increase in value if they built a settlement beside it. Houses, shops, pubs, an institute, a chapel and a post office soon appeared. John Loughborough Pearson, who would later be architect of Truro Cathedral, built a parish church. A brochure promised potential residents 'a southern aspect on a gentle declivity... commanding the most picturesque scenery... few situations present such advantages for the Retirement of the Wealthy, or for the spirited Enterprise of Trading and Commercial Men.'

A canopy of trees turns the road into a tunnel as it approaches Perranarworthal. A Gothic lodge-cottage sits on the edge of the carriageway, the lane next to it leading up to Tullimaar, the house where the novelist William Golding, author of *Lord of the Flies*, lived from 1985 until his death eight years later. The Newquay-born writer was one of a long line of distinguished residents including Sarah Parkin, mistress to George III, the diarist Francis Kilvert, the Romanian-French writer Princess Marthe Bibesco, and General Eisenhower, who stayed there in the weeks leading up to D-Day.

Across the road the narrow channel of the Kennall River runs in the middle of what was once an open creek, long since silted up by centuries of mine tailings, the residue of stone left behind after the precious minerals have been flushed out. Boats sailed up here to unload timber to be used as pit props. The name of the local pub, the Norway Inn, is a reminder of the source of the wood. Large beam engines were built for the mines at Perran Foundry. The business, owned by the Foxes of Falmouth, opened in 1791 and ran for ninety years. Throughout the twentieth century the site lay derelict, an impassive sprawl of crumbling industrial architecture. Now it has been reclaimed for housing.

Soon after the Ponsanooth turn I spot its Methodist palace. Built high on Chapel Hill, the truncated pediment that dresses its façade is visible across the village. It is a building of uncommon elegance, one of the finest chapels in Cornwall, thought to be the work of a local carpenter-architect, John Trevena. The love and care put into cutting the ashlar granite blocks is evident. The upper windows are round-headed with dainty tracery; an imposing flight of steps leads to double doors that sit under a fanlight window with a three-centred arch above. Inside, an oval gallery seems to float above the highly polished pews, its weight borne by delicate Tuscan columns.

The chapel is now a much-loved liability. Chris Trewern, its steward, tells me the village treasures the building, but its running costs are way beyond what can now be afforded. Its Grade II starred status means few changes can be made. 'We had the arts minister come to visit, and we all sat together in the gallery admiring the place. But I told him he was asking a small community to keep a museum for the country, and I'm not sure that's really fair.'

For two years the building was up for sale. Many people came to view but there were no realistic purchasers, and it was taken

off the market. Now the parish council has commissioned a feasibility study into its future. Chris says that Historic England, the body that protects old buildings, has become more open to the idea of changes that would make it suitable for other uses, but it is hard to see what they might be. It is too big to turn into a house. If it was somewhere else it could be a concert hall, its acoustics perfect for chamber music, or an in-the-round theatre, or a place to showcase circus or dance skills. It could become a restaurant; Wetherspoons (cover your ears, John and Charles Wesley) would turn it into a spectacular pub. But all these fantasies quickly wither – the village already has plenty of community spaces, and who would come to performances here? There are near neighbours, no parking, little in the way of public transport, and the cost of heating the barn-sized structure in winter would be ruinous.

Once the heat produced by hundreds of worshippers kept it warm. A rough-and-ready chapel opened on this site in 1807, but was quickly deemed too small for the village. It was pulled down, and its replacement opened in 1813. Within three decades it had run out of space too. The chapel committee met on Christmas Eve 1842, and declared their ambition to build a bigger, grander church. In October 1843 the new building hosted its first service. Even accepting the fervour of 19th-century Methodism, it was a striking achievement. Plans drawn, predecessor demolished, foundation stones laid, stone carved, walls topped out and roofed, interior decorated and furnished – all in nine months. The chapel has space for 600 but in recent years a turnout of twenty has been considered a good weekly congregation. In 2019, it was decided to move the Sunday morning service to the village community hall. For now, Ponsanooth's grand chapel sits empty, awaiting another Methodist revival.

CHAPTER 3

Born of the Sea

Until Mum died, our family routine on a Sunday scarcely varied. Church or chapel took up the morning. A roast lunch was served on the dot of one o'clock. If it was pork last Sunday it would be chicken the following week and then lamb seven days later. Beef only made an appearance on special occasions. There were always plenty of vegetables but my father would exercise tight portion control over the meat to ensure enough was left to have cold with jacket potatoes for Monday-night supper.

The afternoon passed in a gentle haze of boredom, until it was time for Mum and me to visit my grandparents, Agnes and Fred, six miles away in Coverack. The main attraction for me was the chance to watch television. The air was always thick with cigarette smoke; the adults would drink strong gin and tonics while I was served a sugary combination of Mr Kipling Battenberg cake or French Fancies, accompanied by a bottle of Coca-Cola.

In summer the curtains were drawn tight against the glare of the sun on the sea outside. I would perch on a stool, my nose close to the screen, and watch the children's drama. Adaptations of Charles Dickens were my favourite – I sat transfixed through *Dombey and Son, Great Expectations, The Old Curiosity Shop, A Tale of Two Cities*. When *Holiday* started the adults stopped talking. Cliff Michelmore was the host, introducing sunny films from

faraway places, including regular reports from Frank and Nesta Bough who seemed to be on a never-ending road trip through France. The news followed, read by Richard Baker or Kenneth Kendall, the latter soon to become a figure of local interest when he retired to St Martin. The end credits for *Songs of Praise* were normally our cue to leave, though sometimes we'd stay on for a big series like *The Onedin Line* or *All Creatures Great and Small*, or switch over to BBC2 for *Call My Bluff*, which I'd laugh along with even when I didn't quite get the joke.

* * *

Coverack's position, on the south-west corner of the Lizard Peninsula, is near perfect. The crescent-shaped village sits on the edge of a bay that stretches between Chynhalls Point and Lowland Point. At low tide an expanse of sandy beach provides for safe swimming. The two-centuries-old harbour draws the eye, its granite quay protected by Dollar Point and crowned by the village pub, the Paris Hotel. Whitewashed buildings and a high sea wall frame the scene. The cottages near to the quay are the oldest; behind them stand larger Victorian and Edwardian houses, with modern homes lining the crest of the hill. The different periods of Coverack's development seem as clearly marked as the rings that reveal the age of a tree.

Agnes and Fred Blackwood were the local doctors, general practitioners with a surgery up the hill in St Keverne. They knew all their patients well – their names, troubles and concerns. Agnes liked to see hers in the consulting room; Fred would make the house calls in his Rover saloon, a bulging leather gladstone bag left on the back seat, the tube of a stethoscope laced through its handles. Sometimes there would be a late-night knock on the door with a request to attend an emergency. When a baby had been safely delivered, a bag of freshly caught fish or a brace of pheasant would often appear on the doorstep the next morning.

They had met as medical students in Plymouth and married at All Souls Church, Langham Place in London in 1928, the year work started on the construction of Broadcasting House, the BBC headquarters next door. During World War Two Agnes researched diseases in a pathology lab in Sunderland while Fred was the surgeon-in-charge of a hospital in Sedgefield, County Durham. As the fighting came to its end, they settled in Coverack, living at Widegates, a house on the hill that leads down into the village.

On a spring day in 1953, after a service at St Keverne Church, my parents' wedding reception was held at Widegates. A week later the *Helston Packet* ran a photo of my parents using my father's regimental sword to cut their three-tier wedding cake. She was twenty-two; he was four years her senior. They make a beautiful couple – my father handsome and commanding, my mother looking graceful, delicate and extremely young, someone still in the early stages of adulthood.

My grandfather had been introduced to Coverack as a child. His father, a doctor in Camborne, owned a parcel of land on the seafront, where he had installed a military-surplus Nissen hut. The Retreat, as it became known, provided basic accommodation for the family – there was no hot water or heating, the kitchen was rudimentary, the doors opened onto a rough garden running down to the sea. In the 1970s the hut was removed and replaced with a modern house that my grandparents named Landfall, after a novel by Nevil Shute. They retired into the upstairs flat, and rented the one underneath as a holiday let.

Its location was the selling point. Visitors ate off the chipped remnants of various family dinner services, sat and slept on a motley selection of second-hand furniture and tried to find heat on chilly nights from a three-bar electric fire fed by a coin meter. For a while my father took responsibility for letting the place, each January and February advertising its charms in the classified section of *The Lady*. On Saturdays during the summer I would help scrub away at the black mould around the shower surround, move the sitting-room sideboard and sofa to vacuum underneath, and wash pans left greasy by the paying guests.

The holidaymakers who migrate west every year are a vital element of the story of Cornwall. The historical impact of their presence, and the effect it continues to have today, is something that I will encounter multiple times on this journey. Visitors underwrite the Cornish economy and support a vast number of jobs, but many of them are poorly paid and seasonal. While there is a certain pride to be taken from the knowledge that people return here year after year, it is tempered by the understanding that tourism has dramatically changed the ecology of some parts of Cornwall, perhaps forever.

It was the coming of the railway to Cornwall that started the holiday business in Coverack. In 1887 a branch line to Helston made the village even more accessible. The Headland Hotel opened at the very start of the new century, promising 'bathing, boating and fishing' and 'electric lighting throughout'. In 1905 it was destroyed by fire, but its proprietor, George Harvey, quickly rebuilt it, running a horse bus to connect with the train, 'for the convenience of hotel visitors and villagers'. After the First World War he purchased a Ford Model T to serve as hotel taxi.

As Coverack's popularity grew, villagers realised they could supplement their income by offering their spare rooms for bed and breakfast, opening cafés in their gardens, and using their boats to transport those wanting to fish or swim in isolated local coves. But for most of the 20th century the real money was still in fishing, farming and related local trades. In the early 1980s, as I earned my pocket money by helping with the cleaning, Landfall was one of just a handful of holiday cottages. Ben and Georgia Roskilly welcomed campers in their fields at Penmarth Farm; full-service accommodation with breakfast and *table d'hôte* dinner was available at The Bay or the Headland Hotel, but tourism's grip on Coverack had not become even firm, let alone tight.

* * *

It's the middle of January and a team of volunteers are taking down Coverack's Christmas lights. They carefully roll up the multicoloured strings of bulbs that run the length of the sea wall, from the bus shelter to the tip of the harbour pier. The wooden frames that light up to show fishing boats, dolphins, Christmas puddings, tractors, helicopters and crosses, are stacked in high piles ready to go back into storage for another year. A woman walks by and I catch her comment to her friend about how good this year's display has been. 'Better than Mousehole,' she says. I hope the men hear her – there is a long-established rivalry between residents of Coverack and Mousehole, Cadgwith,

Angarrack, Porthleven, Newlyn and other west Cornwall villages as to which produces the best seasonal illuminations.

The Christmas lights team are not the only ones working today. There is a steady hammering as a holiday-let called The Loft undergoes a major refurbishment. A thatcher is unloading bales of reeds as he prepares to renew the roof on Trevarrow; windows are being replaced at the Harbour Lights Café. The first months of the year are the time to make do and mend before the tourists come back at Easter.

Mill Road runs along the top of the beach. As I walk along it recollections of childhood days flood back – there is sand between the toes of my bare feet as I skip along the hot tarmac and dodge the cars to get to Brenda's General Stores to buy an ice lolly with the coins given to me by an elder brother. Brenda Daw opened her shop in 1964, its interior a chaotic cave of tinned, dried and fresh food, wine, beer and pop, and the shrimping nets, cotton hats and sunblock required by the visitors. It is closed today – a few years back the grocery trade was abandoned and now it only opens in the summer, its stock limited to non-perishable items.

In front of the shop, steps lead down to the beach, where a line of shingle soon turns into an expanse of sand. At low tide you can walk across the rocks to the harbour – this morning the tide is in, a boat is unloading its overnight catch. Out in the bay, another fisherman attends to his crab and lobster pots, the gulls wheeling around him in the hope of snatching his bait. There are five fishing boats moored in the harbour, and another six rest on the quayside. These are small craft – a couple have a wheelhouse that offers limited protection from squally seas, but most are completely open to the elements.

The quay that stretches protectively around the harbour basin was built in 1724 – it feels remarkable that it is still used for its original purpose, that after 300 years the fish trade has not been eliminated in favour of the easier buck of tourism. But the future of Coverack hangs in the balance: will it manage to remain a mixed community, a place that is the year-round home to a socially and economically diverse population, or will it shift further towards seaside fantasy mode, with wealthy visitors its primary interest, a new member of a club that includes Helford, Rock, Fowey, and perhaps Padstow and St Ives?

The committee of volunteers de-rigging the Christmas lights indicate that there are still people who want to make a proper community here. Joan Kearsley moved to Coverack half a century ago with her late husband. Today she is to be found leading many village endeavours including a lunch club for single people that meets eighteen times a year at the church hall. She is proud of the quality of the food served and of the mix of diners: locals, whose families have been in the village for generations, long-established incomers like herself, and recent arrivals. 'It is not about being Cornish, it's about buying into village life,' Joan says, citing as another example the retirees who have offered to share their skills and teach basic oceanography, geology and French to local schoolchildren.

New settlers have been arriving in Coverack for decades and the changes resulting from their presence here have unfolded at a gentle pace. But in 2017, an unexpected, violent event prompted a debate about the future. On 18 July a freak storm over the downs above the village saw broad streams of water pour through streets and houses. There was no warning; a flood seemed to build up in a matter of minutes. The main road was blocked by what Parish Councillor Bill Frisken described as 'rocks the size of a double decker bus, pushed by the water as if they were pebbles'. Vehicles were piled on top of each other in the car-park, the enormous hailstones that fell left what looked like bullet holes in the perspex panels on Bill's conservatory.

Half the properties in the village were affected; my aunt Gilly, who now lives in the old Landfall rental flat, spent the night with no electricity and six inches of water on the floor around her bed. The flood happened at the very start of the school holidays, Coverack's busiest period – and many of the summer visitors joined in the great clean-up, shovelling mud, stripping sodden carpets and clearing broken glass from the beach. But others packed up their cars and returned home, locking their undamaged holiday properties firmly shut, and deflecting any gentle hints that they might offer them to those temporarily left homeless.

Joan Kearsley is certainly not anti-tourist. 'A few years back we had a campaign to collect money to improve the school,' she tells me. 'We raised £130,000, and most of that came from summer visitors. But it is a matter of balance.' She raises her eyes when I ask her about the five substantial houses built in the garden of a 1930s residence just up the hill. Most of these new developments become second homes, she says, 'sometimes used for just a matter of nights each year'. All this building puts pressure on services like water, sewerage and parking. 'People bring two cars with them and then the locals come home from work and find there is nowhere for them.' Her village action group went as far as issuing unofficial parking permits to encourage visitors to think about the impact they make.

None of the new-builds are targeted at the local market; there is nothing close to affordable housing to buy or let in Coverack. Joan tells me about several young families who have tried out village life by renting holiday units over the winter months. 'When the spring comes they have to move and there is nowhere else local for them to go.' As a result the village school is down to twenty-five pupils, and its junior class is threatened with closure. 'We have been given two years to improve numbers,' says Joan, who hopes planned after-school activities four nights a week will make the school attractive to working parents in neighbouring villages.

When the local council floated the idea of selling part of the village car-park for market-value housing, many saw red and a meeting was convened to discuss Coverack's future. People were asked to share their opinions, writing on sheets of A2 paper. The page titled 'Housing' attracted the most comments. Joan unrolls it for me, and I read what people wrote. Over and over again the same concerns are expressed – 'No more holiday homes', 'affordable housing desperately needed', 'houses are needed that will be lived in all year', 'homes for young people to bring children and life to the village', 'low cost housing for young people to keep village facilities going, school, Post Office, shops etc.'

* * *

North Corner is the most desirable part of Coverack. Its houses are set along a gently rising road that runs along the top of the foreshore, heading east away from the village. There is no passing traffic other than walkers on the coast path towards Lowland Point. Trophy residences with balconies, conservatories and garden rooms enjoy uninterrupted views out to sea. Planning notices pinned to telegraph poles give details of anticipated new developments to be shoehorned into sites that were once garages or gardens.

Landfall is at the village end, by the bus-stop and the green where stone benches mark Queen Elizabeth's Silver, Diamond and Platinum Jubilees. I have often wondered what it looked like here before my grandparents built their house. In family albums there are a few shots of 1960s tea parties, but nothing that actually shows The Retreat itself. I have pretty much given up on ever finding a picture, when one day I come across images of it online, in footage from a film made in Coverack in 1949.

Caught in a panoramic wide shot taken from the harbour, the tin, wood and breeze-block structure perches on the side of a bluff that seems to rise straight up from the beach. North Corner looks bare; a broad expanse of garden separates Blackwood land from that of the Tregarthens up the hill. Apart from a couple of thatched cottages and one substantial villa, the area is still untouched.

Born of the Sea takes the viewer on a thorough tour of post-war Coverack. Little of the village escapes the camera's eye. The film is no more than a footnote in the history of British cinema – a 42-minute-long B-movie of the kind designed to bulk up a night at the pictures. In the trade these films were known as 'three weekers' – the length of time they took to make. The format was often used to break in new talent, though director Anthony Mavrogordato never seems to have made another film.

The plot is simple but compelling – a stricken ketch fires its emergency flare and the lifeboat is launched. The only survivor of the shipwreck is a tiny baby, and when no relatives can be traced, he is taken in, named George, and raised by the village. He grows from infant to boy to man, and as soon as he is eighteen, he joins the lifeboat crew himself. Soon after, in the course of another mercy mission, he is lost at sea.

The opening scenes paint a vivid picture of daily life, much of it set out in a clunky voice-over delivered in RP accent by the film's one professional actor: 'To me high tide and low tide just mean the level of the water but to these fishermen they are more important than the 8.30 to town.'

We watch the men laying crab and lobster pots, or heading further out in search of grey mullet, a fish that fetches a good price from the Newlyn merchant who visits each Monday. At the bottom of the slipway a fisherman guts a haddock for the postmistress; above the harbour Ben Polglaze thatches his cottage with help from his boy Adam; up the hill at Trenoweth farm, girls from the village do back-breaking work picking the daffodil crop. The launch of the lifeboat is captured in minute detail: the crew mustered and ready to sail in five and a quarter minutes. The chains are released and the craft slides majestically down the slipway, a camera on board capturing a halo of salty spray as the boat hits the water.

It is not difficult to imagine what life must have been like in a Cornish fishing village three-quarters of a century ago, but it is thrilling to be able to see it for real. Though the film is a curious mix of fantasy and reality, drama and documentary, the staged and the spontaneous, it is a rich piece of archive. 'All the players are natives in the fishing village of Coverack', reads a slide at the start. 'They have been filmed going about their everyday work with its hazards, disappointments and rejoicings.' The amateur cast help drive home the idea of a community bound tightly together. The infant survivor is welcomed without question; Mrs Penlee sends over the family cradle in which she raised her seventeen children, pupils from the school bring warm clothes, eccentric Charlie Jarr gives the item he values most, a ship-in-a-bottle that he made as a boy. As the narrator solemnly tells us, each person in Coverack has a two-hundredth share in young George – he is the village's son. One scene takes the viewer along the road that leads from harbour to church. Neighbours are in and out of each other's houses, front doors are left wide open, revealing to the camera low beams, smoke-stained walls and heavy furniture.

Today these same rooms are painted in bright pastel colours with pale pine tables dressed with red gingham or duck-egg-blue oilcloth. Blue-and-white striped Cornishware mugs sit on sideboards, and above the nooks that once housed Cornish range stoves are positive signs, 'Live life in flipflops', 'Kitchen Closed, I'm at the Beach' – generic holiday-home tat.

When the film was made these cottages were the homes of locals whose families had lived in Coverack for generations. Now, between Coastguard Cottages and the top of the hill by the church, I count nearly a dozen homes kitted out like this. Others wear their contemporary identity even more overtly – eleven have key safes to facilitate easy access for new arrivals, another seven have discreet notices in the window with details of websites where a weekend or week's rental can be arranged.

Towards the end of January I take an early-evening walk through Coverack. A football match or film is playing on the odd television, but most of the houses are dead, empty, locked shut for the winter. There is no chance of finding the villagers needed if one wanted to reshoot *Born of the Sea* today.

It is dangerous to idealise the past; for some the arrival of the movie crew will have been a brief moment of happiness in a generally tough, unrewarding life that offered few opportunities for escape or advancement. Maybe even in 1949 there was something unreal about the fantasy of a village coming together as one in the face of a crisis. Or perhaps some of the sense of community shown on screen has survived, as indicated by the proud Christmas lights display and the mutual aid many offered each other after the flood. But watching the film again, it is hard not to conclude that something has been lost. The incomers should not take the blame alone; the children and grandchildren of some of the actors will have helped change the village themselves by cashing in and selling their cottages to be turned into holiday homes. Open doors and burning lights don't automatically signify happiness, but they feel more encouraging than key safes and dark windows.

*

In the opening frames of *Born of the Sea* the waves crash over the rocks beyond the harbour – an ever-present, uncontrollable force that the villagers treat with gratitude, respect and fear. The last scene finds the community coming to terms with the loss of its adopted son. In church the congregation sing the sailor's hymn, 'Eternal Father Strong to Save': 'O hear us when we cry to Thee / For those in peril on the sea.'

If the picture has a hero it is the lifeboat coxswain Archie Rowe. He was already cherished before the film, having led a clutch of successful RNLI missions, including a rescue operation in March 1941 after the bombing of a Polish steamer, *Cieszyn*. Rowe and his men saved the crew despite the real threat from enemy aircraft that still lurked in the skies above.

He became even more famous in 1958 when he was chosen as a subject of the television series *This Is Your Life*. A BBC researcher used the cover of a family holiday to come to Coverack and sniff out stories about Rowe. A fake trail was laid to get him to London from where the show was broadcast. Summoned to an urgent meeting with the lawyer of his recently widowed sister, he was looked after by a Coverack man living in the capital, who happily had managed to secure a couple of tickets to be in the studio audience at the BBC Television Theatre in Shepherd's Bush. On arrival Rowe was cornered by the avuncular host Eamonn Andrews, who waved his red book and announced the coxswain was to be that week's subject. In front of a cloth painted with a picture of the Paris Hotel, a line-up of locals and rescued sailors appeared on stage to praise Rowe's seamanship and bravery, one awarding him the title 'Uncrowned King of Coverack'.

Vera Lynn, Anna Neagle, Norman Wisdom and Barbara Cartland were among other *This Is Your Life* subjects that season. Rowe stood in sharp contrast, a man who was doing no more than what he saw as his duty, never seeking fame or fortune.

He looks a bit bemused in photographs from the night, but his integrity and shy warmth shines through just as it had in *Born of the Sea* a decade earlier.

The lifeboat seen in the film was the 36ft Liverpool Class vessel *The Three Sisters*. It was replaced in 1954 by the 42ft *William Taylor of Oldham*. Just under two decades later the RNLI downgraded its Coverack station and *William Taylor* was transferred to Arklow in County Wicklow. An inflatable inshore craft, so small it was not considered worthy of a name, was the village's last lifeboat, its final operation on 30 July 1978 – the rescue of someone who had drifted too far from the beach on an airbed.

Today all-weather RNLI boats at the Lizard, Falmouth and Newlyn offer support to mariners in trouble off Cornwall's far-south coast. The barnacle-encrusted slip at Coverack rusts gently away, the boathouse opening in summer to serve fish and chips to crowds of visitors.

CHAPTER 4

The Manacles

It was raining hard last night and the wind is still up as I walk towards Lowland Point, half an hour east from the harbour at Coverack. The ground is sodden and several times my feet sink deep into the mossy, springy soil. Out to sea the rolling waves are topped with a fine head of white foam. Two ships pass along the horizon. One is a bulk carrier that sits high in the water, its holds empty of the cargo of steel, cement or grain it might normally carry; the other is a long, thin vessel stacked high with containers that from this distance look like grey, green and rust-red Lego bricks. A soft drizzle gently kisses my cheeks and my ears process the unceasing white noise of the ocean. Looking back towards the village I can just see the lifeboat slipway. Coverack got its first rescue boat in 1901 – *Constance Melanie*. It was a century late.

The Manacles lie just beyond Lowland Point, a treacherous rake of rocks that run a mile and a half out to sea and stretch out two miles wide. Some of the stones and clusters stand proud of the water, others break through when the tide is low, many are submerged and hidden. They are the wreckers of hundreds of ships and the killers of untold numbers of people. On a map showing all the craft that have foundered here, there are so many names that they jostle for space, blocking each other out.

I walk down to the water's edge, stones replacing grass underfoot, the noise made by the impact of my boots rising and getting shriller as the pebbles get smaller. From this distance the tips of the visible rocks look almost benign, shining black stone polished smooth by the swell. It is hard to imagine the chaotic scenes that have played out where I am standing – the fading lights of ships lying prone; survivors scrabbling for dry land, too exhausted to cry out; human bodies and bits of cargo and maritime flotsam and jetsam washed ashore by the never-ceasing, crashing waves.

On 22 January 1809, two separate wrecks killed in excess of 200 here. The transport ship *Dispatch* was the first to be breached, at about 3.30 a.m. It was sailing home from Coruña in Spain, carrying 70 men and three officers of the 7th Light Dragoons. They were survivors of the Peninsular War, ragged and weak after fleeing Napoleon's French soldiers. Conditions were appalling as they approached the Cornish coast, with snow falling and winds running at hurricane force. Caught on the Manacles, the ship quickly broke up and all but seven of the soldiers died.

An hour and a half later His Majesty's Brig of War *Primrose* was sunk. It had 120 officers and men, and six passengers on board; 'only one poor lad was preserved from the dreadful catastrophe' – John Meaghan, rescued by a boat manned by six Porthoustock fishermen. Some maritime historians suggest that, including the crews of the two ships, as many as 270 drowned that morning; only 110 bodies were recovered.

While poor weather conditions were to blame for the wrecking of the *Dispatch* and the *Primrose*, gross negligence did for the emigrant ship *John*. It had left Plymouth at lunchtime on 3 May 1855, bound for Quebec. Its manifest listed 279 on board – 149 adults, 98 children, 16 infants in arms and 16 crew. As the ship prepared to pass Lizard Point it was far too close to land. At 9.30 p.m. the able seaman at the helm shouted, 'Fishing boats ahead', but what he had seen were not smaller craft, but the Manacles. A minute later the *John* was on the rocks, control of its rudder was lost, and water soon started leaking in.

Despite being no more than 500 yards from land, the captain, Edward Rawle, refused to launch the large lifeboats, telling passengers repeatedly that they should stay put, as help would soon come. Several survivors testified as to his panic-stricken demeanour at the time. 'He said he was a ruined man, and should not see his owner any more,' recalled Michael Stadden, a cobbler from Launceston. Captain Rawle was at pains to point out that he had not been drinking before his ship collided with the rocks. 'You see that I am not drunk,' he demanded of one passenger, who noted: 'no one that I had heard had spoken to him on that matter.'

Fishermen from Coverack and Porthoustock soon reached the scene and managed to save as many as 50, but at least 190 died. The crew put their own interests first. The arriving rescue boats found them calmly awaiting collection, carrying their bags with them and seemingly oblivious to the panic of the passengers still on board.

In the aftermath, the bodies of scores of children were laid out just above the high water line, awaiting identification. Many of the passengers were Cornish – labourers and skilled crafts-men including masons, shoemakers, and carpenters emigrating with their families in the hope of escaping poverty at home and making a new life in Canada. The Board of Trade inquiry that followed criticised the captain and his company for their callous behaviour. They were also condemned by the press: 'We cannot understand how a ship that left Plymouth at 2 o' clock should at 9 30 p.m. come plump upon the Manacles', observed *The Times*. 'There must have been the very grossest carelessness – the most utter absence of ordinary nautical skill, to admit of such a result.'

The great chronicler of the Manacles' wrecks was Canon William Diggens, vicar of St Keverne between 1896 and 1913. He had started his ecclesiastical career as a curate in Hulme, Manchester. Eleven years in Australia followed, as rector of Rockhampton, Queensland, and then six in Dunedin, New Zealand. During his years in Cornwall he dedicated much time to writing an account of the history of his parish, detailing its traditions, its people and its shipwrecks. Two years after he took up his post, he became part of the story himself when he conducted the funerals of some of those drowned in the sinking of the SS *Mohegan*.

Built in Hull, the Atlantic Transport Company liner had made its maiden transatlantic journey in July 1898 as the *Cleopatra*. The crossing exposed a long list of faults on board that needed to be fixed. With the work done and a new name, it sailed for New York, leaving Gravesend on 13 October, with fifty-three passengers, ninety-seven crew and six or seven cattlemen on board, the latter returning on a free passage after escorting their bovine stock from America to England.

There was a mixed cargo in *Mohegan*'s holds, including tin, antimony, lead, creosote, church ornaments, artificial flowers, spirits, beer and prunes. After dropping the pilot at Dover it continued down the English Channel. Early the next evening, as the ship prepared to skirt around the southern tip of Cornwall, there was no sense of anything unusual about the course it was taking. The passengers, dressed in elegant gowns and formal evening wear, were just sitting down for dinner when at 6.50 p.m., *Mohegan* ploughed into the Manacles.

At the subsequent inquiry, a survivor remembered the first impact 'not as a solid shock, but as a grating noise, more like a cable running out than anything else.' The Vase Rock tore off the ship's rudder; immediately it hit another rock, the momentum pushing the vessel a further 450 yards into the inner Manacles, where finally another set of stones ripped out much of the starboard side. Within minutes the ship was listing. Water poured in and quickly reached the dynamos, extinguishing the electric light. As there was no time to locate the emergency oil lamps, the ship was left in darkness. It is not hard to imagine the immediate panic that followed.

The disaster had already been anticipated by the coxswain of the Porthoustock lifeboat, James Hill, who had been mystified when he saw the lights of a large ship heading directly towards the shore. He had mustered his crew and had his boat launched within twenty-five minutes.

Hill was able to pick up several people from the ship's own lifeboats; more were saved when a line was attached to the sinking vessel. The inquiry heard that John Juddery, one of *Mohegan*'s quartermasters, swam out to the rescue boat, and after drinking some brandy swam back with a line around him, over which sixteen people sheltering in the mizzen rigging were safely evacuated. With Coverack yet to receive its lifeboat, rescue

83

vessels from Cadgwith, Lizard and Falmouth were all launched, though only the Falmouth crew found any survivors, a man and a boy.

The dead included Charles Duncan, father of the dancer Isadora Duncan. Five members of one family perished – Thomas Worthington King, his wife Gertrude, their sons Rufus and Anthony, aged eleven and seven respectively, and Gertrude's mother, a Mrs Weller. They were returning from their summer residence at Carbis Bay to their home at Saratoga, New York. Mrs King's English maid Ellen Elliot also died but Mr King's valet Joseph O'Rourke avoided death by climbing high up the rigging.

Other survivors included Amelia Compton Swift, an amateur actress 'well known in Chicago society', and Maude Roudez, an opera singer. Her mother, who was travelling with her, was not so lucky. Having survived the initial stages of the disaster, she died when she was accidentally struck by an axe being used to free another passenger. 'Ship wrecked. Mother Dead. I am alright', her daughter wrote in a cable home. Roudez had spent the previous two years singing in the company of the Royal Opera House, Covent Garden. Subsequently her stage costumes were among the lots offered in a London auction of goods salvaged from *Mohegan*. Despite the shock she must have suffered, she ploughed on with her career – on 12 November 1898, less than a month after the shipwreck, she made her Chicago debut singing Flora in *La traviata*, and a month later was Mercédès in *Carmen* at the Metropolitan Opera New York.

SS *Mohegan* was a new ship in good order. Richard Griffiths, its captain, was a highly experienced mariner who had crossed the Atlantic 200 times. His crew were hard-working and committed, and unlike the men of the *John*, did not abandon their vessel. 'Seldom had gone to sea a ship better equipped, both as regarded herself and as regarded her crew and officers,' noted the Board of Trade inquiry, which went out of its way to praise their 'bravery and unselfishness'.

The main question for investigators was why had *Mohegan* been anywhere near the Manacles? The inquiry concluded the ship had simply taken the wrong course. Inevitably few were satisfied with that analysis, and numerous theories were presented, often in letters to newspapers. Many related to the ship's compass. Could it have been skewed by some magnetic attraction from the Manacles themselves, or affected by the ship's on-board electric system? Captain Griffiths had lost his right eye some years previously – did he simply misread his instruments? The master was presumed drowned along with all the senior officers who might have born witness to what had happened; the surviving sailors simply spoke of Griffiths' good seamanship and skill at maintaining discipline.*

At least 106 died. The survivors were taken in by locals in Porthoustock, St Keverne and Coverack, the crew given sanctuary at the Royal Cornwall Sailors Home in Falmouth. Many of the

---

*Did Captain Griffiths actually drown that night? In his highly detailed study *Mohegan – the Cornish Titanic* Chris Holwill notes that after the sinking there were many rumours and conspiracy theories about what had happened to the captain. According to some locals he was seen climbing out of a lifeboat, dressed in either a boiler suit or evening dress. Did he have a grudge against the company and sink the ship deliberately? Others reported seeing him in New York; an American newspaper reported that he was a naturalised US citizen. Several months after the shipwreck the headless body of a man wearing the uniform of an Atlantic Transport Company captain was found in Caernarvon Bay by a fisherman. It was assumed to be that of Griffiths, the tides having carried his corpse from Cornwall. Or had he actually made a secret return to Wales to find sanctuary and later died by suicide? This, and many other strange tales relating to the *Mohegan*, make for good reading.

dead were first laid out in St Keverne Church. It was reported that one shop in Penzance was doing a good trade in photographs of the corpses.

There was a sense of morbid fascination about much of the press coverage; representatives of major British and American publications were quickly dispatched to the scene. The *Graphic* published a special supplement, with an illustration of the process of identifying the dead on its cover. The *North-Eastern Daily Gazette* told of 'one poor lad of seventeen, who had come to identify his mother (and) spoke of her as the last relative he had in the world.' A dramatic illustration of *Mohegan* dropping beneath the waves, with tiny boats heading to its aid, graced the front page of the *Christian Herald*. Soon after, the much-mocked Scottish master of doggerel poetry, William McGonagall, made the wreck the subject of one of his last poems:

> *For God's sake, boys, get clear, if ye can,*
> *Were the captain's last words spoken like a brave man;*
> *Then he and the officers sank with the ship in the briny deep,*
> *Oh what a pitiful sight, 'tis enough to make one weep.*

Before the 19th century was done, one more ship ran aground at Lowland Point. SS *Paris* had started its journey at Southampton at noon on 20 May 1899, with nearly 800 passengers and crew on board. After a brief stop at Cherbourg it sailed for New York. At just after one o'clock the next morning it hit a hidden rock and came to a sudden halt. The passengers were woken and called to the deck, where all was calm, stewards distributing coffee, biscuits and stimulants. Passenger David Goldberg of Butte, Montana told the *Western Morning News* that 'there was an entire absence of actual disorder and no shrieking and supplications on the part of the passengers. A boat from Coverack was first on the scene, its crew were cheered as they came alongside the big liner.'

First light revealed the alarming sight of the masts of the *Mohegan* sticking out of the water nearby. But though the hold was flooded, SS *Paris* did not sink. *Dragon*, a tug from Falmouth, helped collect the passengers; later the mail bags were recovered and transported to Southampton, from where a German ship took them to America. Crowds from across west Cornwall travelled to Lowland Point to see the spectacular sight of the vast beached liner, 'like a great town', according to one local farmer. The Liverpool Salvage Company failed in its attempts to refloat the ship, despite bringing six tugs; a German firm finally freed it some weeks later. After major works in Belfast, the vessel saw another two decades' service.

With no funerals to put on, this time Canon Diggens could organise a service of thanksgiving. A few years later when the Redruth Brewery built a new pub on Coverack harbour in 1907 they named it the Paris Hotel. By then the village had finally got its own lifeboat, a direct result of the *Mohegan* and *Paris* incidents.

My grandmother Agnes once took me to visit Parc Behan, now the Coverack youth hostel. Together we ascended its grand staircase, salvaged from the Mohegan, the bannisters and panelling once admired by passengers making their way to dinner in the grand saloon. Many houses in Coverack had something from the ship – bits of metal or wood, fixtures and fittings, plates, deckchairs or lifebuoys washed up on local beaches or bought at salvage sales – a simple way of remembering those who had died in the tragedy.

At Lowland Point there is no commemorative marker to the hundreds of passengers and crew lost from ships broken by the Manacle Rocks. For that you have to head to St Keverne, two and a half miles away by road, little more than a mile by foot. Its church contains a series of memorials to those drowned here. For me it is a place freighted with family memories.

The Manacles' name is a transliteration of two Cornish words, *meyn* meaning stones, and *eglos* meaning church. Church Rocks. Even though satellite information is now used for maritime navigation, nautical charts still show the tower of St Keverne Church. From the spire the sea can be seen on three sides. To the north there is a clear view towards the castles at Pendennis and St Mawes, guardhouses of Falmouth's harbour and river estuary. The coast of Cornwall's Franco-Celtic sibling Brittany lies a hundred miles south-south-east. The Manacles are immediately due south.

The church sits in a corner of St Keverne Square, which it shares with two pubs and a general store. Several simple cottages used to stand in the centre, demolished to create space for the war memorial. Before their wedding breakfast at Coverack, this is where my parents got married. 'Military Wedding – Archway of Swords at St Keverne' was the headline in the *West Briton*, accompanied by comprehensive descriptions of the dresses and flowers of the bride and bridesmaids, a list of the principal attendees, and the detail that three clergy had officiated: two local rectors, and Canon J. J. Griffin of Glengariff, County Cork, my mother's uncle.

I don't think my father returned to the church for more than half a century – his next visit was in May 2004, when it was the location of my brother William's funeral. I read a poem. Afterwards, as I stepped down from the lectern, I looked across to Dad sitting in the front pew. His face was set firm and revealed nothing, the model of a stiff-upper-lipped ex-army man, deter- mined to keep his emotions to himself. Now I understand his mastery at building walls to keep his feelings safely contained – or

at least to stop others seeing in. I suspect some close to me would say I have inherited that skill. On that spring day most of us failed to contain our grief as the ritual of William's funeral was acted out. But not my father. A bit of me admired his absolute refusal to play along – why should anyone else get an insight into his thoughts about being back at the place where he had wed his late wife – and was now burying their eldest son?

I loved coming here as a child. Mum and I would often stop for a few minutes on the way to Coverack. A particular delight were the three sets of rood steps, little stairways carved into the wall that now lead nowhere. Once they would have taken priests up to balconies from where they would have addressed the congregation; they may have also led into the tiny chapels of the monastery first established on the site over a thousand years ago.

Today tea and coffee is served after the Sunday service, on

the very spot where the bodies of drowned *Mohegan* passengers were laid out awaiting identification. One of the pictures sold in Penzance shows around twenty victims fully dressed, boots and shoes still on their feet, their corpses half-wrapped in white shrouds. In subsequent images coffins are piled high behind the pews.

Some of the dead were embalmed by the village undertakers and then shipped to America for burial. Joseph O'Rourke's final task as valet to Thomas Worthington King was to accompany the bodies of his master and his family home to New York. More than forty victims were buried together in the churchyard in a mass grave, 13ft across, 20ft long and 10ft deep. A photograph shows six gravediggers at the bottom of the pit. Posies of flowers rest on the coffins around them, a crowd of onlookers gawp down from above. *Mohegan* is the only word inscribed on the base of the Cornish cross that marks the site.

Benjamin Franklin Fuller, a Boston timber merchant, was buried in an individual grave, as was twenty-three-year-old assistant deck steward, Charles Brownjohn, the mournful inscription on his gravestone reading: 'The devoted and only son of a widowed mother. He never said an unkind thing to her in his life.'

Nearby a small round-topped stone, not three feet tall, indicates the burial spot of the 120 drowned when the *John* sank, the flaking relief-carving showing the three-mast barque being thrown around on steep waves. Just behind, another stone marks the mass grave of those lost on the *Dispatch*, and to the left a Cornish cross stands in tribute to the dead of the *Primrose*. Together these graves form a significant maritime memorial, a simple tribute to hundreds who lost their lives at sea.

Above the wall that separates the church and the square sits a cannon salvaged from HMS *Primrose*. The ship's gudgeon, the socket that enables the rudder to move freely, is mounted inside the church. Above the main altar is a stained-glass window donated by the Atlantic Transport Company, owners of the *Mohegan*. A small slate plaque notes the death of James Hill, Porthoustock's heroic coxswain, and a man who knew the Manacles better than any other sailor.

Twelve decades have passed since the loss of the *Mohegan*; visits to this churchyard by descendants of its dead, or those of the other 19th-century Manacle wrecks, are rare. The gravestones are encrusted in lichen; some of the inscriptions have become hard to read. Today the sea off Lowland Point is a prime site for divers, who come from around the world to explore the wrecks lying just below the waterline.

I wonder how many walking the coast path around the point today think much about the terrible events that once happened here? Coverack, St Keverne and Porthoustock lent their sons to man the boats that helped save lives; villagers carried corpses from the sea; the parish church was used repeatedly as a makeshift mortuary, its clergy overseeing the funerals of a parade of victims who had no previous connection with the place; its residents opened their homes to give warm hospitality to both shocked survivors and grieving relatives. The names *Dispatch, Primrose, John* and *Mohegan* remain part of the history of this stretch of Cornish coast.

CHAPTER 5

Helston

Henry Trengrouse invented a remarkably simple way of reducing the death toll of shipwrecked sailors. On 29 December 1807 he was working in his carpenter's shop on Meneage Street in Helston when he heard of the loss of HMS *Anson*. He immediately set off on foot for nearby Loe Bar to see what he could do to help. The forty-four-gun man-o'-war had sailed from Falmouth bound for Brest, where it was to help enforce the blockade of the French port. Poor conditions at sea forced it to turn back. After failing to reach Falmouth the captain decided to await calmer weather and moored off the Bar. The winds did not abate, and one by one, *Anson*'s anchor cables snapped. The ship soon started to break up. Even though it was within shouting distance of the shore, the high surf prevented local boats from reaching the wreck. Trengrouse helped rescue a child and a man, but a conclusive figure for the number who died that day has never been established; estimates vary from 60 to 190.

Deeply frustrated at the rescuers' inability to assist the stricken sailors, Trengrouse determined he would find a way of ensuring such a disaster would never be repeated. He came up with the idea of a life-saving device that used a rocket to fire a lightweight line between ship and shore. Once secured, a length of heavy hawser rope would be dragged across the divide. In turn this would support a cradle seat – a *chaise volante*, as Trengrouse called it – that would be used to evacuate sailors.

Trengrouse dreamt of the equipment being part of the manifest of every British ship, and set off for London in 1808 hoping to interest the Admiralty in his invention. He soon discovered he had a rival, an inventor from East Anglia, Captain George Manby, who had had a similar idea when he witnessed HMS *Snipe* run aground off Great Yarmouth. The Manby Mortar and the Trengrouse Rocket were in direct competition. The Admiralty gave the Cornishman short shrift, with questions raised about whether his idea was even original. Dejected, Trengrouse returned to Helston, and spent a decade perfecting his apparatus, before trying to raise fresh interest. This time he was successful, a naval committee reporting that his was the 'best mode of gaining a communication with the shore for saving lives'.

But once again Trengrouse was to be disappointed by the London maritime bureaucrats, who announced they would purchase just twenty sets of equipment from him, after which the Ordnance Department would take over the manufacturing process. He would be paid just £50 compensation. Determined not to give up, he staged a demonstration of his machinery in Hyde Park, with rockets fired across the Serpentine, and a man drawn twice over the water, all this 'in the presence of the Duke of Sussex and several persons of distinction'. The Society of Arts awarded him their silver medal and 30 guineas, and Tsar Alexander I invited him to Russia, presenting him with a diamond ring.

Despite his energetic self-promotion, Trengrouse received little return on the £3,500 he had spent developing his invention. Shortly before his death in 1854, aged eighty-two, he told his son: 'if you live to be as old as I am, you will find my rocket apparatus all along our shores.' His prediction was correct. His invention, and variations on it, saved thousands of lives.

*

Henry Trengrouse is Helston's most famous son. His memorial stone in the church graveyard is topped with an anchor, the text noting that in his life's work he gave 'signal service to humanity'.

Nearly a century after his death he was cast back into the town's consciousness. In 1947 it was decided Helston deserved a post-war makeover, with a grand entrance leading into the town, an avenue sweeping down to Meneage Street, lined with much-needed social housing, and called Trengrouse Way.*

In the interests of the new a row of cottages was demolished, and a new estate laid out, with Cornish Unit houses, their pre-cast panel walls made of concrete produced from china clay spoils. A product of the Central Cornwall Concrete & Artificial Stone Co., at first the homes seemed to exemplify urban modernity and early tenants were delighted with their new accommodation. Tens of thousands were built, across the country. Decades later the problematic nature of the design became clear – the panels were vulnerable to decay, the houses started to suffer from damp, and they were hard to keep warm. In the 1980s, when the new Right to Buy legislation saw local authorities selling their housing stock, tenants found it was near impossible to get a mortgage on a Cornish Unit.

----

*Trengrouse also lent his name to a care home in Helston built by the county council in 1972. At the time the council's in-house architect's department was exploring how modernist architecture might sit within the dramatic Cornish landscape. Trengrouse House was the work of Mike Way, whose most celebrated building was a gloriously brutalist police station in Truro with a gently ascending entrance ramp, a wall of glass made of four tiers of floor-to-ceiling windows, and a briefing room perched high on concrete pillars. Inexplicably it was never listed, and was demolished in 2017. There is a gallery of pictures of the building on the Truro Civic Society website: trurocivicsociety.com

The ones that stand off Trengrouse Way are immediately recognisable; the slatted concrete panels have gone, replaced with a double layer of brick, but the distinctive, overhanging mansard roofs remain. They take their place alongside 16th-century doorways, Georgian mansions, Victorian memorials and 1930s shopfronts in Helston's rich architectural history. Though at present down-at-heel, this is one of Cornwall's finest towns.

Helston was once rich. Its prosperity can be traced back to 1305 when it became one of Cornwall's first stannary towns, where miners had to come to pay tax on the metals they had harvested from the ground. Assayers would cut a tiny corner from a smelted block and assess its tin content in order to calculate how much tax was owed. Once the levy was paid, the ingot would be stamped with an official mark and could then be sold. This business happened in the Coinage Hall, which gave its name to the street on which it stood.

Other stannary towns – Lostwithiel, Bodmin, Truro and Liskeard – were far away, making Helston the most important centre in the west of Cornwall from the 14th until the 17th century. Until Penzance became a coinage town in 1663, miners from as far away as West Penwith had to lug their heavy blocks of tin to Helston to have them valued.

When the writer Daniel Defoe visited Helston in the first decades of the 18th century, he described it as a large and populous place with a handsome church, a good trade, and four spacious streets.* The streets take the shape of a slightly misshapen cross –

---

*Helston has had other famous visitors over the years. Svetlana Alliluyeva, daughter of Joseph Stalin, did her shopping here when she lived in nearby Mullion in the mid 1990s. *Daily Mail* journalist David Jones tracked her down, and she granted him a twenty-minute audience in one of the town's cafés. Jones recalls that she made it clear when the interview was over, instructing him that 'when we walk out of here, you go left and I

Wendron Street drops down from the north-east with Coinagehall Street continuing along the same axis; Meneage Street comes from the south-east, terminating on one side of the Guildhall, with Church Street continuing north-west from the other.

For 500 years the Angel Hotel has crowned Coinagehall Street, its 16th-century arched granite doorway sitting behind a pillared Georgian porch. Before it became a coaching inn, it was the town house of the Godolphins, whose eponymous country estate was five miles out of town. One of the first Cornish families to grow rich mining and processing tin, they used their wealth to build a political power base.

In 1544 the soldier William Godolphin took a company of miners from west Cornwall to France where they brought about the end of the Siege of Boulogne by digging tunnels under the castle walls. He was subsequently appointed Bailiff of Boulogne, eventually returning to Helston with his face badly scarred from his military endeavours. As Richard Carew noted in his *Survey of Cornwall*, published half a century later, his injuries contributed 'no lesse to the beautifying of his fame, then the disfiguring of his face'.

Godolphin had become a justice of the peace by April 1548 when the government agent William Body was sent to Helston to remove statues of saints and other 'popish' images from the town's church. A hated, deeply distrusted figure, Body's reputation came before him. In events that presaged the Prayerbook Rebellion the following year, he was met on arrival by furious protestors led by men from St Keverne and Constantine. Body tried to find

---

go right'. In 2011 Hollywood stars Brad Pitt and Angelina Jolie decamped to the town, secretly residing at the Nansloe Manor Hotel as Pitt shot the apocalyptic thriller *World War Z*.

safety in a house by the church, but was dragged out and killed by the angry mob.

Body's death did not calm the town's anger; within a few days 3,000 protestors had gathered, and there was talk of rebellion. The job of pacifying the crowd fell to Godolphin, who soon organised a militia of gentlemen and constables to ensure such sedition would not happen again. His loyalty to the government surely helped him when he applied for a lease to farm the Isles of Scilly in 1558; his descendants continued to hold the title Governor of Scilly until 1834.

After his death, the estate passed to his nephew Francis Godolphin, who was at his Helston house in July 1588 when the news arrived that the Spanish Armada had been spotted off the Lizard.

Cornwall became directly involved in the Anglo-Spanish War seven years later, when four Spanish ships landed at Mousehole. A raiding party of 200 set fire to the village and the church at nearby Paul, killing four Cornishmen along the way. Godolphin rode west to investigate, and then mustered a band of Helston men to defend the coast. By the time his militia arrived, the unperturbed Spanish had returned to their vessels and weighed anchor for Newlyn. There 400 of them came ashore and began to attack Penzance. Godolphin's forces were massively outnumbered. The Spanish calmly celebrated mass before returning to their ships and sailing for Marazion, where finally there were enough Cornish forces to prevent them coming ashore.

Sidney Godolphin was one of the last members of the family to live in the Coinagehall Street house – not that he was there much, spending most of his time at court where he wrote poetry and became a trusted servant of Charles I. Aged eighteen when he was elected as a Member of Parliament for Helston in 1628, he was the last Royalist to speak in the House of Commons before the Civil War. He died aged just thirty-three, victim of a skirmish with Parliamentarian forces in the Devon town of Chagford, his demise causing an outpouring of public grief in Helston.

The property remained in the family, through its descendants, the dukes of Leeds, until 1921 – but the Godolphins had moved out by the end of the 17th century. The house became an inn, and quickly established itself at the centre of town life. A pit for cock-fighting was an early attraction, though later the place became associated with more sedate pursuits. A bowling alley was established in 1760, and a Georgian ballroom complete with a minstrels' gallery became a meeting place for the town's gentry. In 1833 works by Beethoven and Mozart were performed at the first concert of the Helston Harmonic Society. The Angel was central to business life in the town too, hosting an excise office and a Freemasons' lodge, servicing the mail coaches, laying on grand civic lunches and dinners, and providing a focal point for Helston's colourful political scene.

It was a truly rotten borough. Until the changes introduced as a result of the Great Reform Act of 1832, Helston sent two representatives to the House of Commons. Until the late 18th century they were elected by the town's freemen, of which there could be no more than twenty-four at any one time. By 1774 there were just six electors, and a new charter was introduced, allowing for an infinite number of freemen. The old guard were horrified at the prospect of the franchise being extended and appealed success-fully to Parliament to overturn the change. Fifteen years later just one freeman survived – Richard Penhall, who enjoyed complete control over who Helston returned to Westminster. Finally the terms of the 1774 charter were adopted, though they represented a mere tiptoe towards any sense of representative democracy. In the early 19th century, the duke of Leeds paid the entire Helston rate bill in exchange for the right to choose its parliamentarians.

After an election in 1865 was declared void due to bribery, a by-election was called. William Balliol Brett was the Conservative candidate, with Australian-born Robert Campbell representing the Liberals. The result was tied, both men receiving 153 votes, so the returning officer, Mayor Thomas Rogers, gave his casting vote to Campbell. Brett appealed to the House of Commons, which concluded that the mayor (who happened to be the father of Campbell's political agent) had no right to a casting vote, and as it had been a tie, he should have returned both men to Parliament.

Local satirists relished these political shenanigans. In 1867 a bill displayed on hoardings across Helston advertised 'Rogers's Menagerie at the Angel Hotel'. It promised a unique collection of animals, 'their odour rather bad and their natural propensities somewhat peculiar'. Locals were invited to see Sly Reynard the Fox, famous for his artifices, the Cape Flying Jackal and the Laughing Hyena. There would be a further selection of 'snakes, reptiles, carnivorous and creeping animals. It is very amusing to see the animals feed, as they are all fed in one den.' Local politics at this time may have been messy and chaotic, but the fact that Helston elected its own Member of Parliament ensured lively local discourse that kept people engaged and meant the town's name was spoken of at distant Westminster. In 1885 Helston's connection with the decision-makers of Parliament became more distant when it was absorbed into the Truro county division. Today it is part of the St Ives constituency that stetches across fifty-five miles from Manacle Point in the east to St Agnes in the Isles of Scilly in the west.

Helston was where I went to secondary school. My friend Alan Treloar and I would often lunch at the Angel on Fridays. Its staff seemed relaxed about the presence of under-age drinkers. We'd sit in the bar and order chicken-in-a-basket, meat and chips served together in a faux-woven bowl made from moulded plastic. Freddie Worrall, our headmaster, would raise his hat as he passed by, bound for the smarter restaurant at the back where he would eat after a morning doing his weekly duty as a justice of the peace at the town's magistrates' court. As long as our pints, or glasses of heavy Australian red, were downed no later than ten to one, we would be back at school in plenty of time for our 'A' Level English class at five past.

Lessons took place in a sprawling campus on Church Hill, opened in the early 1970s by the then Secretary of State for Education, Margaret Thatcher. The building seemed to epitomise the dream of non-selective, comprehensive education set out by her Labour predecessor Anthony Crosland. Traditional subjects were taught in classrooms with blackboards and overhead projectors or well-equipped science labs, a gas tap to fuel a Bunsen burner at every desk. Alongside were spaces where pupils could learn practical skills – cookery, metalwork, woodwork and commercial studies, each room equipped with the requisite ovens, lathes and typewriters.

This brave new world of steel-framed glass walls, quadrangles, language labs, sports halls and lecture theatres was ours from the age of thirteen. Our first two years of classes took place down the hill in the old grammar school. Until a decade before I started at Helston, a pass or fail in the eleven-plus exam meant the difference between a place on the academic fast track, with the prospect of university at the end, or consignment to the secondary modern school on Penrose Road. There lessons were squeezed into small classrooms; there was little outdoor space and no playing fields, unlike the grammar school, which was surrounded by acres of rugby, football and cricket pitches.

Although in theory it was possible to be 'promoted' from secondary modern to grammar, the reality was few pupils made the leap. The cruelty of casting children's futures in stone at the age of eleven comes clearly across in a local history film interviewing adults who had been pupils in the 1960s at what was known as the Green School.

While some talk fondly of kind-hearted teachers doing their best to help their charges progress, others remember a place where failure hung in the air and bullying was rampant. A woodwork teacher would floor members of his class and then lock them inside cupboards. In the gym a physical education master created an atmosphere of 'fear and terror'. One teacher entertained himself by making his charges fight each other. 'It was just so sadistic,' recalls one former pupil. ' "Gather round, everyone!"

he would say. "I want to see one of you knocked out or I want to see blood." '

I became very familiar with the Penrose Road site, as it was where my father worked. After he left the army and returned to Cornwall, he found a job as Education Welfare Officer for Helston, responsible for tracking down truant children, ensuring provision of school meals and arranging transport. The former school had become a community centre, and Dad's office was on the first floor.

He ran it like a military campaign post, with lists of pupils and their requirements on clipboards hung on the wall, one for each school. Large-scale maps enabled him to work out who was entitled to free transport. 'More than three miles distant' was the rule; the mother of my friend Ann Roberts claimed her daughter was 3.1 miles from school and therefore qualified; my father turned to his detailed maps and announced that Ann's house was 2.9 miles away and thus she had to pay. Thankfully our friendship survived.

I spent many teenage hours in that office, with its scuffed brown carpet tiles and suspended ceiling, making use of Dad's Imperial typewriter and seemingly lavish supply of A4, Tippex and carbon paper, or listlessly doing my homework and hoping he would soon finish for the day so we could go back to St Martin.

Today his office is a clothes-maker's workshop, one of a series of artists' studios that fill the building with energy, creativity and colour. Teresa Gleadowe, an art curator and former staffer at Tate Britain and the Royal College of Art, moved to Helston in 2007 and became curious about the old school, a short walk from her home in Cross Street.

Gleadowe managed to get inside the locked-up, abandoned building and saw its potential as the base of an artistic community. Putting to one side thoughts of the leaking roof and the antique wiring and plumbing, she started fundraising. Today there is a long wait for a studio at CAST – the Cornubian Arts and Science Trust. A cinema displays a programme of digital art, there is a ceramics studio and the hip café means the smell of freshly ground coffee permeates the space that was once my father's office. And children are back in the building, taking part in workshops and art projects that local schools can no longer afford to fund themselves.

As I walk down Wendron Street, CAST's new slate roof stands out. Few of Helston's commercial buildings seem as well maintained. Moss and weeds are commonplace on roofs, walls are in need of fresh paint, glass is cracked in upper windows, frames around rot gently. It feels as if the light that illuminates this beautiful town has been dimmed a little; fresh energy is needed to make the place glow again.

Between them Meneage Street and Coinagehall Street hold over eighty listed buildings. The former is narrow and tightly packed with shop-houses and cottages, the latter is a confident broadway, sweeping upwards and bending almost imperceptibly towards the Guildhall, with deep pavements, fine houses, wide shopfronts and the imposing limestone façade of a late-Victorian Methodist chapel, built to seat a thousand.

Move the cars out the way and Church Street is ready for the filming of a costume drama. The road drops sharply down from the Guildhall before climbing again as it approaches the church. Tiny workers' cottages sit hugger-mugger aside middle-class Georgian dwellings. It is not a wide street, but two-way traffic is still allowed, motorists at risk of losing a wheel to one of the open kennels that run down either side of the road. These carved granite channels, a foot wide and eight inches deep, were laid out across the town at the start of the 19th century to aid sanitation. Water still gurgles its way along them, today moving at furious speed after a period of heavy rain. The source is the River Cober, the supply diverted from a weir two miles north-east at Wendron and then fed down a leat to the town; after its urban adventure, the water is returned to the river by the municipal boating lake, from where it feeds into Loe Pool and the sea.

Helston is quiet this afternoon; the Trengrouse Way car-park is nearly empty, a man driving his mobility scooter down the pavement of Meneage Street has a clear run. The lights are off at Lloyds Bank. When I look more closely I notice a sign in the elegant bay window of the banking hall informing customers that the branch has closed and recommending that they go instead to Camborne or Truro, ten or seventeen miles away.

The bank was the work of the prolific Truro architect Silvanus Trevail, who was responsible for hundreds of Cornish buildings in the last three decades of the 19th century. They included institutes, libraries and hospitals as well as grand projects like the Headland Hotel in Newquay, King Arthur's Castle Hotel in Tintagel, and a 250-bed extension to the County Lunatic Asylum at Bodmin.*

In Helston he presented his clients, the Cornish Bank, with plans for an impressive building rising over four levels. If it had

---

*As well as being an architect Silvanus Trevail was a property developer, local politician and campaigner for improved public health and sanitation facilities. He did not live to see the completion of the Foster Building at the Bodmin Asylum. On 7 November 1903 he set off by train from Truro to attend the funeral of his Uncle Joseph at Luxulyan. He had purchased a ticket as far as St Austell, but did not disembark there. As the train approached Bodmin Road Station (now Bodmin Parkway) he went to the train lavatory and shot himself. Writing in the *St Austell Star* the following week, the editor described Trevail's suicide as 'a pitiful ending to a life that was so big'.

been built it would have dominated the centre of the town but ultimately, a simpler, two-storey structure was chosen, which opened for business in 1891.

Today there is not a bank left in Helston and most of the stores that sustained our family have gone too. Woolworths, where I bought 99p pop singles and bags of pick-and-mix, is now a Poundstretcher. The shop where the peninsula's newlyweds got their beds, sofas and dining suites, has become a sprawling Wetherspoons. Barnett's, the men's outfitters on Wendron Street – where I was taken to get my school uniform of grey trousers, aertex shirt and navy-blue polyester jersey – has shut, as has Rowe's Fruit where in the summer of 1988 half a dozen of us skipped class to picket outside, holding home-made signs calling for a boycott of fruit from apartheid South Africa. Today it is a Bet Fred bookmaker.

The Gaiety Bookshop, Hydrovolt Electric and the local branch of Dingle's department store – where my mother would buy gingham and flowered dress fabric cut with a flourish from great bales of cloth – are no more. Estate agents occupy the sites of Oliver's and Eddy & Son. The former was the Harrods of Helston, with displays of Continental meats and cheeses, tins of quail's eggs, dressed crab and stoneless black cherries, and a wine department that offered a enticing range of port, sherry, madeira and colourful liqueurs alongside its racks of clarets, hocks and burgundies. The new owners of Eddy & Son's premises have had the sense to keep the art-deco shopfront that has graced Meneage Street since 1936. Black vitrolite surrounds the display windows; a neon sign hangs over the pavement; underneath a green wooden noticeboard has the family name carved at the top. On frosted glass the store's offerings are listed in elegant outlined type – Stationery & Toys, Fancy Goods, Crafts, Decorators.

I find myself launching into a nostalgic reverie about old Helston when I meet David Turnbull in the CAST café. I realise he is getting bored when he gently rolls his eyes. 'You can't turn back time,' he chides. 'Saying things aren't what they used to be achieves nothing.'

Raised in County Durham, another area of abandoned mines and shuttered Methodist chapels, he moved to Cornwall fourteen years ago, and has since become one of the leaders of the community interest company charged with reviving Helston.

Turnbull's optimism and energy is heartening, and it is more than just talk. He and his colleagues, all of them volunteers, have already revitalised Coronation Park and the boating lake, which they now manage, having paid the local council a pound for a ninety-nine-year lease. They raised £1.8 million to redevelop the site of the old cattle market, where offices let at commercial rents fund a community hub, home to the town's oversubscribed farmers' market. The museum is now under their control too – a decade ago it was threatened with closure under local government cuts, now it is considered one of the best in the county.

Helston's situation is not unique – at least a dozen other Cornish towns are in a similar position, with high-street shops forced out of business by the vast superstores set up on the ring roads. Only market forces will drive full-scale renewal; Turnbull is pragmatic about the limits of what local activists can achieve. But they can at least encourage people back into the centre – as tenants in the empty, abandoned units above shops, and as clients of the businesses below.

'Helston is a town people pop into, and only then when they have a specific reason. We need them to stay longer, to make two or three purchases rather than one. Fourteen thousand people live here, but most housing is in a doughnut shape around the edges. Once people have got into their car, they will drive to one of the big superstores or to Falmouth, Penzance or Truro. Better public transport and a network of safe paths and cycleways are key. We want to encourage people into our town centre, rather than out of it.'*

As I walk back to my car the sun is low, the golden-hour light adding an extra magic to the streetscape. It is easy to imagine Helston as it could be: the shopfronts tarted up again, and accommodating the mix of small businesses and national chains that a town needs; the flats above refurbished and providing affordable accommodation; the pavements traversed by enough people that occasionally someone has to step back to allow another to pass. Helston has been a rich, proud, inventive, mercantile town – it was still a place to spend a day when I was a child. Its physical beauty seems undiminished – one day economic prosperity will return too.

---

*After a four-decade interregnum Helston once again has a bookshop. Located at the top of Meneage Street it opened in November 2023. With space for events, a children's play area and coffee machine next to the till, it styles itself as 'the southernmost bookshop in mainland Britain'.

CHAPTER 6

The Flora Dance

Helston is most famous for Flora Day, the riotously joyful celebration of spring that takes place at the start of May each year. Visitors pack the town's pavements, queueing early for a good spot, but only locals can actually take part. May the 8th is when Flora Day happens, unless the date falls on a Sunday or Monday, in which case the celebrations are held the previous Saturday. It is a day when the town's shops, pubs and cafés do spectacular business – but it is about more than just good trade. It has become a statement of Cornish identity, something that, unlike an old fisherman's cottage or a heart-stopping coastal view, cannot be bought at any price.

I treasure a crumpled old postcard of Flora Day. It is a composite of three pictures taken in 1989. In one the town band lead a parade of children all dressed in white; in another women in long frocks and men in top hats and tails hold their hands high as they dance; in the third a party of costumed players look on as a plump teenager wearing white britches, frock coat and jabot holds a handbell high. Just after the camera shutter had clicked, he would ring the bell, and announce, in Cornish and English, the start of the Hal-an-Tow.

The young man in the picture is me, town crier for a day, just a few weeks shy of my eighteenth birthday. My friend Alan is dressed in green as Robin Hood, across from him stands an orange dragon, and a man playing the bass drum that is hung across his chest – Andrew George, who eight years later would become the local MP. It is half-past-eight on a perfect May morning and we are about to give the Hal-an-Tow its first outing.

Drums, whistles, horns and bells have signified the arrival of the procession of players. I have called the audience to order, and welcomed visitors from near and far. It is time for the assembled cast to break into lusty-voiced song:

Hal-an-tow, jolly rumble, O. For we are up as soon as any
   day, O
And for to fetch the summer home, the summer and the
   May, O
For summer is a-come, And winter is a-gone O.

In the five minutes or so that it takes for the Hal-an-Tow to play out, St George slays the dragon and St Michael does the Devil to death. When the first performance is complete, the cast and their followers move on to the next location, presenting the piece seven times in little more than an hour. This life-enhancing pageant, and the series of dances that follow, mark the green shoots and long days of late spring, a reminder that we should revel in the hope and potency the season promises.

Traditionally the Hal-an-Tow gave Helston's working-class population a chance to subvert the natural order of affairs and claim power for the day. Celebrations would start in the early hours with a trip to nearby woods to gather greenery to dress up already elaborate costumes. Participants wove foliage into their headdresses to help ensure anonymity – flirtatious glances could be exchanged, as all were safe in the knowledge that if a pass was rejected, the disguise would save players from humiliation.

What had started out as a bit of light fun, a letting-off of steam after the darkness of winter, became something disturbing to later generations. The thought of what these young people might get up to in the woods, let alone their bawdy, licentious, uncontrolled behaviour when they returned to town, troubled Helston's Victorian morality keepers. In 1885 the *West Briton* described the Hal-an-Tow as being 'little other than a prescriptive nuisance'. Two decades later the paper claimed the event had fallen 'into great disrepute'.

To the relief of some it disappeared in the opening years of the 20th century, only to emerge again in 1930 – no longer the property of working-class Helstonians, but now sanitised and reinvented, a tradition safely supervised by the custodians of the Cornish Celtic revival. Once the Hal-an-Tow had been a subversive event that offered an annual moment of joy to those living hard, demanding lives. Now it had been remade as something quaint and prettified.

By the time I made my appearance as town crier, the Hal-an-Tow had recovered much of its noisy egalitarian past. I was the understudy, called for duty after the regular crier, Howard Curnow, careers master at Helston School and committed Cornish nationalist, had gone to Australia to educate the diaspora about their homeland. There was no question of him not returning to a role he would eventually play for forty-one years, part provost calming down the crowds, and often the performers too, part fairground barker building up the tension before the drama began.

His speech was always bilingual; when he started in the 1970s it would have been a rare opportunity to hear someone speak *yn Kernewek*. Ironically the drama that the crier introduces is curiously un-Cornish, reflecting folk traditions found across England. The Hal-an-Tow verses feature Robin Hood and Little

John, the humiliation of the Spanish, the slaying of the dragon by St George and requests to 'send us peace in merry England'. St Piran, Cornwall's patron saint, did not get a look-in until 2005 when a new verse was added – and a new costume, featuring a replica of the coracle that had brought the saint ashore at Penhale Beach.

* * *

The Hal-an-Tow is the morning's second event – Flora Day begins outside the Guildhall at seven o'clock sharp. Helston Town Band starts playing the familiar tune, and those taking part in the first of four dances set off on a steady progression around the town.

The event's roots sit in the tradition of ancient pagan fertility festivals.* Davies Gilbert, early-19th-century Helston MP and collector of Cornish folk tunes and carols, suggested that the name of the day's 'elegant amusements' was a 'fanciful allusion' to the Roman festival of Floralia. One helpful legend provides a local twist – an account of the Devil hurling a red-hot boulder at St Michael, the town's patron saint. The rock misses its target, and lands in the waters of Loe Pool, the lake a couple of miles south of the town centre. The saving of the saint, and the avoidance of Helston's fiery destruction triggers a bout of extreme religious fervour, the citizens offering their thanks by processing through the streets in what has subsequently variously been called the Furry, Faddy or Flora dance.

Whatever its origins, it soon stretched beyond Helston – considered Cornwall's national dance, our version of the Catalan *sardana*, an opportunity for people to express joy together, hand in hand. Often the excuse for a turn would be a local one – a

---

*Padstow Obby Oss is another, held each year on the 1st of May.

good harvest, a propitious wedding, lives saved at sea, but on occasion the dance could be lent out to mark broader causes. When Napoleon was defeated there were extended Furry dances in Truro, Falmouth and Penzance; the people of Chacewater danced together when Victoria became Queen; in St Mawes in 1842 villagers saw their victory in a dispute over fishing rights as a good reason to dance; the historian A. L. Rowse recalled a Furry on the streets of St Austell and Fowey when he was a teenager at the end of World War One. Today, while other Cornish towns and villages try and maintain the tradition, it only truly flourishes once a year in Helston.

In the 18th and early 19th century an early-morning alarm call of drums, fifes and fiddles signified the start of the holiday. Townsfolk pinned sprigs of lily of the valley and bluebells to their suits and dresses. At ten a squad of soldiers fired three volleys from a position on Coinagehall Street. 'The town now began to fill with visitants in their holiday cloaths, who with the town's people, faddied at intervals thro' the streets and regaled themselves with their friends til evening', the *Royal Cornwall Gazette* reported in 1802.

A century later a *Times* correspondent described an event that was 'open to anyone, if the spirit of festivity moves him, and he is within earshot of the band, to improvise a procession of his own ... the town is full of such little trains of merriment, colliding with each other.' This feels like a visiting London reporter determined to file a romantic dispatch. While there were breakaway moments of informal dancing, much of the day was tightly organised, with divisions strictly maintained along social lines, the schedule of dances specifically arranged to keep the classes apart. The first was commonly known as the 'Servants' Dance'. It started at six, an hour earlier than now, to ensure that participants had plenty of time to return to their employers' homes after, ready to first serve them breakfast, and then help them dress for their big moment.

The 'Quality Dance' left the Guildhall at noon, led by the mayor, followed by members of the town's leading families, representatives of the business community and important visitors. It became a particularly social experience when it passed through the interiors of the villas and town houses lining Cross Street, Helston's most elegant road, the dancers breaking for refreshment in the spacious gardens of Lismore, its grandest house. Suitably rested, in the evening the wealthy would attend the Flora Day Ball, where dancing continued until five o'clock the next morning. Those still standing then joined the Helston Hunt for its last meet of the season.

* * *

The ball is long forgotten – replaced by a more egalitarian form of entertainment, a raucous funfair held at the bottom of the town. The Servants' Dance is now the early-morning dance, its route the longest of the day, going up and down Meneage and Wendron Streets, into Penrose Road, Church and Cross Streets, dropping down past the Freemasons' Hall, touching the Penzance Road and ending with a climb up Coinagehall Street. Once done, its dancers have surely earned the right to party – but perhaps in moderation; they are expected to regroup in the afternoon for the dance that ends the day at five o'clock.

What was the gentry's moment is now simply called the midday dance, though the mayor, the local MP, the commanding officer of RNAS Culdrose and other prominent local citizens still take leading positions, and participants must wear morning suit and top hat or long dress and bonnet. New residents of certain houses on Cross Street can expect an early visit from a member of the Flora Day Committee, come to politely remind them of their duty to allow the dancers to pass through their hallways and gardens.

Another dance was added to the day's programme in 1922 – the children's dance. I was twelve when I took part. In the weeks beforehand we rehearsed our steps in the school sports hall, the music played off loudspeakers from a cassette recorded for us by Helston Band. Lined up in our groups of four, we would carefully count the beat until it was time to swap partners. I found the required combination of steps and hops tricky to master, though most of my friends seemed to grasp it straight away. More counting, and then time to return to our original pairs.

The uniform we had to wear spoke of summer days – white trousers, white plimsolls, white shirt and blue-and-gold-striped school tie. We shivered a little as we mustered on Wendron Street. Helston School brought up the rear of the long snake of 1,000 children, so the band was already far away and faint as we set off, our teachers walking alongside counting in hushed tones, lest their charges missed the distant beat.

* * *

Helston Band play the dance nearly a thousand times on Flora Day, its senior members walking sixteen miles over the day. The tune has never been formally published, each generation of Helston musicians passing it on to the next. This secrecy has ensured that it has remained the town's exclusive property, but it also means some visitors are surprised at what they hear on May the 8th, having got to know a similar, but slightly different tune created by an Edwardian singer, violinist and entertainer.

Katie Moss was a light soprano who delighted London audiences in recitals of songs by Schumann and Tosti – she was described as a 'gifted and talented' singer with a 'refined and intelligent manner' by the critic in *The Queen* magazine who heard her perform at the Bechstein Hall in February 1905. Her talent at accompanying herself on violin helped add to her fame.

But her legacy was defined by the song she wrote after she spent a holiday in Cornwall in 1911, visiting Flora Day and watching the midday dance. An unshakeable earworm, the tune lodged itself in her mind and on the long train journey home to London she created her own song, inspired by what she had heard and seen in Helston. It was soon published, and the next year the first recording was made by the Australian baritone Peter Dawson, for whom it became a signature piece.

The words Moss gave 'The Floral Dance' were as flowery and colourful as the day itself; on the page there is the sense of doggerel about them, but sung or spoken out loud they make for a well-told ballad – her story of being captivated by this 'quaint old Cornish town' and thrilled by the sound of the band: 'Fiddle, cello, big bass drum, / Bassoon, flute and euphonium', the last syllable of 'euphonium' requiring a heavy stress to make the rhyme work. The protagonist becomes caught up in the music and is desperate to dance, but has no one to pair up with – until she spots an old friend in the crowd, who she quickly pulls into the 'merry throng' of dancers.

Dawson made multiple recordings of 'The Floral Dance', which soon became a light-music classic. In his rich and detailed account of the song's history, Ian Marshall cites names of other stars who performed it – a list that includes Kathleen Ferrier, Julie Andrews, Moira Anderson, Stanley Holloway, The Yetties and the Romanian panpipe virtuoso Gheorghe Zamfir.

The most celebrated recording was by Brighouse and Rastrick Band, an arrangement made in 1977 by music director Derek Broadbent. It spent six weeks at number two in the pop singles chart in December 1977 and January 1978.* An appearance on the BBC's *Top of the Pops* helped maintain its popularity, as did airplay by Radio Two presenter Terry Wogan, who would sometimes leave his microphone switched on as he sang along using Moss's original words. Soon he was in the recording studio laying down his version; his own visit to the *Top of the Pops* studio followed.

The performance is available to watch on YouTube – a couple of minutes that help debunk the idea of a television golden age. Dressed in a wide-lapelled beige suit and flowery shirt and clutching a bunch of pink flowers, the Irishman appears woefully under-rehearsed. The young audience seem confused as to why he is there, and soon Wogan is laughing nervously as he realises he is losing the room.

Despite his dire performance he spent five weeks in the charts, although twenty-one was the highest position he reached. Helstonians kept a respectful distance from the whole affair, pointing out that while Katie Moss had created a nice tribute in her 'Floral Dance', it was an ersatz reinvention; the authentic 'Flora Dance' had been kept safely away from the grasp of outsiders.

---

* 'Mull of Kintyre' by Wings concurrently held the number-one position.

Today temporary car-parks are set up at the rugby club and showground to accommodate the Flora Day crowds. Visitors, and the money they bring, are warmly welcomed – but as guests at an event that is still entirely about Helston and its people, something that places Flora Day apart from many other events in Cornwall's annual tourist cycle. The children's dance is restricted to pupils of Helston's schools; the leading pairs must have been born in the town. The midday dance is by invitation, the early-morning dance by application. Despite Katie Moss's intervention, only the musicians of Helston Town Band know the proper 'Flora Dance' tune. Come and enjoy, take pictures, post videos – but Helstonians respectfully ask you to remember that this is their day, not yours.

CHAPTER 7

Falmouth Bay

Many of the men and women who taught me at Helston were veterans of the old grammar school. Some seemed shell-shocked at the realisation they were now on the staff of a boisterous, home-to-all comprehensive. Some hung onto the past, wearing academic gowns at daily assembly, which took place in a parquet-floored hall, its walls lined with wooden boards bearing the gilt-lettered names of old Oxbridge entrants and former head girls and boys. One legacy of the days of grammar-grandeur was a system of school houses. Cups were handed out annually to celebrate victories in rugby, cross-country or cricket by pupils in Trevenen or Vyvyan. I was in Godolphin, named after the family of Angel Hotel fame. I was no sportsman, so my contribution was limited to helping out with occasional prizes for poetry reading and student drama. We had a good chant – 'God-ol-phin, God-ol-phin,' shouted with equal stress on each syllable – but we always seemed to be beaten by Grylls, who managed to combine cultural interests with sporting acuity. My Hal-an-Tow colleague Alan Treloar typified the house's flexibility – he was the Shakespeare-reading star of school plays who decided he was not interested in exploring a career in professional football, despite circling scouts trying to talk him into trials. The house system had a certain charm, but it was abandoned not long after we left, the boards taken down, put in storage and soon forgotten.

The victorious Grylls name lives on in a fine memorial monument at the bottom of Coinagehall Street in Helston. It is one of the last markers on the Flora Day route, with dancers passing under its arch before making their way up Coinagehall Steet and back to the Guildhall. The monument is a splendid Gothic folly, with octagonal pinnacles stretching up from a castellated parapet. Built in 1834 and funded by public subscription, 196 tons of best Cornish granite were used in its construction.

Humphry Millet Grylls was a prominent Helstonian who had attained hero status after saving a nearby mine. During a financial crisis local banks were about to call in loans they had made to the business; Grylls used his influence to persuade them to wait, thus protecting 1,200 jobs. He was just forty-five when he died; his funeral on 24 April 1834 drew in Flora Day-sized crowds, the procession of mourners two miles long.

Grylls lived and died at Bosahan, a house perched on a bluff overlooking the mouth of the Helford River. Old sketches show a solid-looking manor house, dressed up in Georgian times with double sets of bow windows. Impressive though this dwelling was, it was not substantial enough for a subsequent owner. Sir Arthur Pendarves Vivian bought the estate in the early 1880s and immediately set about demolishing the existing house and building in its place what was to be the grandest Victorian residence in Cornwall.

When complete its footprint covered nearly 22,000 square feet, with twenty-six bedrooms to accommodate family and guests. It was a landmark, visible from Falmouth Bay, a heavyweight architectural statement from an industrious, successful man. Yet this new Bosahan stood for just seven decades before it too met the wrecker's ball. Today a few black-and-white photographs are

all that survive as proof of the existence of one of the great lost houses of Cornwall.

Arthur Pendarves Vivian was an industrialist, traveller and politician. His grandfather John was a Truro-born mining entrepreneur who in 1809 opened a smelting works in Hafod near Swansea. By 1820, his company was the second-largest producer of copper in Britain.

His son, John Henry, studied at the prestigious Freiburg Mining Institute in Germany before joining the family business. He became an active Whig politician, Member of Parliament for Swansea and supporter of the new Cornish newspaper the *West Briton*, which had been launched to challenge the Tory-supporting *Royal Cornwall Gazette*. His position in the trade was confirmed by a statue that still stands in Ferrara Square in Swansea's docklands; the mineral Vivianite was named in his honour.

Arthur followed his father into politics, elected in 1868 as one of two Liberal MPs for the Cornwall Western Division, representing the seat unopposed for seventeen years until the 1885 Redistribution of Seats Act created six new single-member Cornish constituencies.

Three years before he left Parliament, he sold a property he owned on the cliffs at Newquay and purchased Bosahan. The new house that he built had ornate Dutch gables and broad chimneys; the copper guttering and drainpipes were specially made at the family's Swansea works. A castellated tower with a flagpole hid a water tank. Grass banks and gentle granite steps led down to the gardens below.

When Arthur died aged ninety-two in August 1926, his coffin was carried the mile from Bosahan to Manaccan Church by twelve of his workers, drawn from a vast retinue of gardeners, gamekeepers, woodmen, carpenters, cooks, maids and footmen, his terrier Sona trotting behind.

By the end of the Second World War, maintaining such a grand existence was no longer possible. Harry Graham-Vivian, who had inherited the estate, concluded that the house was unsustainable, simply too big to survive. He oversaw its demolition in the 1950s, and built a new residence on the same site, which occupied less than a quarter of the footprint of his great-grandfather's pile.

Today Richard Graham-Vivian and his wife Christine live at Bosahan. I go to see them, taking Cornish pasties which we eat in their modern kitchen before we go into the dining room where on the table Richard has laid out the plans of the Victorian house.

On the ground floor there is a billiards room, library and drawing and dining rooms, along with kitchens, pantries, wine cellar, butler's bedroom and servants' hall. Guest bedrooms dominate the first and second storeys, many with connecting dressing rooms. There are multiple lavatories marked, but only one bathroom on each floor.

The most noteworthy feature is the great hall, which extends up the full height of the building. At one end is an organ, the pipes reaching the roof, the keyboard placed in the midst of a minstrels' gallery. The plans, and the surviving pictures, suggest this was a space for nocturnal use – the roof was made of dark oak; little light would have penetrated the twenty-six-pane stained-glass window with its panels showing coats of arms and other heraldic devices. Huge logs would have been consumed by the fire under a mantelpiece specially carved in Verona, 14ft long and 9ft high. Richard recalls a cousin telling him he found it a frightening place, with heads of buffalo, moose, elk, bear and antelope hanging from the walls alongside ancient weapons and Flemish tapestries.

Bits of the old survive in the new, a 1950s architect making neat notes in pencil on the plans, instructing workers what they should remove and store – chimneypieces, marble surrounds, doors, architraves and the kitchen range, all to be recycled. Richard points down to the polished floorboards underfoot, some of which are now in their third home, having been laid first at a house on London's Pall Mall before their move to Cornwall.

As we leave the house and walk outside, I have a sense that someone has their eye on me. I look up and spot a carving of a soldier, resting in a niche. 'Hussey Vivian,' says Richard. 'Arthur was very proud of his uncle.' Reportedly one of thirty-two siblings, Richard Hussey Vivian was born in Truro 1775. His father thought he should study law but he decided a military career would be of greater interest. A hero of both the Peninsular War and the Battle of Waterloo, he rose to the rank of lieutenant-general, commanded the forces in Ireland, and in October 1819 was sent to Newcastle to quell riots that had broken out following the recent Peterloo massacre in Manchester. In 1841 he was ennobled for his military service and his subsequent duty as a politician. Miniature statues of the first Baron Vivian appear above the door of the lodge, and on the wall of the former pumphouse.

These buildings, along with the stable block, give a clue as to the vastness of the edifice that once stood here – but I still can't quite get my head around its scale. Christine scrolls through her phone and finds a picture that she took during a recent hot summer. The grass has thinned, leaving the foundations of the old house clearly visible, a ghostly map of what is no more.

* * *

I look up towards Bosahan from a boat on the Helford River. The house is framed by subtropical gardens, fern-carpeted woodland stretches down to the shore. It is four o'clock on a weekday afternoon in early May and the water's surface is completely still. There is scarcely any wind so my brother Andrew is having to use the motor of his 31ft yacht *Stardust*, in order to get us over to Falmouth.

Our journey started in Helford, once a centre of smuggling. The river's hinterland, with its creeks and quays, provided ample spots where spoils could be unloaded unnoticed. Cognac, tea, tobacco, salt and silk were the favoured goods of the area's 'free-traders', whose business continued well into the 19th century. As late as 1840 Helford's Custom House came under attack from thirty men who managed to escape with 126 kegs of untaxed brandy, seized a few days earlier by revenue officers when they intercepted the lugger *Love* arriving at Coverack from Roscoff.

Helford is the prettiest village on the Lizard Peninsula, its white-limed cottages built up on stone quays on either side of a stream that flows down to the river. Many of the houses, including the pub, the Shipwright's Arms, are thatched, some have boathouses and private landing stages at the foot of their gardens. This was one of the first villages to become dominated by second homes and holiday lets. In the early 1980s, when my father and one of his grown-up sons headed to the Shipwright's for a pint, I would wheedle my way into the party. This was a time when children were not allowed into pubs so I would be left outside, sitting on a bench with a bottle of ginger beer and a packet of crisps. After a while, sensing that I had been forgotten by those enjoying the smoky, blokey camaraderie of the bar, I would take myself off for a walk. In autumn and winter it could seem like the village had been abandoned. I would peer through windows and spot dust covers laid over furniture and the plugs of electrical equipment lying disconnected on the floor. There was no one around to tell me off for being nosy. It felt as if Helford was half dead, punished for its sheer beauty.

When I revisited last winter there was not a single light from the houses on the east side of the stream. Bridge, Creek, Hope, Christmas, Dowr Penty, Wednesday, September – two-up, two-down cottages built originally for fishermen and farmhands, now sitting empty. The houses are clearly well looked after, window frames recently painted, gardens carefully tended – yet they exude the feeling of a theatre set, a bit of Cornwall carefully primped and preened; fetching, neat and clean, but not quite real.

On board *Stardust*, Andrew's wife Alison puts the kettle on, eventually passing up mugs of tea and slices of home-made fruit cake from the galley below. We reflect on Helford's fate, and the conversation broadens out to jobs and the economy. Alison says that she recently drove past the still-standing headframe of South Crofty mine at Pool. I tell her about the celebrated piece of graffiti painted along the perimeter fence soon after the mine closed: 'Cornish lads are fishermen and Cornish lads are miners too. But when the fish and tin are gone, what are the Cornish boys to do?'

There are around a dozen fishermen still working out of Helford – six of their boats are anchored around the visitors' moorings today. *Lady Hamilton* FH214 is the most elegant, its pale-blue body trimmed with dark-blue and red stripes. The two letters of its code indicate it is registered in Falmouth; there are Padstow (PW) and St Ives (SS) plates too, though some of the craft have further-flung origins. One is from Beaumaris on the Isle of the Anglesey (BS), another has Berwick-upon-Tweed (BK) as its home port.

But no fishermen live in Helford any more; indeed it is not entirely clear if they are welcome to work here. There is no harbour, so they are forced to land their catch by tender, loading nets and fuel the same way. It is exhausting and potentially dangerous work. In 2009 the fishermen applied to build a small jetty and roadway behind the pub, standard facilities in most places where fishermen work. Kerrier District Council* approved

---

* Kerrier Council had its main offices in Camborne and was one of six district councils abolished in 2009 when Cornwall Council became a unitary authority. The others were Caradon (Liskeard), Carrick (Truro), North Cornwall (Wadebridge), Penwith (Penzance) and Restormel (St Austell).

the scheme, triggering an immediate outcry from the Helford Village Society, a group that claimed to represent 80 per cent of local homeowners.

Two hundred letters were written opposing the plans; an investigation by BBC South West revealed that almost half of them came from outside Cornwall. The society funded a judicial review, which overturned the council's decision to award planning permission and left the fishermen forced to decide whether they continued to use their tenders or landed their catch elsewhere. A victory for part-time villagers wanting to preserve the quiet charm of their adopted home, and happy to forget the brutish – sometimes dirty, noisy, smelly – reality that had brought the village into existence in the first place.

* * *

The date for our voyage to Falmouth has kept shifting as we wait for the perfect combination of wind and sunshine. In the end we get fed up with hanging around and decide to go for it. The rain has stopped, but the sky still feels heavy with water, the clouds a catalogue of greys, dark-stained around the edges, like ink spilled on blotting paper.

The engine is virtually silent as we slip the mooring, leaving the cluster of fifty or so yachts anchored on the river or resting alongside the pontoons of the sailing club. A bright, circular sign appears on a small concrete quay at the tip of the village – someone is calling the ferry. At Helford Passage, the hamlet on the other side, a boatman keeps half an eye out for the distant signal, a red semicircle flipped into a large yellow disc when a traveller needs collecting. The ancient ferry was once one of the business interests of the bishops of Exeter; today it is part of the South-West Coast Path, giving weary walkers a brief chance to rest their legs.

To the left of the Ferryboat Inn, tall Monterey pines surround Ridifarne, one of a series of substantial houses built on the north side of the river in the 1920s on land that had previously been used for potato farming. In World War Two it was requisitioned by the Special Operations Executive, who used the river as a discreet base for its small-craft operations. A fleet of two trawlers and eight medium-size French fishing boats was used to deposit or exfiltrate undercover agents in and out of remote coves on the Breton coast; 'lardering' operations saw caches of arms, communications equipment or medical supplies left hidden in lobster pots or among rocks, ready for collection by the resistance. The beach at Praa Sands, fifteen miles from Helford towards Penzance, was used to test 'surf-boats', a new rowing boat designed by the SOE to reduce the chances of its operatives being detected as they approached the French shore.

There were briefly American forces here too, as the Trebah estate became a staging post for soldiers on their way to the Normandy Landings. Part of the garden was turned into an ammunition store, and the beach was covered with concrete to make a flat apron from where, on 1 June 1944, men of the 29th US Infantry Division, and their guns, vehicles and related materiel, departed on ten landing craft.

The Isle of Wight was their first stop, and from there they continued to Omaha Beach. Contemporary photographs offer incongruous views of American troops in transport lorries passing thatched cob cottages near the estate. It has proved impossible to remove all the concrete from the beach; now it looks out of place against the backdrop of well-tended mature gardens, a reminder of the chaos, the noise and the scent of fear that once briefly lingered here.

Trebah is one of the magnificent gardens laid out by the

Foxes of Falmouth. First and foremost ship agents, their business interests also included mining, timber, heavy engineering and pilchard fishing. As they grew richer, members of the family started to buy land around Falmouth, building substantial houses, and laying out exotic gardens.

Robert Were Fox was a scientist as well as a businessman; his research into underground heat and terrestrial magnetism led to correspondence with Alexander von Humboldt and Michael Faraday. His dipping-needle compass was used by Sir James Clark Ross on his polar expeditions. He settled close to Falmouth at Penjerrick, where he planted 180 different varieties of conifers in the garden. His brother Charles Fox bought Trebah in the 1830s, and immediately set about creating a twenty-six-acre woodland garden lining both sides of the valley running down to the water.

A couple of fields separate Trebah from Glendurgan, where in the mid 1820s another brother, Alfred Fox, started to lay out his garden. Trees were cleared, a maze laid out, a pond built and filled with trout, orchards were set with apple and pear trees, and beds were filled with exotic plants, perhaps some of them brought back to Falmouth from afar by friendly sea captains. Alfred's wife Sarah established a school in the woods at Glendurgan in 1829, and they built themselves a thatched cottage in which they lived happily for a decade until it burned down in 1837.

Alfred was in Falmouth when word of the fire reached him, and immediately rode there with his nephew Barclay Fox. But they arrived too late to do anything useful: 'We found the tragedy concluded & the four smoking walls with a smokeless chymney [*sic*] at either end all that remained of its former magnificence', Barclay wrote in his diary. His uncle, now homeless, kept his upper lip stiff: 'He was the merriest of the party, looked on the bright side of it all and gave the operatives some porter, which was the finest trait of all.'* They needed a new house in any case, to accommodate a growing family which eventually stretched to six sons and six daughters. The estate stayed in the family until 1962 when Cuthbert Fox and his son Philip donated it to the National Trust to mark the bicentenary of his great-great-grandfather George Croker Fox launching his Falmouth firm of ship agents.

Just after Bosahan the mouth of the Helford narrows, tightening its jaws before it spits us out into Falmouth Bay. I clamber over the deck for a better view of the south bank, where a promontory forms a barrier between the river and Gillan Creek. Andrew gently tucks the boat around Dennis Head and we slide up towards St Anthony Church. My aunt Barbara lived in a cottage at Carne at the top of the creek, but today the tide will not allow us to travel that far up. Bits of the church were built as early as the 13th century; a shingle beach and a boatyard separate it from the water. Behind a sloping graveyard rises up, Barbara now one of its resting residents.

Across the creek, towards the sea, is Gillan, where I would swim after school on hot June and July days, always wary of the strong currents brought about by the meeting of river and sea. As I emerged from the cold water and wrapped a towel around my shoulders, I would look up at a house in the woods above – Machan, a rare example of Cornish-Moderne architecture. Today the white walls of this early 1930s art-deco treasure

---

* Barclay Fox was an inveterate diarist who started a journal at the age of fourteen in 1832 and continued with it until he got married twelve years later. It provides a rich insight into the lives of Cornwall's wealthy merchant class. Barclay was named after his mother, Maria Barclay, a scion of the Quaker banking family. His maternal grandmother was a Gurney, of the Norfolk banking family, who merged their business with that of the Barclays and the Backhouses to form Barclays Bank in 1896.

stand out against the grey sky, its four decks giving the impression that an ocean liner has somehow left the water and become beached on the hillside. It became a nursery school in the 1950s, and then a summer camp for boarding-school pupils whose parents' distant locations meant that they couldn't return home for the holidays. When Machan was up for sale in the mid 1990s my brother William and I pretended to be potential purchasers and got an estate agent to show us around. I felt a shiver of excitement at being inside – it still exuded the magical glamour that had seduced me as a child. Damp had stained the walls and lifted the parquet tiles off the floor, the electric wires and switches looked unchanged in half a century, cold draughts poured through rusty Crittall frames. But its bedrooms, each with its own terrace, and the ten-windowed circular dining room were glorious statements of intent. As a boy I had fantasised about the parties I might throw here, the gatherings I might facilitate, my inspiration coming from a variety of sources, including Agatha Christie and Truman Capote. I saw the place as a Cornish Hearst Castle, a building that seemed to come from a different world, yet occupied its landscape with ease and elegance. If I could live here, I would have made something of my life. The agent seemed to take us seriously as she patiently showed us around, but the asking price was at least ten times more than any mortgage offer I might get. Never mind the building works. Eventually it found a saviour in the form of a British-born American businessman, who had stayed there when it was a children's hostel, and determinedly set about restoring it to its old splendour.

Soon we are back on course for Falmouth. I look again at Dennis Head, the colours getting darker as the land gets closer to the water, green to gold to brown to black; trees, scrub, and then on the shore, rocks covered with lichen and barnacles, or polished clean by the ebb and flow of the tide. The name Dennis comes from the Cornish word *dynas*, meaning fort, and there have been fortifications here since at least the Iron Age. The promontory's position made it an effective location for anyone wanting to control access to the Helford.

It is possible there was a Roman base here. A command post was established at Isca Dumnoniorum, now Exeter, around AD 55, from where the Romans controlled their western territory. A forward operating base at Nanstallon, near Bodmin, was well located in the middle of the county between the Fowey and Camel Rivers. How much further the Romans came, and how passive or aggressive their day-to-day control of Cornwall was, is still a matter of conjecture.

William Borlase, the 18th-century pioneer of Cornish geology, archaeology and history,* was convinced Roman soldiers were posted to Dennis Head, citing as proof the remains of a vallum, or rampart that ran from sea to creek across the western side of the headland. Richard Polwhele, in his seven-volume *History of Cornwall*, published at the start of the 19th century, offered further evidence – the discovery in 1735 at nearby Condurrow of twenty-four gallons of coins from the era of the 3rd-century Roman Emperor Constantine the Great. 'Their small size', Polwhele explained, meant they would have been 'incommodious for trade, or for any other purpose than paying the common soldiers.'

Dennis Head was fortified in the 1570s as Spain built up its naval power, a move that 'awakened fear and roused to vigilance all Cornwall'. In 1643, during the Civil War, Royalist forces,

---

*Science was in theory Borlase's hobby; his principal occupation was being vicar of Ludgvan, a post he held for fifty years from 1722 until his death in 1772. He also tried to arrest John Wesley (see Chapter 2).

led by Richard Vyvyan of Trelowarren, constructed a square, bastioned fort with a battery facing north-east towards the mouth of the Fal. It was manned for three years by a garrison of soldiers drawn from St Anthony, St Martin, St Keverne and other local villages – one lieutenant, one master gunner, five other gunmen, one porter, and forty rank and file.

The soldiers were paid by Vyvyan himself, whose commitment to the cause saw him created a baronet in February 1645. But a year later local support for the King had virtually collapsed – this was one of just three garrisons still holding out along with Pendennis Castle and St Michael's Mount. Dennis Head finally fell on 17 March, its strategic importance made clear by the fact that the surrender was accepted in person by Thomas Fairfax, the Parliamentarian commander-in-chief.

It is easy to imagine the Cornish soldiers in their camp, knowing the game was up, waiting for the inevitable end. Their ranks included men called Hill, Jenkin, Tonkin, Stephens and Phillips, still surnames around here today. Fairfax was a Yorkshireman, well travelled thanks to his military life. As he led his men to the Royalist fort, did he appreciate the beauty of his surroundings, did the unfamiliar Cornish names register, did he sniff the delicate scents of early spring? Or did he see his journey here as just another part of a long and bitter campaign?

* * *

The boat is rolling more – we are free of the river and in open water. I spot the marker spire of St Keverne Church. As we head further out, I borrow Alison's binoculars and focus them on the reassuringly distant Manacles. There is a military-looking building on the headland at Nare Point, hard to spot at first against the dark sea. Today a National Coastwatch lookout, it was built by the Ministry of Defence as part of a torpedo-testing range that was in use until 1993. This station, and another a mile and a half south at Porthkerris, were equipped with cameras that tracked the range and trajectories of missiles launched by aircraft based at Culdrose.

In World War Two Nare was the location of one of a series of decoy sites designed to stop bombing raids on Falmouth Docks. A row of signal lights simulated the town's railway yards; cordite was used to create mini-infernos suggesting burning ammunition stores; from high above a muted lamp appeared to be a window left uncovered during a blackout. The idea was that German pilots would be confused, and dump their deadly cargo early, bombing undeveloped coastline rather than the port, and the town around it.

Andrew slowly turns the tiller 90 degrees, putting us on a direct course for Falmouth. Tiny flagged buoys mark lobster and crab pots. A lighthouse stands on St Anthony Head, its tower, keeper's cottage and outhouses built on a granite plinth on top of the rocks. In the 18th century sailors were warned off these rocks by a red flag flown from an elm tree by the Killigrews of Arwenack. Their maritime lineage was impeccable – members of the family had been pirates and privateers in the 15th and 16th centuries. In 1546 John Killigrew became the first captain of Pendennis Castle, one of two new forts built at the command of Henry VIII to guard the entrance to the Carrick Roads, the other standing opposite at St Mawes. It was a highly prestigious job, a hereditary post that should have passed down the generations alongside the family estates, but it was lost after barely half a century. In 1597, with panic in the air about the weakness of Cornish defences in the Anglo-Spanish wars, John Killigrew III was removed from his command. His son, John, tried to reinvent the family business by building the first lighthouse at Lizard Point in 1619. But the project caused anger in the village, with locals furious about their potential loss of earnings if the light stopped ships wrecking themselves on the rocks. Any goods washed ashore in such circumstances were regarded as common property, to be appropriated and then used or sold on by villagers. On occasion, the wreckers, as they were known, fed up with waiting for the wind to drive ships ashore, are said to have lit lamps above remote, rocky cliffs, in order to convince sailors they were near a harbour. But rather than finding safe haven, their ships would be lured to rocky destruction.

The Killigrews had nothing to do with the current St Anthony Head lighthouse, which was built in 1835 by Trinity House, the national lighthouse authority. Mariners can use the St Anthony and Lizard Lights together to plot a safe route around the Manacles. Until 1954 a huge bell hung outside, rung by the lighthouse keeper when fog obscured his lantern. Now an automated foghorn has taken its place.

* * *

Behind us the Lizard Peninsula now appears as a shadowy grey-green line of land sitting between two tarnished sheets of silver, sky reflected on sea. Ahead, the sun has found a gap between the clouds over Gyllyngvase and Castle beaches, theatrically lighting the string of black-and-yellow beach huts, ambitious new apartment buildings, guest houses turned into care homes, and the Victorian stucco of the Falmouth Hotel, built for railway passengers in 1865 on what was previously undeveloped farmland.

A tall crane stands above the hotel's roofline of chimneys and dormer windows; it is part of the docks, whose wharfs and quays are protected by the strong arm of Pendennis Point. *Stardust* seems to bounce in the water; we are crossing the wake left by a blue-hulled harbour authority boat which has just delivered a pilot to steer a fuel tanker safely to its berth.

An elegant wooden speedboat has left a line in the water which I trace to a superyacht moored off St Just in Roseland. *Cloudbreak*, I later read, will set sail the next day for the Maltese capital Valetta via Gibraltar. With six guest cabins, a gym, a cinema, an 'eagle's nest observation tower', an extensive selection of 'water toys' and a crew of twenty-two, it is available to charter for €750,000 a week.

Perhaps the ship was fitted out by Pendennis, whose hangar-sized sheds cover an expanse of Falmouth docks. Established thirty years ago, it is a Cornish business success story, employing hundreds of workers to build boats from scratch, refit existing craft and install new engines, navigation equipment, galleys and bespoke interiors. Andrew looks up the Pendennis website on his phone. It is rich with glitzy luxury, a far cry from the cosy cabin of *Stardust*, with its faded upholstery and unpredictable pump-action lavatory. Here are pages of dark-wood finishes, pale leather panels with nickel trim, parquet floors, chandeliers that stretch between decks, jacuzzis and infinity pools. The 'finding us' section reassures potential customers wanting to visit the shipyard that there is a private helipad available for them.

As we make a final turn into the marina that is *Stardust's* home, a wall of naval grey looms above us. RFA *Argus* was a commercial ferry and container carrier when it was called up for duty in the Falklands War. Now it is operated for the Navy by the Royal Fleet Auxiliary as a 100-bed hospital ship. Falmouth is its home port. In the next berth is the survey ship HMS *Scott*, which spends its long deployments scouring the floor of the world's oceans to provide information and charts for naval and civilian mariners. At 430ft, *Scott* is the largest of the Royal Navy's survey ships. It turns out we just missed two of its smallest vessels, HMS *Example* and HMS *Explorer*, 70ft training craft attached to university naval units, that sailed in the morning bound for the Ulster ports of Belfast, Portrush and Derry.

Andrew cuts the engines and we glide slowly towards our berth. 'Leap off,' he instructs me, 'and secure her as we come alongside.' The steel of the army officer he once was has returned to his voice. Once *Stardust's* ropes are tied, I look up and marvel at the seemingly unplanned way Falmouth's buildings rise up from the shore, in places seven levels of tightly packed streets. Workers' cottages, sea captains' villas, chandlers, ship agents, civic buildings, pubs, churches and chapels, all of which have at some point had a connection to the sea.

CHAPTER 8

From Cornwall to the World

There were two particular reasons why I was always excited when my parents planned a trip to Falmouth. One was the assured visit to what was then Cornwall's only branch of Marks and Spencer. The other attraction was more abstract, a somewhat niche concern, but one of particular appeal to a boy determined to see the world – Falmouth was the base of Cornwall's international diplomatic community. There was no embassy quarter, no row of eye-catching mission buildings, but rather a single office, where a prominent local businessman represented the interests of a handful of European nations. I looked up the countries represented in an old copy of the Diplomatic List that I had once acquired. Should I ever meet the honorary consul, would I address him as 'Your Excellency'? It all felt thrilling to the eleven-year-old me.

Despite having one number, 48 Arwenack Street is actually an elegant pair of houses, built of red brick, a column of bay windows at the centre of their symmetrical façade. Delicate wrought-iron handrails lead the visitor up gentle granite steps, the front doors crowned with cobwebbed fanlights. But as a boy it wasn't the rich architectural detail that delighted me, but the row of consular medallions that hung under the first-floor windows. The symbols of countries far away across the seas, their governments represented here in Falmouth.

This was the building from which the Foxes conducted their affairs. The houses were still new developments when G. C. Fox and Company moved in at the end of the 18th century. For the next 200 years they remained the headquarters of the family's eclectic and extensive business interests.

I knew the Fox name thanks to their small chain of travel agents. A neat row of airline stickers decorated the windows of their branch on Wendron Street in Helston – the slightly faded logos of British Airways, Pan-Am, Dan-Air and Aer Lingus. The staff were happy to give out colourful brochures selling cruises, fly-drive holidays to America or package tours to Cyprus and Yugoslavia. Once when I asked for information about the new, high-lux iteration of the Orient Express, I was rewarded with a set of glossy leaflets presented in a thick cardboard folder, the paper bearing a slight hint of sweet scent.

Finally, at the age of thirteen, I made a purchase – or rather my father did – a rail ticket for my first solo trip to London. My heart beat as the assistant wrote out the docket by hand, carefully checking that his pen was reaching through the layers of carbon paper, before giving the document an official stamp of validation. Dad suggested he might keep the ticket safe himself, but I wasn't going to give it up. Every day I would carefully take it out of its envelope and check it once again; the words 'London Paddington' imbued with rich possibility.

The writer, poet and painter Charles Fox was the last member of the family to practise consular service. At his home, Glendurgan, he shows me the handwritten papers confirming his ancestor Robert Were Fox as American consul to the Port of Falmouth. George Washington himself signed the document on 30 May 1794, in Philadelphia, the city that was serving as temporary capital while Washington DC was being built. Another certificate shows Alfred Fox's name inserted in handsome copperplate,

Abraham Lincoln's signature at the bottom. The family served the United States for 115 years. Opening a velvet-lined box, Charles shows me a heavy metal disc, an inch and a half wide, with the words 'Consulate USA Falmouth' around the edge, and a bald eagle in the centre – the consular seal used to stamp American authority on documents and papers.

Over two centuries the Fox family provided consular services to thirty-six countries. In 1822 Alfred Fox used the *West Briton* to publicise new shipping regulations sent from St Petersburg by the Russian Department of Foreign Trade. Six years later, as representative of both Germany and Brazil, he had to address the plight of a party of 350 German emigrants stuck in Falmouth after their Rio-bound ship was wrecked.

Alfred's son George Henry Fox became Ottoman vice-consul in 1875, and in 1939 his son Cuthbert Fox refused to become Nazi Germany's envoy after being asked to sign a document confirming that neither he nor his father, nor their wives, were of Jewish origin or descent. Some of the states the family served no longer exist – Prussia, Mecklenburg, Sardinia and Tuscany; still extant nations that were represented include Venezuela, Honduras, Mexico and Colombia.

By the time Charles took control the group had shrunk to half a dozen European nations – France, Germany, Norway, Spain, Greece and the Netherlands. He recalls being invited to conferences abroad, when he and his fellow consuls were treated like royalty with outriders on the way from the airport, grand dinners and trips to the opera. Back in the office, reams of press releases and government information would arrive by post each week. 'I tried to absorb it all,' he says 'but in reality, the main duties were crew repatriations, issuing life certificates, organising the occasional drinks party for a visiting ship and making sure the right flag was flown on each country's national day.'

Increasingly the work of the Falmouth honorary consul became focused on the mundane – advancing money and providing passports. By the late 20th century, email, mobile phones, credit cards and electronic bank transfers had made much of the job redundant. One by one the flags were lowered for a final time, and the consular signs were removed from the front of 48 Arwenack Street, carefully packed up and returned to foreign ministries across Europe.

* * *

No more than a rudimentary grasp of geography is needed to see why Falmouth is one of the world's great natural harbours. The outcrops of land at Pendennis Point and St Anthony Head form a mouth that protects the Carrick Roads, and an estuary running four miles inland and well over 100ft deep in places.

It offers a haven that can accommodate hundreds of ships in its extensive network of inlets and creeks. In December 1814 the *West Briton* reported that the Royal Navy's entire West Indian fleet had taken shelter from a storm, riding out heavy gales 'with scarcely any damage; a thing unprecedented in any other port in Great Britain'. Falmouth was the obvious place for a centre to service a profitable maritime trade, a settlement tucked safely into the bottom left-hand corner of a lake-like expanse of water. But by Cornish standards it is a new town, not settled until the mid 17th century. It is curious that Henry VIII's forts did not prove an immediate catalyst for the place's development. A map drawn around 1580, four decades after the castles at Pendennis and St Mawes were built, shows the Killigrew family home at Arwenack Manor and a small, waterside community called Smythycke as the only other settlements. The rest of the peninsula is largely covered in fields. Finally, at the end of the 16th century Sir Walter Raleigh sailed into the harbour, and made the suggestion that it would benefit from a town at its mouth, an idea that John Killigrew IV decided to act upon.

Until this point Penryn, two miles upstream, had been the principal local town. Incorporated as a borough in 1236, it had become one of Cornwall's major ports – its ships traded as far as Constantinople and it was the last English victualling stop for vessels bound south or west. It was not going to relinquish its position without a fight. Killigrew made his first move in 1613, securing permission from James I to open four inns. Penryn made furious protests, supported by Truro and Helston. The town suffered further humiliation as six more inns and a market were established, and a resident customs officer was appointed.

Development started to move even faster when Peter Killigrew inherited the estate from his brother in 1648. Raised at court, he had become a rich man, and devoted much of his fortune to the new town.

In 1660 Penryn thought the Restoration might be a good moment to appeal against its neighbour's growth, but was thwarted a year later when Smythycke was renamed Falmouth and received a royal charter from Charles II. A mayor and corporation quickly followed, giving new authority, and meaning the place had good reason to reinvent itself. A port settlement rife with heavy drinking, prostitution and violence was quickly to become a respectable and ambitious borough.

Penryn realised it was going to have to exist alongside its new neighbour, building a new wharf, Exchequer Quay, and exploiting its proximity to the rich mining lands that lay between the town and Redruth. It remained the favoured home for wealthy merchants and sea captains throughout the 18th century, but soon after entered a period of long and slow decline, caused by both the collapse of the tin industry and the development of Falmouth. In 1870 Penryn was declared 'poverty stricken and insanitary' in a Board of Health report; in 1975 the local council declared it a 'housing action area', a designation usually reserved for inner cities; 330 dwellings in the town centre were declared 'squalid', with 43 per cent having no fixed bath and 32 per cent no running hot water.

* * *

Falmouth evolved fast. By the late 1660s it had shipyards capable of building large vessels. Related trades flourished as those who made ropes, sails and candles all found new customers. Two decades later the town's trading fleet boasted twenty-seven craft. Incoming cargoes included timber from Scandinavia, salt from Portugal and France and wines from Spain and Madeira; exports were dominated by tin and pilchards. The fish were caught by boats working the coast between Penzance and Fowey, then salted and shipped to Mediterranean ports.

Fish was soon replaced by a new cargo – international mail carried on board the General Post Office's packet ships. For much of the 17th century letters and parcels bound for mainland Europe and beyond had been taken by sea to Calais, and then carried overland to their final destinations. But this system ground to a halt when William III joined the Grand Alliance against France in 1689.

Mails for northern Europe and Habsburg and Ottoman territories could be routed through Harwich and the Hook of Holland, but a new system was needed to serve Spain, Portugal, the Caribbean and the Americas – one that avoided the now dangerous English Channel. At first Plymouth was considered as a possible base for the new service, but Falmouth's position, and the ability of its harbour to protect shipping from both bad weather and enemy attack, gave it the edge.

The first packets sailed in November 1689, bound for the city of Coruña, known to English speakers of the time as The Groyne. With Spain about to join the allies, diplomatic hands must have been involved in the naming of the first ships, *Spanish Allyance* and *Spanish Expedition*. They started a service that was to give Falmouth an international role for 160 years.

Money poured into the local area as the demand for ships' supplies and victuals increased exponentially. A reservoir was built across the water at Flushing to supply the thousands of gallons of fresh water which vessels needed for their journeys. New hotels were constructed for rich passengers – in the early 19th century a passage to Lisbon was priced at £23 (around £2,100 today); a ticket for Brazil cost £107 (nearly £10,000).

One unexpected benefit which delighted Falmouth's more inquisitive citizens was that they came to hear about international affairs, diplomatic intrigues and general gossip up to a week before such information reached the coffee houses and newspapers of London. In the early days of the service, it could take that long for letters unloaded at Falmouth to reach the capital. The 273-mile journey was made on the King's Post Road, for much of its length barely more than a cart track. Individual parishes were responsible for their own stretches of the route, meaning the quality of passage was highly variable. Gradually conditions improved, and by the end of the 18th century mail posted in London on a Wednesday could be dispatched on ships sailing from Falmouth on Saturday. The Packet Service brought about improvements for those trying to trade in Cornwall too – a new turnpike route from Falmouth to Grampound via Truro and a Truro–Launceston road, the basis of today's A30.

In theory packet cargo was limited to mails, official consignments and gold and silver bullion. In reality ships set sail heavily laden with goods – there was a lucrative market for wool and cotton products in Portugal; boots, shoes, cheese, potatoes and fighting cocks sold well in the West Indies and North America. Vessels returned with wine, gin, tobacco, sugar and silk – a trade estimated to be worth £4 million a year at the end of the 18th century. Many of the packet captains were in on the trade themselves, and those that were not tended to turn a blind eye, knowing that the extra money made amends for the paltry wages they paid their crew – as little as twenty-eight shillings a month, barely enough to keep their families fed.

In August 1815, crowds lined the waterfront hoping for a glimpse of Napoleon. The deposed French emperor had spent a week aboard a ship moored in Plymouth Sound while the British government decided what do with him. Having concluded that he should be exiled to the remote South Atlantic island of St Helena, he was transferred to HMS *Northumberland*, which made a stop at Falmouth to take on supplies ahead of its ten-week journey.

Napoleon's defeat, and the subsequent peace with France marked the beginning of the end of the Falmouth packets. The first big change came when the Navy took command. Although historically the Post Office had run the service, the ships themselves were privately owned, control ultimately resting in the hands of often mercurial captains. It was a state of affairs that had long caused the government worry. With the war over, the Navy had a surplus of ships and sailors for which it was keen to find employment, and in 1823 control of the service passed to the Admiralty.

An advertisement from 1827 lists thirty-seven Falmouth ships, including *Magnet*, *Swallow*, *Rinaldo*, *Sheldrake* and *Calypso*. There was a weekly departure for Lisbon, with other regular services offering direct sailings to the Caribbean islands of Barbados, Jamaica, Cuba, St Lucia, Gaudeloupe and Antigua, Veracruz and Tampico in Mexico, the South American cities of Rio de Janeiro,

Salvador da Bahia, Montevideo and Buenos Aires, the Atlantic Ocean territory of Bermuda, Halifax in Canada and the European ports of Cadiz, Gibraltar, Malta and Corfu. It was an impressive list of destinations, but one that was soon to shrink.

Falmouth's biggest problem was that long journey to London. If shipping could now safely navigate the Channel, why not use a port more conveniently situated for the capital? A route between London and Seville was launched in 1823, and though not an immediate success, it showed that Cornwall could no longer expect to maintain a monopoly on packet services.

The contract to carry the Lisbon mails was awarded to the Southampton-based Peninsular and Oriental Steam Navigation Company (later P & O) in 1837. From then on Falmouth's fall was quick. A direct railway link might have bolstered the port's position. In 1839 a committee led by the earl of Falmouth proposed a service to Exeter, where trains would connect with other routes being built to London. The line was to be the HS2 of its day: speed was all that mattered; it would take the most direct path, even if that meant bypassing and thus foregoing business from major towns on the route. The directors reckoned 80 per cent of income would come from packet traffic. The plans came to nothing, and it was another twenty years before Cornwall was connected by train to London. Falmouth had to wait until 1863 before it joined the network.

In 1840 the Post Office published a notice stating that 'the Packet Mails for North America will in future be despatched by Steam Vessels from Liverpool', carried by what became the Cunard Line. That same year the first train ran between Southampton and the capital. Fast services could cover the route in just three hours. Two years later the Royal Mail Steam Packet Company secured the contract to serve the West Indies, Mexico and Cuba from the Hampshire port. For a short while Falmouth kept its right to load and unload international mail, forcing ships to make an extra call at the start or finish of their voyage, but soon the game was up.

The final Falmouth Packets ran in 1851. *Seagull* was one of the last to dock. As the *Royal Cornwall Gazette* reported, it arrived from Rio after forty-seven days' passage. The hold was nearly empty – 'She brought only a small parcel of letters, and but three packets of diamonds on freight.' There were also eight passengers: two Misses Weitman, Master Le Febre, four members of the Fowler family and a Mr Manuel. Their ascent up the gangplank marked the end of a business that had made Falmouth a centre of global trade for 150 years.

* * *

Arwenack Street forms one end of Falmouth's elongated main street. I follow the road along, until it kinks and becomes Church Street. Raised up above the pavement is the Church of King Charles the Martyr, built immediately after Falmouth had received its royal charter. Further along the road bends north-west, and assumes another name, Market Street. The buildings on the right form a barrier, an extended lip of shop-houses and commercial premises that seem placed to keep town and waterfront apart. Occasionally the line breaks to allow traffic to reach Fish Strand Quay, Custom House Quay and Prince of Wales Pier, but otherwise the harbour is kept out of sight, the ever-present hard yell of the gulls a reminder of its proximity.

'Ope' is a word used in Cornwall to describe narrow lanes or passages that run under buildings or between high walls; here they appear on either side of the road. Some have steep stairs that lead to tiers of terraces above, others are half-lit alleyways that drop down to neglected moorings, landing platforms and flights of granite steps that eventually peter out under the water.

The café at the back of Marks and Spencer had one of the

best views of maritime Falmouth. For half a century it was the retailer's only Cornish branch, and drew customers from across the county, including my parents. Dad's favoured weekend smart-casual was a check shirt and a pair of their corduroy trousers; my first jacket came from the store, bought when I was ten for my brother Andrew's wedding. Its pullovers, in claret red or dark green, were reliable Christmas gifts, their squidginess making them easily identifiable to an inquisitive child poking at the presents under the tree.

When I went with Mum, any impatience felt while waiting for her to try on a bra, blouse or pair of slacks would be tempered by the knowledge that a visit to the food hall lay ahead. She cooked most of what we ate from scratch; there was a racy excitement about a Marks' supper of warmed-up quiche Lorraine followed by sherry trifle served from a plastic tub. The company added sandwiches to its retail range in 1980. A few years later I recall sitting on a bench by Custom House Quay, relishing eating one of the cardboard-packaged offerings – bacon, lettuce and tomato on brown bread – my father managing to spoil the moment by working out how much he would have saved had he made the same sandwich at home.

Marks and Spencer opened in Falmouth in December 1933; previously its network of shops stopped at Plymouth. It has never been clear why it chose this town for its solo incursion into Cornwall. One local story is that a prominent shareholder in the business, perhaps even a member of the founding Marks/Sieff family, kept a yacht in the harbour or had a holiday property nearby, and thus wanted a convenient store. When I ask the company archivist for information, she tells me that she has heard variations on the same story, but says surviving official documents shed no light on the reasons for the decision. Marks and Spencer plc closed the store in January 2019. The *Falmouth*

Packet featured a multi-page spread of photographs and memories of the staff, some of whom had spent their whole working lives in the company's service.

Today the only reminder of its near nine-decade presence is the old black-and-gold company clock, still hanging over the abandoned shopfront as I write.

* * *

The shopping street ends with a gentle climb to the top of High Street. On the left, wide granite steps lead into an art gallery. It was once the town hall, but was originally built as a congregational chapel around 1710. Along with the Quaker meeting houses at Marazion and Come-to-Good near Truro, this is one of the earliest nonconformist church buildings in Cornwall. A modern mezzanine floor cuts across the middle of the round-headed windows, and the double front doors are distinctly workmanlike, but the building retains an elegant lightness, lifting the spirits of this passer-by, just as it must have done to its first worshippers three centuries ago.

I duck through an ugly modern arch across the road at the summit of High Street, and the town opens up again. Across the lower reaches of the Penryn River sits Flushing, where many of the captains and officers of the packet ships chose to live. While some enjoyed the peace, calm and distance from the harbour, others wanted a livelier existence in Falmouth itself. Canny local builders quickly spotted an opportunity and started building on this side of the river. Dunstanville, Stratton and Tehidy Terraces sprang up, offering properties with high-ceilinged, light-filled rooms, and fine views across the water. The spiritual needs of this maritime elite were soon catered for too when one of the so-called Commissioners' churches, churches built with public money, was constructed in 1827. The castellated Tudor Gothic building of St Michael's Church sits discreetly between a pair of comfortable-looking villas on Stratton Terrace.

I wander back towards town and walk the length of the Prince of Wales Pier, departure point for both summer pleasure boats and the year-round ferries to Flushing and St Mawes. Seagull muck has stained the simple plaque that marks the visit in 1903 of the future George V to lay the first stone.*

An ope across from the pier leads me up a flight of steps to Smithick Hill, its name a rare reminder of the old settlement of Smythycke. Near the top stands a simple but striking building that is now a house. The side walls are rendered and painted pink, two arched windows adorn its red-brick frontage. For seventy years in the 19th century, this was Falmouth's synagogue.

Alexander Moses, or Zender Falmouth as he became known,

---

*The Prince of Wales's Falmouth duties came two days after the heir to the throne had inspected Marconi's radio station at Poldhu (see Chapter 10), a day that also included a visit to Arthur Pendarves Vivian at Bosahan (see Chapter 7).

was one of the town's first permanent Jewish residents. He was an immigrant from Alsace who arrived in 1740 and quickly established himself as a successful silversmith. Jewish traders had long visited the town; in the preceding decades local inn-keepers had taken to keeping stores of kosher cooking utensils in locked cupboards, ready for their arrival. Moses encouraged some of the visitors to stay and open businesses, and gradually a settled community took shape. In 1766 he became president of a congregation that appointed a rabbi and built a synagogue on the waterfront at Fish Quay; fourteen years later he secured land on the Penryn road for a Jewish cemetery, where he was buried himself in 1791.

By the start of the following century many of Falmouth's chandlers, sailors' outfitters and ship agents were Jewish, and a larger synagogue was required. The new building was completed in time for the 1808 Rosh Hashanah and Yom Kippur holy days. At the start of the 1840s there were fourteen Jewish families, but almost all of them left in the downturn that followed the end of the packet trade, with those that remained forced to rely on the community at Penzance – also in decline – for supplies of kosher meat. The synagogue closed in 1880. Nathan Vos, a Dutch-born hotel proprietor, was the last person buried in the graveyard, in 1913.*

* * *

---

*The Jewish Cemetery and adjacent Dissenters' Burying Ground are being restored and can be visited. Penzance's Jewish Cemetery is considered one of the best preserved provincial Georgian Jewish cemeteries in the country. It is now owned by the Board of Deputies of British Jews and maintained by Penzance Town Council. The New Street Synagogue in Penzance opened in 1768, was rebuilt in 1807 and was closed and sold by 1906.

After the Packets, Falmouth found new sources of revenue, swapping mail and passengers for cargoes of grain, timber, coal, granite, china clay, copper ore, rope and fish. When the railway eventually came it helped the port become a well-connected and important regional trading centre, with a spider's-web of sidings stretching out alongside its wharfs and warehouses. In 1855 just one steamship was registered here; by 1900 the number had increased to forty-four. In the 1920s two dry docks were built; another was added in 1958 – the Queen Elizabeth II Dock, one of the largest in the country. These ensured Falmouth became a centre for the repair of big ships, a business that continues today.

The economy recovered more quickly than the town's self-esteem – a sense of humiliation lingered. Falmouth had lost the international prominence that came with being Britain's principal mail port; after the Packets ceased sailing, its name appeared only rarely on international shipping timetables and route plans. In 1895 Arthur H. Norway* published a history of the service, noting that it had been forgotten by historians: 'no one has collected the facts or given any labour to preserve them from perishing. One by one as survivors of the service died their memories died with them.'

His call to arms prompted first an exhibition of memorabilia and then a drive to raise funds for a monument honouring those who had served. It sits in the midst of a roundabout at The Moor,

---

*Norway was a descendant of John Arthur Norway, a packet captain killed on duty in 1813 when his ship, the *Montagu*, was attacked by an American privateer off Madeira. Norway's other books included an early piece of south-west travel writing, *Highways and Byways in Devon and Cornwall*, published in 1898. As well as being a prolific writer, he was also a senior civil servant, secretary to the General Post Office in Ireland at the time of the 1916 Easter Rising. His son was the novelist (and aeronautical engineer) Nevil Shute.

the town's civic quarter. To read the inscription on the 38ft-high obelisk, I have to dodge buses and taxis, and climb over rings of bricks and cobbles. The wording is simple: 'To the honour of the gallant officers and men of H. M. Post Office Packet Service'. It is an impressive tribute to generations of seafarers, many of whom gave up their lives while carrying out their duties. But it feels as if the memorial also stands for something bigger. These sailors helped shape the idea of this county as a place that looks out to the world. The Falmouth Packets were the first of a line of services that helped turn Cornwall into a vital staging post for global communication.

CHAPTER 9

Under the Sea

It was surely Cornwall's place as a hub of international communication that inspired me in the career choices I have made. 'Nation Shall Speak Peace Unto Nation' were the words adopted by the BBC as an official motto in 1927. Cornwall can lay claim to playing a vital role in facilitating that global conversation. Long before the BBC we were already key to world communication, thanks first to the Falmouth Packets, then to undersea cables and more recently to wireless masts and vast dishes staring into outer space.

My journey today takes me to the very end of the A30. The ten miles that stretch towards Land's End are the last gasp of a route that starts at an unprepossessing roundabout in suburban London, the conclusion of a long march south-west. Beyond Penzance there is little sense of this still being a major road. Up country dual carriageways are long forgotten, reflective black-and-white chevrons warn of hard bends, 30mph speed limits slow me down as I pass through the communities of Drift and Catchall and Sennen. The last trunk road sign, white and yellow type on a green background, points east to Penzance and west to Land's End. From here the road gently descends towards the sea, ending at the place where the English Channel and the Atlantic Ocean meet.

Beyond the famous signpost ('John O' Groats 874 miles') is the Longships Lighthouse, built on a rock a mile and a half off shore. Eight miles out to the south-west, the Wolf Rock Light rises defiantly from the sea. Both of these towers had resident keepers until 1988; now they are controlled from the headquarters of Trinity House, the English lighthouse authority, at Harwich in Essex.

Sometimes the visibility has been so good here that I have been able to see St Martin's, the closest of the Scilly Isles, nearly thirty miles off the mainland. But today conditions are not promising, and mist threatens to block the view of Longships, let alone the Scillies. The BBC weather app suggests an 86 per cent chance of rain for the next few hours. My friend Tatiana and I planned our walk to Porthcurno more than a week ago. We spoke earlier on the phone, moaned about the weather and danced around a bit, but neither of us was going to blink first and postpone the expedition.

Sudden squalls make it hard to get out of the car and Tatiana struggles against the gusts as she pulls on her waterproofs. I am not so well prepared and my jeans are soaked through before we reach Pordenack Point. At least I have remembered a plastic bag to keep my phone dry.

On summer days a constant trail of walkers passes here, many ticking off another stage of the South West Coast Path, their routes carefully planned, with specific destinations that must be reached in time for pre-booked pub suppers and B&Bs. Today we are the only people out, and are rewarded for our tenacity. As we pass the cubed rock formations balanced along the cliff like half-made Easter Island statues, the wind blows the precipitation out to sea. Grey changes to blue, and then the sun breaks through, turning the sand on Nanjizal Beach a rich yellow, and illuminating the entrances to the caves behind.

We climb up the steep steps to the Iron Age cliff castle at Carn Lês Boel, where it is calm enough to sit on a rock and eat our sandwiches. But not ten minutes later the skies darken again, and the clouds start dumping vast quantities of water into the sea. The downpour is soon over our heads, and we duck behind finely built stone walls in an attempt to find protection from the driving rain that whips our faces. At Gwennap Head the volunteers scanning the sea at the National Coastwatch station look cosy and warm behind the glass of their well-placed lookout.

The path briefly breaks away from the coast and follows a narrow lane, its high hedges blocking out the roaring sea. By the time we reach Porthgwarra it is dry and mild again. An arched tunnel leads down to the beach, its floor left shiny and slippery by rain and sea spray. Miners from St Just blasted this passage through the cliffs in the 1890s to enable fishermen to land their

catch more easily. Just beyond the rocks a seal surfs in the swell. Today the hamlet is quiet, the woman running the Porthgwarra café has sold just a handful of hot drinks. The only drama as we pass through is the arrival of the postman, who issues a cheery wave as he opens the free-standing cast-iron post box, which he finds empty.

St Levan Church sits inland, comfortably sheltered by gentle hills. Less protected on the edge of the sea are a holy well, and further down a little pathway, a tiny chapel built in the 7th or 8th century in honour of the saint. Until the 19th century water drawn from here was used for baptisms – and was considered to be efficacious for anyone suffering from eye problems or toothache. There is another climb out of Porth Chapel, the coast path steering us upwards to the Minack headland, the name from the Cornish *meynek*, meaning a rocky place.

In 1923 Rowena Cade bought the land here for £100 and set about building a house. She began to stage plays in her garden, before deciding to turn a natural amphitheatre on the cliffs into an outdoor auditorium. With the help of her gardener, Billy Rawlings, and a local craftsman, Charles Angove, she flattened an area for the stage, gathered sand from the beach, salvaged wooden beams from the sea and carved terraces and rows of hard seats out of the stone. The Minack Theatre opened with a production of *The Tempest* in 1932. Now professional and amateur companies, many of them based in Cornwall, appear as part of its twenty-week annual season. Every actor who walks out onto the Minack stage is well aware that their performance must compete with a majestic backdrop of sea and sky, a glittering star cloth made of real stars, and perhaps a cameo performance from a fishing boat returning home or a passing pod of bottlenose dolphins.

Beyond the theatre the coast path drops down steeply treacherous steps to the beach at Porthcurno. At the back of the cove, almost hidden by the sand dunes, is a small, flat-roofed shed. It has little architectural merit, but it warrants a prime place in the history of communication.

This hut was where fourteen international cables came up from under the sea. Tatiana and I peer inside and see two rows of old junction boxes. Each is labelled with the name of a place. There are markers for lines to Gibraltar and Vigo in Spain. Out of sight in the darkness are the ends of wires that reached Fayal in the Azores, Brest in France, Bilbao in Spain, Carcavelos in Portugal, and Newfoundland, across the Atlantic.

I imagine leaning in and taking one of the cables in my hand, pulling it so it tautens and rises a little from the seabed, my faraway tug felt in another distant shed by the side of the Mediterranean, or in the New World. A thin, delicate coil of copper wrapped in rubber, sharing the ocean floor with creatures of the dark deep, carrying onwards a never-ending current of information.

* * *

When the Falmouth Packets stopped sailing, Cornwall's time at the heart of global communication might have seemed over. But within two decades the county had found itself another vital role, as the starting point for a cable that linked Britain with its greatest colonial possession, India.

John Pender was a Scottish textile merchant who had established a successful business based in Glasgow and Manchester. His extensive trade with the Near and Far East made him realise that the global economy could become much more efficient if information could be exchanged at near-instantaneous speed, rather than the weeks it took to send letters, bills and other documents by sea. He had invested in the first transatlantic cable companies, and in the late 1860s he started working with a consortium that was planning a link with Bombay.

At first the cable was to land at Falmouth, but when Pender saw how busy the harbour was, he started to worry about the risk of ships' anchors slicing through his fragile link. Porthcurno provided a perfect solution – an almost uninhabited valley leading down to a quiet beach on a bay that commercial shipping had no reason to disturb.

An engraving shows a three-masted brig laying one of the first cables. More than twenty men are on the beach, looking like a tug-of-war team as they work to drag the line ashore. The picture is a curious juxtaposition of the old and the new – against a backdrop of the Treryn Dinas headland, a classic sailing ship installs cutting-edge technology still used in the 21st century.

The connection to India was completed on 23 June 1870, using a series of cables linked in a chain, the first section running between Porthcurno and Carcavelos near Lisbon. Pender threw a party at his house in London's Piccadilly to celebrate. 'How are you' was the first signal; 'All well' came the reply. A message that would have taken six weeks to reach India could now be sent in just nine minutes.

Pender went on to create the Eastern Telegraph Company, bringing together many smaller operators to form what eventually became the world's largest operator of submarine cables, with over 73,000 nautical miles in its system. In 1877 Porthcurno, or 'PK' as it was identified in transmissions, handled an average of 600 messages a day. By the end of the first decade of the new century it had 150 operators and direct links to coastal and island outposts across Europe. Associated companies took messages further. The Eastern and South African Company had 10,000 miles of cable around the African coast, Western Telegraph reached South America, the Eastern Extension Company carried signals to China and Australasia.

A message from London to Bombay would first be telegraphed from the capital to Porthcurno, where it would be processed and sent by cable to Gibraltar. There an operator would resend it to Malta, from where it would be forwarded to Alexandria. A line carried it across Egypt to Suez, where an operator sent it on to Aden. The final stage was a 2,000-mile-long cable under the Arabian Sea to the west of India. Most urgent communications with the British Empire and its trading partners passed through this remote Cornish valley; only cables to central and northern Europe and North America were routed through other stations.

Junior telegraph operators worked split four-hour shifts; senior members of staff did eight hours at a time, with overnight duty every sixth week. Workers needed to be constantly alert as they received and transmitted messages. The sheer length of the cables meant that incoming signals were often very faint by the time they reached Porthcurno; the telegraphers were well aware of the potential significance of a missed dot or an extra dash.*

The operators were recruited as cadets at the age of sixteen or seventeen. They would spend twelve months training in London, before being sent to Cornwall as probationers. At first facilities were basic; many had to lodge with local families. But gradually the company took over the valley and filled it with the buildings it needed – a telegraph hall, large houses for managers, a block of apartments, a hotel for visitors and quarters for single staff. In between the new-builds, a pair of traditional granite-faced two-up, two-down cottages survive, a reminder of what the place was like before the arrival of the cable. They sit in the shadow of what was an accommodation block on one side, and the station's

---

* An example from 1878 relates to a cable transmitted from Brisbane that celebrated the official launch of a new railway by Sir Arthur Kennedy. 'Governor of Queensland turns first sod' was the message transmitted from Australia. It reached London as 'Governor of Queensland, twins first son'. The next day's newspapers reported the exciting news that Lady Kennedy had delivered two children at Government House. An apology to Kennedy, a sixty-seven-year-old bachelor, soon followed.

social club on the other. Membership of the Exiles Club cost four shillings a month and gave staff access to a billiard room, a library and a theatre, as well as associated cricket and football clubs. Spiritual needs were met by the church up the hill at St Levan, where pews were reserved for those working at the station.

Though the place was run on quasi-military lines, staff were allowed freedom in what they wore while on duty; one operator regularly worked night shifts dressed in a colourful dressing gown and a flowered, tasselled smoking cap. 'Cut off from the outer world as they undoubtedly are, the staff... are thoroughly contented with their lot', noted an article in the January 1911 edition of the *Syren and Shipping*. 'In the midst of one of the grandest and healthiest districts of the British Isles, it is natural that their constitutions should be of the robust order and their spirits irrepressibly buoyant.'

The valley's remote location helped toughen up staff for future postings – once fully qualified, the former probationers could expect to see service in far-flung international stations, which included the Cocos Islands in the Indian Ocean, the Portuguese island territory of São Tomé, and Ascension, where cables linking Rio de Janeiro, Buenos Aires, St Vincent and Cape Town met in the middle of the Atlantic Ocean.

The strategic significance of the network became immediately clear with the start of World War One. In the early hours of 5 August 1914, the day after Britain had declared war on Germany, the cable ship CS *Alert* was dispatched to the Channel. Its task was to locate and then destroy the enemy's undersea wires. Within a few hours most of Germany's fixed links to the outside world had been severed; a British cruiser cut two more cables near the Azores. Berlin was then left with little choice but to send its messages on the British system or by radio transmission. Either way, supposedly secret communications could easily be intercepted.*

That year Walter Bell was a young man working at the telegraph station on St Vincent, an island in the north of the Cape Verde archipelago, 500 miles off the West African coast. He later recalled how, 'crowded round the PK (1) circuit,' he and his fellow workers saw 'the fateful words of the declaration of war spurted out on a Long Distance Recorder.'

When the Second World War began, the Eastern Telegraph Company had become Cable and Wireless, and Bell was back in Cornwall, about to be appointed local manager. The station was soon vital to the war effort. In 1938 official government communications through Porthcurno ran to 12 million words. By 1944 the traffic consisted of 266 million words. The place had to be protected at all costs. Within a few days a small guard of special constables were assigned to protect the site's key buildings. It was quickly realised that this was not enough. Porthcurno might be hidden away but it was still vulnerable to attack and the consequences of it being sabotaged or destroyed were unthinkable.

At first the beach was seen as the most likely route in. Pillboxes were built at sites overlooking the bay, with 300 infantrymen billeted locally, assisted by the 12th Land's End Battalion of the Home Guard. In case the enemy got past their sniper fire, machinery that would create a terrifying wall of fire was installed, its flaming jets fed from a large petrol tank halfway up the hill.

---

* Four hundred Eastern Telegraph staff were killed in action during the war; the number would have been far higher but for the fact that work carried out by the company's operators and engineers was deemed so important, they were actively discouraged from joining up.

Barbed wire was stretched across the valley, there were hidden tank traps and fake haystacks and bus stops were built to hide military materiel. The valley became a 'Protected Place', with strict rules on who could enter and passes issued to Cable and Wireless staff and farm labourers alike.

The real threat was from above. Bell's predecessor had noted this the year before the war began, writing to the managing director of Cable and Wireless on 8 June 1938, pointing out 'the extreme vulnerability of this branch from the air'. 'Bearing in mind the existing international situation,' wrote Owen Langley Hart, 'it is interesting to note that Porthcurno is less than 500 miles, across water, from Nationalist Spain, and that a direct hit from one moderate sized high-explosive bomb would cause irreparable damage to our apparatus.' A contemporary aerial photograph shows how exposed the site was – its technical buildings and accommodation blocks neatly framed by the hills, a set of tennis courts providing a helpful target marker.

The fall of France meant the enemy was little more than 100 miles away. On 5 July 1940 key staff received a typed memo stamped 'Secret' announcing that a bomb-proof shelter would be built. A special 'Porthcurno Emergency Account' was opened to pay for it, and a workforce of several hundred assembled, including three gangs of labourers brought in each day from Penzance and experienced rock drillers from Geevor, the tin mine at nearby St Just.

In just ten months 15,000 tons of granite were removed and two tunnels were blasted into the rock behind the cable station. An unexpectedly large volume of water leaked through from above, and there were concerns over the strength of seams in the rocks, so the walls and ceilings were lined with concrete, more than 2ft thick in places. Finally partition walls were installed and trenches were dug to run the wires linking the coding and receiving machinery with the transmitters and long-distance cables. On 31 May 1941 the tunnels were opened by Lady Wilshaw, wife of Sir Edward Wilshaw, the managing director and chairman of Cable and Wireless, a man who had started his career aged fifteen as a boy clerk.

Three weeks before the tunnels were opened, enemy bombs fell on Cable and Wireless's principal London office, Electra House on Moorgate, home to its central telegraph station. Staff were moved to another office on Victoria Embankment. Should that have come under attack, the headquarters would have moved to Porthcurno. Plans were put in place for the evacuation of operators, and routes were mapped for the motorcycle messengers who would carry signals between the capital and Cornwall if the telephone lines went down.

The messages sent through Porthcurno included troop and ship positions, briefings from senior field officers, lists of the dead and missing and occasional reports of surrender or capitulation. When Japanese troops took control of Singapore in February 1942, Cable and Wireless operators continued to transmit messages for as long as they could. One of the last read: 'Goodbye. Most unlikely able to evacuate. Please inform wives.'

In 1944 the station handled 139 million words from correspondents filing reports for newspapers, agencies and broadcasters, and 49 million words were included in personal telegrams, up from just 3 million before the war. Those wanting to send greetings to or from the field were encouraged to 'ease the burden' on wartime communications by using set phrases, three of which could be sent for two shillings and sixpence. They ranged from the grateful: 'Parcel was just what I wanted many thanks', to the desperate: 'Anxious welfare no news recently'. Some might be sent by parents or lovers: 'Glad and proud to hear of your decoration everybody thrilled'. Others were brisk and businesslike: 'Consult lawyer before taking action'. The ups and downs of normal life continued amid the chaos, but with conversation reduced to a series of cold, impersonal codes.

* * *

Now the tunnels are open to visitors, part of a museum with an eclectic collection that stretches from Victorian telegraph machines made of polished wood and brass, with delicate cogs and ebony and ivory piano keys, to the monogrammed silver toast racks and porcelain coffee services supplied to staff working at distant company outposts. The main entrance to the tunnels is still guarded by blast doors, thick hinges supporting their enormous weight.

On my visit I have the bunker to myself, but there is still a sense of energy and activity thanks to the constant click-clack sound of still-working machinery kept running by a group of volunteers, many of them former engineers here. It is easy to imagine these tunnels when they first opened, filled with staff who rarely got the chance to leave the valley, snatching sleep and food in between their long shifts. Any opportunity for entertainment was seized upon: occasional visits by troupes of ENSA performers,* a weekly organised 'hop' dance night, and a canteen run by the Women's Voluntary Service.

In the decades after the war the tunnels remained in use, their racks and bays restocked with new machinery – the high-tech of the time with keyboards made of plastic and rows of flashing lights held in steel frames painted in shades of utility grey. On

---

*ENSA – the Entertainments National Service Association, formed in 1939 to provide entertainment for armed forces personnel. Some of the biggest stars of the day gave their services, though that didn't stop the organisation gaining the affectionate nickname 'Every Night Something Awful'.

the wall is a map of the Cable and Wireless network in 1965. It looks like the route plan of a major airline. Tristan da Cunha, Palau and the Marshall Islands are among the few places not connected by the steady red or blue line denoting a cable, or the red dots of a radio circuit. But impressive though the map is, it reflects a company in decline.

Most delegates at the 1945 Commonwealth Communications Conference were keen to bring about the end of the monopoly that gave Britain effective control over international connections. American interests wanted New York rather than London to be the world's telegraphic capital. In Africa, the Indian subcontinent, the Middle East and the Caribbean, nations looking forward to their independence were keen to start planning their own systems. What was still needed was a supply of highly trained engineers, system designers and operators, so Porthcurno reinvented itself as a college. For three decades the place flourished – with hundreds of students enrolled in the early 1980s. But with 70 per cent of them coming from abroad, Porthcurno's isolation, once so attractive, became a problem. The college closed in the early 1990s.

* * *

I am on my own a week later when I return to Porthcurno, this time using its car-park as the starting point for a walk towards Lamorna. Today the sun shines brightly and the patches of mud along the cliff path have turned solid underfoot, thanks to three consecutive nights of frost. The sea is absolutely clear and as the tide goes out an island of sand appears in the midst of Pedn Vounder beach. It can't actually be an island, as there is someone in the middle, dressed in loose orange clothing, doing their morning ta'i chi.

I am still mulling over in my mind the achievements of the early cablers when I reach Treryn Dinas, or Treen Fort, a rough promontory with the Logan Rock as its centrepiece. The 80-ton boulder tops an outcrop of cubed granite, its central weight so perfectly balanced that it can be rocked backwards and forwards. They say ancient Druids came to worship here, cherishing what they believed were the rock's supernatural powers. It is a richly romantic thought that Iron Age Celts were responsible for placing the stone, but surely that would have been an impossible task, a far greater challenge than laying cables on the seabed. The more prosaic explanation for its gentle movement is that it is the result of erosion caused by thousands of years of wind and rain.

The historian and priest William Borlase was the 18th-century pioneer of Cornish geology, archaeology and history. He described the Treen stone as being 'so evenly poised that any hand may move it to and fro'. It doesn't move quite so freely now. Borlase reckoned that no 'lever or indeed any force however applied in a mechanical way' could remove it. His words were taken as a challenge in the early 19th century by a Lieutenant Goldsmith of the Royal Navy, who, with the help of nine men from the revenue cutter he commanded, managed to roll the stone off its base.

The local community was furious and demanded answers from the Admiralty. Goldsmith was publicly shamed, in his own words, 'being held as little better than a murderer'. His Navy superiors told him he must restore the stone to its original position, or forfeit his commission. On 2 November 1824, seven months after it had been dislodged, it was back in place. Goldsmith went from villain to hero, albeit one £124 10s 6d poorer. His new popularity may have been in part due to his generosity. Many enjoyed his largesse – his bills included £6 paid to sixty St Just men 'who did nothing but drink beer to the value of 13s 6d'.

I wonder if the men enjoyed this vista of the sea as they sipped their bitter. I can see right across the mouth of Mount's Bay to the Lizard. Newlyn, Penzance and St Michael's Mount are out of sight, round the corner after Mousehole. But if I had a pair of binoculars, I could make out Loe Bar, Poldhu, maybe even the sun shining on one of the dishes at Goonhilly.

Both sides of this bay have provided a safe place for tech pioneers to go about their business; a haven where they could develop new ways for the world's citizens to talk to each other. Over on the Lizard Peninsula brilliant minds looked up to the skies; here they laid their cables on the bottom of the ocean. I look back to Porthcurno and for a second visualise an un-ceasing flow of ticker tape stretching out towards the sea, a dense traffic of words: great affairs of state, military orders, financial instructions that might make people rich or bankrupt, news of births and deaths and love, every message passing through a small window-less hut on this Penwith beach, a construction barely worthy of note, an unremarkable concrete cube through which the world communicated.

CHAPTER 10

Through the Air

In his 2014 *Lizard Exit Plan*, the artist Paul Chaney imagines the Lizard Peninsula as independent, self-sufficient land. The work's subtitle explains why this might need to happen – either to survive an 'unspecified apocalyptic event', or as the consequence of a decision to 'decouple from the economy of global capital for no particular reason'.

In a series of poster-size cyanotype blueprints, he provides detailed plans to help local residents survive the change. There are comprehensive lists of farms and their stock and a survey of former military positions that could be returned to service. Outsiders are considered the main threat; the charts include details of a protective barrier to stop unwanted incursions – using the metal fence that surrounds the perimeter of RNAS Culdrose, repositioned to form an outer palisade, to be later strengthened by the planting of 48,000 willow whips.

Chaney's work echoes a recurring fantasy of my childhood in which the Lizard breaks its bonds with the rest of the United Kingdom. For some reason I became fascinated at an early age with tiny countries, micro-nations, enclaves and exclaves. I would track down detailed maps of Gibraltar and the Sovereign Base Areas of Cyprus, read about landlocked Lesotho or the remote French archipelago of Saint Pierre and Miquelon. If

Tuvalu and San Marino could be sovereign nations, why not the Lizard?

It has always felt like an island, with the sea marking out the boundaries east, south and west. Often the air tastes salty, in the winter wet gales blow above, speeding from coast to coast. The land border that Chaney envisaged is short, little more than three miles from Loe Pool on Mount's Bay to Gweek Quay, the upper limit of the navigable Helford River.

Presumably a frontier post would stand at the roundabout by the cottage hospital at the top of Helston, from where the A3083 forms the peninsula's spine, first skirting the edge of the military airfield and then running almost straight from Cury Cross Lanes to Lizard village – the fast route to the far south.

* * *

Lizard Point gets the medal for being the British mainland's southernmost tip, but its lead over adjacent Bass Point is barely 1,000 feet. My piano teacher, Mrs Siday, lived here in a wind-licked house high on the cliffs. A Steinway parlour grand took up a fair chunk of her sitting room, scores piled high on occasional tables arranged around the instrument. Normally she came to St Martin to give me my lessons, but as exams got close I'd visit her for extra tuition, praying that a few sessions of cramming would make up for months of indolence. As I stumbled my way through Clementi sonatinas and simple works by Beethoven, the windows would rattle in the wind. The sea was heard, not seen – the glass left opaque by layer after layer of sticky sea spray.

Mrs Siday was an enigmatic figure. Betty was her first name, not that I ever considered using it. She told me of a career as a concert pianist in India in the years after independence. Once she showed me a picture of her in concert dress, smiling as she stood next to a handsome Indian man in a smart white dhoti. She did not explain who he was, but there was a definite sense that he had been important to her. It was never clear how she ended up living alone at this remote Cornish extremity.

Each of our lessons would start with me assuring her as to the amount of practice I had done that week, a statement revealed as a lie almost as soon as I started playing. I was not a natural musician – the ability to create beautiful sounds at the piano keyboard did not come easily to me. How disappointed she must have been in me, how bored our lessons must have left her. And yet she managed to sow a seed; years later I realised that something of her passion for Schubert sonatas, Brahms songs and Beethoven quartets had lodged in my subconscious. Sometimes at the end of our lessons she would play herself, leaving me with a wondrous appreciation of the truly talented, and their ability to create music that seemed capable of slowing time.

* * *

I park up where Mum used to leave our red Renault 4, just in the lee of Landewednack Church. St Winwaloe is named after a cleric who established a monastery in his native Brittany in the 5th century. The tower, built a thousand years after the saint had done his good work at Brest, is made of blocks of granite and serpentine – Cornish marble.

At nearby Kynance Cove, jagged rock formations on the beach provide an impressive display of the reddy-brown stone in its natural state. Worked and polished, it became highly collectable – a serpentine bowl, clock, chimney piece or set of carefully shaped ornaments were staples of the Victorian home. At the height of its success the Lizard Serpentine Company, formed in 1853, had a London showroom at 20 Surrey Street, just off the Strand.

There is a surfeit of polished serpentine inside St Winwaloe – the pulpit, lectern, even the columns that support the font's ancient bowl. It bears the name of Richard Bolham, a priest who relinquished his post here in 1415, the year of the Battle of Agincourt. In the 1660s another incumbent of Landewednack, the Revd Francis Robinson, is thought to have preached the last ever Cornish-language sermon here (at least until modern times).

The lane towards Church Cove leads me towards the coast path. The wind is behaving like a capricious child, one that refuses to give in to exhaustion. My legs brace involuntarily against the strong gusts; fifty yards below, the water churns violently around the cubes of smooth rock at the cliff's base. Almost hidden in a narrow slit at Kilcobben Cove is a lifeboat station. The boathouse rests just above the high-water mark on a concrete platform, its foundations sunk ten metres into the seabed. Exposed wooden beams support the building's curved copper roof, the metal slowly turning green in the salty air.

There has been a rescue boat stationed at the Lizard for more than 150 years. Its current home, an impressive piece of civil engineering, was completed in 2011: 170 stairs lead down from the cliff-top car-park, ascending alongside a funicular railway that can carry injured people to a waiting ambulance. The lifeboat, *Rose*, is an all-weather Tamar Class vessel, capable of rolling and self-righting while carrying up to 44 rescued people. *In extremis* up to 118 can squeeze on board.

Today a sea mist comes and goes; I spot a dolphin in the water, and a small colony of grey seals, but there is not a single boat to be seen. I reach my teacher's old house, and immediately remember the squeaking gate, and the sense of panic provoked by its call.

An old coastguard station stands between the house and the sea. Mrs Siday would take Tupperware boxes containing home-made cakes and biscuits to the salaried officers who were stationed here around the clock. Then in 1992 the government made a decision to save money by closing coastal bases like this one, and replacing them with ten computerised regional operations centres – Falmouth was the nearest, Lerwick on Shetland the most northerly.

Two years later Peter Williams and Tony Culmer, fishermen from Cadgwith, were lost at sea. They had not gone far off shore; their boat *Karen Marie* was found off Kennack Sands, just a few miles away. It was possible that whatever disaster had befallen the men, it had played out within sight of the lookout. The thought that an old-fashioned visual watch might have saved two lives prompted the reopening of Bass Point, with volunteers using powerful binoculars to scan the sea, while at the same time monitoring radio emergency frequencies. Bass Point was the first of what has become a chain of fifty-seven National Coastwatch stations, thirteen of them in Cornwall, from Boscastle to Cape Cornwall and Rame Head.

A brick wall a couple of metres high, painted red with a white stripe, stands in front of the lookout. It warns mariners they are close to the Vrogue Rock, its tip just five feet below the surface at low tide. Ships are set on a straight course for the rock if the sign triangulates with two other nearby markers, one on the wall of a distinctive two-storey building that went up here in 1872. Its roof is lined with battlements, the ropes of a flagpole sing shrilly in the wind. Three words are spelt out in black capitals on the west side: 'LLOYD'S SIGNAL STATION'.

This was another business concern of the Foxes of Falmouth. Lookouts on the roof would watch for semaphore signals from ships inbound to Channel ports. News of impending arrivals could be sent ahead, meaning the process of unloading, loading and replenishing vessels could happen more quickly, thus increasing owners' profits. For the first few months of operation men and horses were kept on standby to ferry information to

the nearest telegraph station at Helston, from where it would be relayed by wire to owners, ports and the shipping press. When a cable reached the signal station itself, near real-time communication became possible, with signallers on the roof passing messages back from land to sea.

The system was not flawless – communication was hard at night or in poor visibility, and the rocks around the coast near the station were a hazard. *Queen Margaret* had left Barry in South Wales at the end of July 1912. It carried coal to Montevideo, then progressed to Sydney, before returning heavily loaded with wheat. In May 1913 the four-masted steel barque arrived off the Lizard and was immediately instructed to sail on to Limerick to unload, and then to Glasgow, where its crew would be paid off. The captain demanded extra information, but while he was waiting for a reply, his ship struck the Maenheere Rock in the Stags reef just south of Lizard Point. The crew all survived but the vessel was wrecked – not a good advertisement for the Fox system.

That didn't put off Lloyds of London, who had noticed how the station had helped streamline the maritime trade and started planning a network of similar outposts around the coast. In 1883 Lloyds took charge of the operation at Bass Point, running the service for nearly seventy years, until the semaphore flags were rolled up for the final time in 1951. Today the station is an 'iconic and historic' holiday let, guests encouraged to use the signalling terrace for morning yoga or evening cocktails.

* * *

Beyond the signal station are two wooden huts, now owned by the National Trust. In the winter of 1900/1901 an Italian engineer made a series of pioneering experiments in radio communication here. Guglielmo Marconi reckoned Bass Point was a good place to test his long-range radio equipment. On 23 January he successfully received a signal broadcast from Niton on the Isle of Wight, more than 180 miles away.

It was a good start – but what Marconi really wanted to do was send radio waves more than ten times further, across the Atlantic. This required much larger transmitters and a substantial area of relatively flat, open land where they could be built. He found the right location seven miles away on the west side of the Lizard Peninsula. In fields on top of the cliffs at Poldhu he built a transmitter 100 times more powerful than anything that had come before.

His first successful wireless transmission across the Atlantic happened on 12 December 1901. Three short pips spelling out the letter 'S', sent from a 15kW spark transmitter at Poldhu, were received on a 500ft aerial held in the air by a kite at Signal Hill, Newfoundland. There was no way of transmitting a signal back, so the only way Marconi could tell his Cornish team about their success was with a telegraph message sent on the undersea cable via Porthcurno, the very method of communication the Italian hoped to make redundant.

Born in Bologna in 1874, Marconi had first become interested in the possibilities of radio transmission as a teenager, when he taught himself Morse code. In 1895 he managed to transmit a signal over a distance of nearly a mile, but despite his success he could not convince the Italian government to take his work seriously. He hoped he might find more interest in London. 'Signor Marconi', as the press called him, spoke perfect English, learnt from his mother, a scion of the Jameson family of Irish whiskey distillers. He quickly established himself as a showman. Newspaper readers lapped up reports of his early demonstrations, which included one in the City of London where he sent signals between the General Post Office at St Martin's Le Grand and a bank on Queen Victoria Street. Soon after he impressed the military when he displayed his technology in action on Salisbury Plain.

In 1898 he received royal approval when he was invited to Osborne House on the Isle of Wight to assist Queen Victoria to communicate with her son, the Prince of Wales, who was recuperating from illness on board the royal yacht. The monarch was said to be much pleased with the experiment and Marconi revelled in the resulting publicity. In March 1899 his lecture at the Institution of Electrical Engineers was so popular that 'a large number of persons had to be turned away'. The following month he transmitted a Morse signal across the Channel from South Foreland in Kent to Wimereux in the Pas de Calais. The naval attaché to the Chinese legation in London was one of those who came to watch.

This international interest caused a fall in the value of Eastern Telegraph Company stock, and raised concerns at Porthcurno about what radio might mean for the future of the cable industry. Staff used their binoculars to look across Mount's Bay and observe the Poldhu aerials taking shape.

In June 1902 an engineer was instructed to go to Poldhu – a sixty-mile round trip via Penzance, Marazion and Helston – and report back on what was happening. This was nothing less than industrial espionage, the scale of which increased dramatically when the Eastern Telegraph Company leased a patch of land to build their own aerial, presumably so that they could listen to and closely observe Marconi's experiments. Secrecy was key; in contemporary boardroom documents there is no mention of a reason as to why the land was rented and no reference to the purpose or cost of the mast. As John E. Packer points out in his account of this period, *The Spies at Wireless Point*, this was curious, given that minuted subjects did include the cost of buying new ashtrays for Porthcurno and a ceiling fan for the Suez station.

The cablers were obsessed with bureaucracy and liked decisions made by committee, whereas Marconi nimbly led his business from the front. As a result he found it much easier to get public attention. An exchange of messages between the King and the American President Theodore Roosevelt in January 1903 won new headlines; in July that year a visit to Poldhu by the Prince and Princess of Wales caused more anguished muttering at Porthcurno.

* * *

It would have taken the Porthcurno spy the best part of a day to reach Poldhu on horseback, but he would have been impressed at what he saw once he got there. To the residents of the nearby parishes of Mullion, Cury and Gunwalloe, Marconi's aerials must have seemed like something from another world.

I was ten when my brother Johnny played me Jeff Wayne's concept album *The War of the Worlds*. I listened to it over and over again, and then borrowed H. G. Wells's novel from Helston Library. The idea of the Martians and their tripodular fighting-machines gave me nightmares and reminded me of pictures of the old Poldhu masts. The aerials started to appear just a few years after Wells's story had made its debut as a magazine serial. The first was 60ft high and shaped like a drum, with wires strung between twenty masts arranged in a circle – like a technical sketch of a fully filled city gasometer. As towers were replaced by more advanced equipment or blown down by strong winds, the layout of the site kept changing. One set-up involved four, 72ft lattice masts that formed the corners of a square, with transmitter cables drawn from the top down to a single point in the centre. How incongruous these super-modern structures must have looked, their sinister size and scale defiling the soft landscape.

Marconi and his engineers stayed at the Poldhu Hotel, which had opened in 1899. Today it is a care home offering its elderly residents sweeping views across an ever-changing seascape. The coast path passes the front of the hotel and then runs down one side of the forty-four-acre site where Marconi's masts stood. Their concrete foundations have survived. There are heavy emplace-ments which would have anchored the wooden structures, and smaller plates, some still studded with the hooks that tethered wires in place.

As well as sending messages abroad, these masts also enabled communication with ships at sea. For the first time telegrams could be sent to passengers on board transatlantic liners, who were also offered a comprehensive service of news and information. During the First World War use was restricted to official business, including the sending of orders to commanders of naval ships on active service. When peace came, Marconi attempted to improve the reliability of the transatlantic service by shifting transmissions to a station at Clifden, County Galway, several hundred miles further west. When it was attacked during the Irish Civil War, the service was switched first to Caernarvon, and eventually to Rugby. Poldhu became a research station, engineers experimenting with short-wave transmissions which would eventually sustain a global radio telegraph network. By the time the site closed in the early 1930s, Marconi was living mainly in Italy, a marquess, with a grand villa outside Bologna. When he died in July 1937 Mussolini ordered that he should receive a state funeral.

A memorial quickly went up in Cornwall, overlooking the sea, where his transmitters had once stood. Its shaft is topped with a globe that rests in a double triangular frame – M for Marconi. The words of the main inscription reflect a remarkable period: 'When the Poldhu station was erected in 1900, wireless was in its infancy. When it was demolished in 1933 wireless was established for communication on land, at sea, and in the air, for direction finding, broadcasting and television.'

* * *

Poldhu was a quarter-of-an-hour drive from home. Sometimes we would go there for a Saturday afternoon walk, with an ice cream from the hut on the beach, or a cup of tea and a bun in the hotel if Dad was feeling flush. But the next chapter of the Cornish communication revolution played out even closer to home. At night, safely tucked up in bed, I would look out of the window to check that the red safety lamp on the apex of the oldest and largest of the Goonhilly dishes was gently winking. In the morning as I walked to school I would see the structure's metal frame glinting in the sun. The giant satellite dish had been named *Arthur*, and I felt more than a little pride in knowing that he sat within the St Martin parish bounds.

When Arthur H. Norway visited the Lizard in the 1890s, researching his book *Highways and Byways of Devon and Cornwall*, he wrote of the 'great waste of Goonhilly Downs'. It was, he said, a place 'sufficiently savage to have been a terror to travellers of all ages ... still a perplexity even to natives, when the sea mists envelope it with light wreaths of vapour.'

Today the downs are a nature reserve, a site of special scientific interest. In the dead winter months, when the adders are safely hibernating, it is one of my favourite places to walk Rocky and Belle. They can run great distances here, vanishing from view for long minutes before their heads pop up again, a brief but reassuring glimpse of them as they speed along some distant furrow.

The circular walk we take ends near Dry Tree, a roughly carved standing stone, or *menhir*, that marks the meeting point of the St Martin, Mawgan, Cury, Grade Ruan and St Keverne parishes. Placed there in the Bronze Age to mark the grave of some contemporary dignitary, the stone was knocked over in the 19th century by locals fired up by rumours that gold was buried underneath. In 1927 Dry Tree was set erect once again. Ten feet high, it dominated the landscape here for another three decades. Then came a new, bigger neighbour – a structure that must have first seemed even more out of place than Marconi's Poldhu aerials: a parabolic metal dish 85ft in diameter, resting on a heavy concrete base – the structure that took Britain into the satellite age.

In the late 1950s the Post Office was looking for a suitable site for its first satellite station. Its engineers soon realised that this flat pan of open space was the perfect location. Their antennae could lock onto satellites high in the sky and track them as they descended low on the horizon, keeping contact for the longest possible time before they disappeared behind the curvature of the earth.

The first dish was built in just twelve months, the construction team keeping close tabs on the progress of parallel work underway at the American base station at Andover, Maine. On 10 July 1962 *Telstar*, a 170lb satellite, powered by solar cells and built with 15,000 different electrical components inside, was launched by

NASA at Cape Canaveral in Florida. The first live transatlantic link was planned for the next day. The BBC put on a special broadcast, fronted by Richard Dimbleby. It was not a complete success. 'We'll get this picture if it kills us,' Dimbleby promised those tuned in, but the enthusiastic commentary provided by Raymond Baxter, who was on the ground at Goonhilly, failed to disguise the fact that all viewers saw were a few flickering, unclear images from New York. The French earth station at Pleumeur-Bodou in Brittany had picked up the signal perfectly, leaving GPO engineers mystified and red-faced. They soon identified the problem – the polariser, a tiny but vital component of the vast dish, had been fitted the wrong way round. The problem rectified, the BBC went live again the next night.

This time viewers clearly saw the parallel bars of a test card, followed by the bell logo of the American Telephone and Telegraph Company, and finally a live shot of AT&T's chairman Frederick

Kappell. 'Clear as a bell indeed, clear as a bell,' enthused Baxter. The Post Office had envisaged that the new technology would primarily be used for telephone calls and telegrams, but television executives immediately realised there was a huge appetite for live international broadcasts. A relay of a press conference given at the White House by President Kennedy was an early treat for British audiences, part of a programme that also included images of a buffalo in South Dakota and a rehearsal of *Macbeth* at the Festival Theatre, Stratford, Ontario.

In return the BBC produced a gala with live images from nine European countries. Fifty-four television cameras captured sardine fishermen at Taormina in Sicily, the bells of Big Ben, the horses of the Spanish Riding School in Vienna, and a hovercraft on the Solent. Cornwall was represented with footage of the lifeboat being launched at Lizard Point. Richard Dimbleby anchored once again, introducing US viewers to 'your first view of our continent – one-third smaller than yours in size, one-third bigger in terms of population.' The broadcasts had to be painstakingly planned so as to fit within a time frame of around twenty minutes – after which *Telstar* would drift out of range of the Goonhilly dishes and the signal would be lost. Three years later the technology made a major step forward with the launch of *Intelsat 1*, or *Earlybird* as it was nicknamed. The first geostationary satellite, it followed the rotation of the earth, allowing for continuous pictures.

The Post Office gave their high-tech installations at Goonhilly names drawn from Arthurian legend. The first antenna was *Arthur*, the second dish took the name of his father, *Uther Pendragon*. *Guinevere*, *Tristan* and *Isolde* all followed. Antenna 6 – *Merlin* – came online just in time to feed *Live Aid* around the world to an estimated global audience of 1.9 billion in July 1985. Then the dishes started proliferating at such a rate that it was too complicated to give them more than a number. By 2000 there were sixty-one receivers – some just a few feet in diameter. Of the big antennae, just *Merlin*, *Arthur* and *Guinevere* survive today. *Guinevere* was built in 1972, its base tapered like a windmill, a near-100ft-wide reflector dish standing in for the sails.

Close up, the scale of these machines is almost overwhelming. The superstructure of *Arthur* is held in place by two reinforced concrete pillars. Around them grow a forest of metal beams and riveted plates, on which the dish rests. Underneath sits a great display of early 1960s heavy engineering. The whole 1,100-ton assembly had to rotate to follow early satellites as they moved across the sky. A Brush engine drives chains that move a circular bed of well-oiled rollers, enabling the dish to rotate a full circle. An enormous vertical screw adjusts the elevation, so it can point anywhere between low horizon and the sky directly above. Like a big man able to dance deftly and lightly, this steel-and-concrete behemoth could effortlessly move its bulk, locking onto its target with an accuracy of within a millimetre.

The Post Office, and then its successor British Telecom, kept on investing in Goonhilly. At its height it provided 300 good jobs, many of them highly skilled and well paid. Then in 2006 BT decided to consolidate its satellite operations at its other earth station at Madley in Herefordshire. For a while it seemed that the dishes would be knocked down, and the site turned into a wind farm. Because *Arthur* had been given an architectural listing in 2003 it alone would survive, a final reminder of the role played by Cornwall in the history of satellite communication.* But then a saviour appeared on the scene, Ian Jones, who had studied electrical engineering at university before joining BT at its research institute at Martlesham Heath in Suffolk. He had

---

*Goonhilly Three, Guinevere, is also listed, added to the register in 2008.

worked at Goonhilly in the 1980s, later going on to launch a successful satellite communications business. When he heard BT were leaving, he began to envisage what the site could become: a centre bringing together satellite technology, deep-space communication, and advanced radio astronomy.

We meet in what is one of the oldest buildings at Goonhilly, the control tower built in the early 1960s. It is only one storey above ground, but the site is so flat, there are views to every corner of the base. Ian sparkles with energy; he is passionate about the science behind what he is doing here – but is also determined to create a viable business. 'I saw what this could be, and set out to raise the money,' he explains. 'I did that classic entrepreneur thing of mortgaging my house to help find funds. By January 2014 we'd met our targets and were able to take the whole place over, on a 999-year lease from BT.'

A sign by the gatehouse welcomes visitors to the 'UK's Gateway to Space'. Which, according to Ian, means many different things. His brother is a professor of radio astronomy at Oxford University. 'This is a chance to explore the ideas we have long discussed at the family breakfast table. Satellite dishes can also be used as telescopes, so *Arthur* will become part of a interferometer, a linked network of telescopes that share their signals to produce incredibly high-resolution data. We have invested in building a supercomputer centre so we can work with university partners and the radio-astronomy community in taking earth observation data and applying AI and machine learning. We'll be able to glean more information than ever – it's technology we can use to see through clouds, or chart single-millimetre rises in the height of the world's oceans.'

There something evangelical about Ian's passion for science. He starts talking about the residual radiation left from the Big Bang, 'now super, super cold, and dying at three degrees above absolute zero. We're building supercooled receivers for some of our antennae, chambers about the size of a dustbin. You take the air out and create a very high vacuum, and then use a helium compressor to cool it right down. Temperature is atoms vibrating, which creates noise which blocks out useful information. But this will help us hear these distant signals, and enable us to identify a faint, but potentially dangerous space debris.'

As we talk there is a sudden movement behind Ian's right shoulder. *Merlin*'s 105ft dish is rotating upwards. Ian gleefully recounts the celebrations when it made its first successful transmission to the Mars Express Orbiter, the European Space Agency mission launched from the Baikonur Cosmodrome in Kazakhstan in 2003. 'We are in the process now of working through our qualifications with the European Space Agency so we can take command of their spacecraft. The Elon Musk model for private companies doing satellite launches has proved the role the private sector can play alongside the national space agencies. We have become the world's first commercial provider of deep-space communication services. But it's quite a responsibility. You are talking about projects that scientists have dedicated their lives to. You don't want to send the wrong command.'

* * *

The Goonhilly dishes disturbed many when they were first built, ugly ambassadors of a new world, imposed by the government upon the Lizard, no approval sought. But today they have become familiar, reassuring beacons, integral to the landscape in which they rest, part of the downs, just like the ancient Dry Tree *menhir*.

In 1967 the sculptor Barbara Hepworth made *Three Hemispheres*, a simple geometric triptych of works in plaster – one has a hole running through it, another is hollow, a third is flat. They were inspired by a visit she made to see the Goonhilly antennae. 'I was invited to go on board the first one when it began to go round, and it was so magical and so strange,' she said. 'I find such forms of technology very exciting and inspiring.'

In 1977 Mr Teague took us on a school visit, where we watched engineers in white coats working banks of flickering switches in rooms full of hot, purring computers fed by reels of magnetic tape. Goonhilly had become the epitome of what the Labour Prime Minister Harold Wilson envisaged when he promised a new era which championed technology and celebrated the men and women dedicating their working lives to science. Post Office workers were among those at the top of the list of heroes in his battle to establish a 'new Britain' forged in the 'white heat' of 'scientific revolution'.

That school trip – along with stories told about Poldhu and Porthcurno – led me towards working in broadcasting. Watching the banks of monitors showing incoming television feeds felt incredibly exciting. The technical developments that meant we could watch, live, the inauguration of Ronald Reagan as American president, the launch of space shuttles and the Olympic Games from Moscow and Los Angeles, were impressive enough. The idea that the pictures were landing from space little more than a mile from my bedroom seemed mind-blowing. I built myself a television studio in the old army hut that was my playroom, with cardboard-box cameras, and became obsessed with the idea of capturing information. Words, stories, sounds, music, pictures – to be shared with others by cable, radio transmission or via space. It was the beginning of a journey that advanced to hospital radio and school video productions, on to relief stints presenting at Plymouth Sound, the nearest commercial radio station, and finally to employment with the BBC.

* * *

The cablers won out in the end, seeing off the radio engineers and white-coated satellite technicians. Today at least fourteen undersea lines start and finish their journey from Cornwall. Rubber-wrapped copper has been replaced with polyethylene-clad fibre optic – but these are still just wires, delicate, easily damaged, vulnerable to attack. The consequences of an enemy state or terrorist group cutting a cable are all too imaginable; as a result the exact locations of landing points and onshore exchanges are sometimes hard to establish.

Atlantic Crossing 1 makes its way under the sea from West Penwith to Long Island; Porthcurno is the stopping point for FLAG (Fibre-optic Link Around the Globe) running between New York and Kanagawa. SeaMeWe-3, the 24,000-mile connection between Perth and Ostend, comes ashore on the Lizard and links to the British network at Goonhilly.

But it is the coast around Bude that has biggest concentration of cable landfalls – it is surely no coincidence that GCHQ, the government intelligence and security agency, has an outpost here, its white satellite antennae sitting on cliffs five miles north of the town. From the north coast EIG (Europe India Gateway) runs through the Mediterranean and the Red Sea to Djibouti and then on to Fujairah in the UAE and Mumbai. 2Africa winds its way around the continent, with lines branching off to eighteen African cities, including Dakar, Cape Town and Mogadishu. Glo1 offers an express route to Accra and Lagos. There are also four transatlantic cables, the newest brought ashore in October 2021, the Google-owned Grace Hopper, which the company claims has enough bandwidth to allow 17.5 million people to simultaneously stream 4K video.

The modern cables serve an impressive list of destinations, reminiscent of the glory days of the Falmouth Packets. But today this infinite stream of blinking digital data simply passes through the county, leaving little in its wake that is of direct benefit to Cornwall. The evidence of what was remains – in the name of the Packet Quay's housing development in Falmouth, the beachside cable hut at Porthcurno, the concrete slabs at Poldhu, the dishes at Goonhilly. These are museum pieces to remind everyone of the role Cornwall played in the communication revolution.

'If There Is a Hole Dug Anywhere on Earth, You're Sure to Find a Cornishman at the Bottom of It'

The 1832 Great Reform Act was a key part of my 'O' Level history course. The bill had had ramifications close to home – hadn't Helston lost one of its two MPs? Our classroom discussions, and the essays we wrote after, were rich in tales of corruption, vote fixing and aristocrats keeping control of political constituencies in places that were very familiar. It seemed bizarre that Tregony, West Looe, St Mawes and Mitchell had each sent a politician to Westminster, when Birmingham and Manchester had no dedicated representatives.

But when it came to the Industrial Revolution, the other major topic on the curriculum, there was barely any mention of Cornwall. Great mill towns like Glossop, Halifax, Preston and Wigan featured in the books we read; they contained pictures of game-changing inventions like James Watt's steam engine and Richard Arkwright's water frame. But we never discussed the sprawling parade of mines around Gwennap. We never visited the mines of Penwith, their deep shafts running out under the sea. We never wrote essays about how mining had changed Camborne and Redruth, making them highly prosperous towns, their names familiar to traders on metal exchanges around the world. Cornwall had moved on, reinventing itself as a land of Celtic legends and pretty views, and the dirty business of mining defiled this image. It was as if we wanted to whitewash away a grimy past, a time when our own Industrial Revolution had made us globally important. As a fifteen-year-old it seemed as if we were closing our eyes to a vital part of our heritage, and this was something that felt wrong.

* * *

The road up to Carn Brea is rough and potholed. I creep along, doing less than ten miles an hour, but several times an unpleasant metallic rasp comes from under the car as a hidden stone scrapes the chassis. The view that comes at the end is worth the slow ascent. From 700ft above sea level it is like looking at a living map of west Cornwall. The land gently tapers away, before a last burst of energy blows the final bubble that is the Penwith peninsula. The Atlantic coast is two and a half miles north, Camborne sits to the west, Redruth to the east. Across Carbis Bay the sun shines on St Ives, while Penzance rests hazy in the far distance. Four towns seen from one place. And two seas – there's a sliver of the English Channel visible at Mounts Bay.

The man-made environment below does not complement nature's beauty. The main-line railway runs along the base of the hill. Behind are the unprepossessing industrial units of Pool, a formless sprawl of boxy grey and blue buildings, used as warehouses and distribution hubs, their yards filled with brightly coloured shipping containers. Four red Caterpillar earth movers work clearing space for new foundations as the estate punches further out into green land.

A white fibreglass structure shaped like a golfball houses the military radar at RAF Portreath; from there I run my eyes along the coastline, stopping where the land rises to form the St Agnes

Beacon. In Cornish legend, Bolster, a giant, was so tall that he could stand with one foot on Carn Brea and another on the Beacon. One day, in a foul rage, he hurled handfuls of pebbles from one of his footstools to the other, leaving the rock formations that give this place its name – 'Rocky Hill' – Carn Brea in Cornish.

A soaring memorial tower ensures Carn Brea draws the eye from afar – a tapered octagonal cross rising out of a 40ft-square plinth. Tiny slit windows shed light on a narrow, tightly wound internal staircase; the fenestrations at the top must offer an even better view. No chance for me to find out – the gate across the entrance is padlocked shut and behind it the ground is covered with years of pigeon droppings. I stick my head in between the bars to see if I can spot the base of the stairs, managing to startle two birds; panicked, they beat and bluster their way past me out into the open air.

The memorial, built in 1836, is inscribed 'THE COUNTY OF CORNWALL TO THE MEMORY OF FRANCIS LORD DE DUNSTANVILLE AND BASSET'. Francis Basset had been created a baronet in 1779 and raised to the peerage seventeen years later. After his death in London in 1835, his body was brought back to Cornwall where it lay in state in Launceston, Bodmin and Truro. The Cornish historian Philip Payton describes the sense of state occasion that surrounded his passing. 'In Truro the shops were closed in melancholy deference to his greatness, and the bell of St Mary's was tolled in his honour. Local mines fell silent on the day of the funeral, a procession of some 20,000 people making its way from Tehidy Park to Illogan Church.' The status and respect that the Bassets enjoyed came from their great wealth – and that derived from tin and copper.

Mining may have been overlooked by those who prescribed my school studies in the 1980s, but a century and a half earlier, people made special trips to Carn Brea to gorge themselves on the vast industrial vista below. Visitors would hire horses, or clamber up on foot to reach the summit, then take refreshment as they gazed down at the grand scale of business visible in all directions. George Henwood, correspondent for the *Mining Journal*, described a 'glorious sight', going on to list the works he could see – Tincroft, Dolcoath, Cook's Kitchen, Pedn-an-drea, The Cupids, The Gramblers, and the Gwennap mines – Tresavean, the Great Consols and United Mines. 'All of these may be seen by the mere twist of a heel,' Henwood observed in 1850.

If he looked beyond the smoke-belching mine-engine chimneys, Henwood might have noticed the house where Francis Basset had lived – Tehidy, a Palladian mansion surrounded by parkland – a 'well cultivated garden blooming in the midst of a barren desert', as a visitor in the 1820s described it.

Basset enjoyed a highly privileged upbringing. After an education at Eton and King's College Cambridge, he made the grand tour to France and Italy. In 1778, following in the footsteps of other travelling English aristocrats, he sat for Pompeo Batoni, the leading portrait painter of 18th-century Rome.* Later he was to gather an important art collection himself, and became a patron of the celebrated Cornish-born artist John Opie. While undoubtedly a cultured man, Basset was also an archetypal Cornish mine baron, determined to increase his family's fortune.

He was one of the first to spot the potential of fixed, cast-iron tracks as a way of moving ore – in 1809 he laid the first rail of a tramway that was to run between mines at Dolcoath and the harbour at Portreath. When it suited him, he worked to improve conditions for his miners, though in 1785, during a downturn, he swore in fifty special constables to put down food riots by unemployed workers in Redruth. Three years earlier, he had joined forces with the Welsh-Cornish Williams family to form a cartel to control who could buy and sell Cornish copper ore.

The family's annual income from its mines was already in steep decline by the time of his death in 1835 – from a peak of £24,000 a year to just £8,000. A nephew, Arthur, was the last Basset to live at Tehidy. He chose to ignore financial reality, throwing a lavish ball for his twenty-first birthday in 1894, and betting recklessly on horses. It soon became clear there was no longer the money to support his lifestyle and the cost of maintaining the house and its gardens. In 1915 he sold the estate for £250,000. The extended sale of furniture and effects that followed gave locals an opportunity to come and gawp at the lavish interiors. The family gone, the place became a tuberculosis sanitorium, a fire in 1916 destroying much of the main house.

---

*Today the picture is in the collection of the Museo del Prado, Madrid.

From the summit of Carn Brea much evidence of the old trade can still be seen. I count twenty-one mine chimneys; many more are just out of sight, or blend into the dull browns and greens of the landscape. Some of the engine houses are just stumps, but to the south are a set of old mine buildings as majestic as the ruined abbeys at Tintern or Melrose.

South Wheal Frances was one of the richest of the Great Flat Lode mines. 'Lode' is the geological term that describes veins of metal ore running through a rock formation – here they dipped at an unusually gentle angle, making it much easier to extract their rich bounty.

A metal grille has been laid across the top of the main shaft; gingerly I walk across it to peer into the deep hole below. The grandeur of the architecture matches the value of the mine's output. The perfectly cut bricks that line the shaft were clearly laid with the level of care to be expected of a cathedral mason. The walls that link engine room and compressor house resemble

a medieval cloister, set with neat arches; it is easy to imagine pre-dissolution stained glass in the empty ocular windows above.

All is calm today – nothing drowns out the chorus of birdsong. But when this mine was being worked the noise would have been intense – a roar of machinery, explosions as shot detonators were fired, clanking wagons, steam whistles and sirens. In the 1870s, several thousand worked here. Though the tradition of bal maidens* had largely ended, there would still have been many women working above ground in administration and occasionally management roles, with men, and boys aged twelve or over, providing subterranean labour. As well as being a correspondent of the *Mining Journal*, George Henwood was a campaigner for better welfare, lobbying to end the common practice of boys being sent to work alongside their fathers. Reporting the story of a miner who had told him that taking his son with him made the family an extra pound a month, Henwood wrote of 'a poor child sacrificed to the idol Gain, and for such a paltry sum'.

The mines were dangerous places. The shafts and tunnels were badly ventilated and filled with dust. Workers whose lungs stayed healthy faced a much higher than normal rate of heart disease. The damp, humid conditions often caused severe rheumatism in the legs of older workers. When miners became ill they relied on the services of a doctor chosen by the management, but paid for from their own sick-club contributions. The doctors usually lived some way away, and the fees were not lucrative, so they would often send an inexperienced apprentice in their place. Facing a risk to life and limb every working day, each miner must have

---

*Bal is the Cornish word for mine. Bal maidens were key members of the workforce in Cornish mines until the middle of the 19th century. Their principal role was on the surface, separating minerals from their ore.

convinced themselves they would be the lucky one, the one who would stay healthy and live to enjoy some kind of peace and rest in retirement.*

Miners could earn as much as 50 per cent more than their peers who chose to work in agriculture. But their income was often unpredictable. Most were effectively self-employed, either as 'tutmen', where they were paid by the volume of material removed, or as 'tributers', a riskier but potentially more lucrative arrangement whereby they would be paid an agreed percentage of the final sale price of tin extracted over a specified period. If the quality of the ore was better than expected, the contract could be quickly completed, and the miner could start a new job. But if the metal was poor, they would have to keep on working until they had extracted the required amount. The varying standards of ore and the fluctuating price of tin meant miners could quickly find their income falling to subsistence level, or worse.

The sprawl of mines that Henwood saw from the top of Carn Brea in 1850 suggested a business in good health, but in reality he was observing the last hurrah of Cornish mining. Within a quarter of a century decline had set in. Forty-seven mines closed in 1874, forty-eight the following year, and thirty-seven the year after that. But by then many workers had already addressed the uncertainty of their lives by emigrating. The mines of Wisconsin and Upper Michigan in the United States, Real de Monte in

---

*Even the introduction of modern technology was not guaranteed to improve conditions. A new type of rock drill introduced at the end of the 19th century seemed safer and made work easier, but in the long term proved lethal to the health of its operator. Between 1900 and 1902 not a single driller was killed in an accident in the mines of the Redruth district, but 103 men, most of them aged between twenty-five and forty-five, died of lung disease, the result of the fine dust the new drills pumped into the air. The tool was quickly nicknamed 'The Widowmaker'.

Mexico and Lake Huron in Canada were big draws in the 1840s. Miners sailed from ports including Padstow, St Ives and Falmouth, knowing their departure was probably permanent.

As the century progressed, a global demand for skilled miners gave Cornish workers much greater agency. Those going to America and Canada could expect to earn a daily rate potentially three times higher than what they would have received at home. Living conditions became much more sophisticated and family friendly, encouraging many men to take their wives and children with them. 'Little Cornwalls' emerged around the world – townships with familiar names, pasties to eat, Methodist chapels to worship in, Cornish associations and bars and temperance houses where the conversation would lead with the latest news from the old country, gleaned from well-thumbed, several-month-old copies of *The Cornishman*, the *West Briton* and the *Cornish Guardian*. Cornish accents were common in the mining districts around Witwatersrand in South Africa, Bendigo in Victoria, Australia and Otago in New Zealand. Others went to Minas Gerais in Brazil or to the silver mines of Pachuca, Mexico, where it was standard practice for the British-owned companies to pay part of their employees' salaries directly into their Cornish bank accounts.

The numbers of those who left are staggering – in the last four decades of the 19th century 118,500 people departed Cornwall, approximately a third of its population. Some moved elsewhere in the UK, but most went overseas, to work as carpenters, masons and agricultural workers as well as miners. The statistic for one generation in particular is startling – 44.8 per cent of the male population aged between fifteen and twenty-four left to work abroad – an exodus of 'the very bone and sinew of the country', as an editorial in the *West Briton* noted in 1863. It is easy to imagine the void these young men left in their wake. Some would become rich and return to Cornwall, buying up farms and houses for their extended families, but most were lost for good, choosing to forge new lives in the New World.

By the start of the 20th century just nine tin mines were still operating. Cornwall's greatest asset was no longer its own reserves of tin and copper, but its miners. They were considered the finest in the world, their international travels prompting a saying that remained true for a century: 'If there is a hole dug anywhere on earth, you're sure to find a Cornishman at the bottom.'*

* * *

If the lands around Carn Brea were one of the great battlefields of the Cornish mining industry, the twin towns of Camborne and Redruth were the command centre. Redruth's history can be charted back to 1333, when King Edward III granted the lord of the manor William Basset a charter for a market and fair. Its name attests to a long connection with the extraction of metals. *Rys* or *rhyd* is the Cornish word for ford, *rudh* means red – a ford over a red river – the water brightly stained by the metal-laden, acidic discharge of ancient mines and smelting plants.

The 19th-century mining money that flowed through Redruth left the town with an architectural legacy that belies its size. The centre of the town fans out from the clock tower. The current

---

* The saying remains accurate today. In 2016 I visited the construction site of the new Crossrail station at Whitechapel in London. Having donned heavy boots, high-vis jacket and helmet, and been taught how to use an emergency respirator, I was taken down the shaft into the hole where today trains disgorge their passengers. The chief engineer was a Cornishman from St Just, a graduate of the Camborne School of Mines. Founded in 1888, the college is now part of the University of Exeter and has moved to its campus at Penryn. It remains one of the world's leading institutions for the study of mining, tunnelling and geology.

structure, perhaps the third on the site, was completed in 1828, and was raised in height several times that century. The surviving façade of the West End Drapery Stores provides a reminder of what was once one of Cornwall's grandest emporiums, its multiple departments spanning both sides of the street. Around Alma Place and the railway station are a series of buildings where tin and copper traders once carried out their business: the Malayan Tin Dredging Co., the Lamb and Flag Coffee Tavern, the Redruth & District Bank, the post office, the offices of Wheal Peevor mine, and the Mining Exchange. The Exchange's name remains today, carved into the stone parapet above a door that leads into a cavernous room where mining shares were bought and sold and telegrams reporting London metal prices arrived twice daily. Any mine captains caught swearing were fined, with monies donated to the town's Miners' Hospital. Immediately behind the exchange is the Butter Market, which despite its name was west Cornwall's main pork market for most of the 19th century. After decades of neglect it is now owned by a forward-thinking community interest company, Redruth Revival, who plan to turn its impressively colonnaded courtyard into a space where musicians can perform and local chefs and food producers will showcase their work.

In the late 16th century Camborne was still a village, described by the mapmaker and surveyor John Norden as little more than 'a churche standing among the barreyne hills'. But by the start of the 19th century it was a bustling town – 'a place fast riding into opulence and consequently importance from the valuable mines of tin and copper surrounding it.' The author of this enthusiastic write-up in Pigot's 1830 *Directory of Cornwall* continued with praise for local town planning: 'Several new streets have been added within these few years . . . the modern erections are light and neat, nor has that pleasing and judicious feature in street building, uniformity, been neglected.' Eight years later the author, scientist and politician Davies Gilbert described Camborne as having 'risen more rapidly into wealth and importance than any other parish in Cornwall'.

The houses on and around Pendarves Road reflect the town's former prosperity. Tregenna is one of a series of substantial Victorian villas. There is a Cornish crest over the door and fussy detailing around the windows, but little sense of anything cosy or welcoming. It feels like a place built to show off its owner's wealth, a home where the door would have been opened by a cowed maid in a black pinny, the sort of house that brings to mind a man of industry in a play by J. B. Priestley. Today it is a care home for the elderly; for much of the 20th century it was where my maternal great-grandparents lived.

Tregenna was built by the Thomases, a prosperous Camborne mining family. Josiah Thomas was born in 1863. He was the son and grandson of important mine agents, but was to discover early on that the leadership class was no more exempt from the vicissitudes of metal prices than those who worked underground. As a boy Josiah spent time in Mexico where his father had had to move to find new employment. He was in his early twenties when he emigrated himself – to Australia where he ran a mine near Broken Hill. He became a prominent advocate for the health and safety of his staff, and encouraged union membership. Later he became a Member of Parliament for the Australian Labor Party, rising to become Minister for External Affairs, one of those behind the establishment of the country's first diplomatic mission, Australia House in London. Raised a Cornish Methodist, Josiah Thomas insisted that hotels in Canberra, the new federal capital, did not serve alcohol, spoke out against plans to adjourn Parliament for the Melbourne Cup horse race, and established a Christian radio station.

My great-grandfather, William Blackwood, was twenty-four and a newly qualified doctor when he came to Camborne in 1902. Born in Moffat in Dumfriesshire, he studied medicine at Edinburgh University. He married an Irish actress and dancer, Agnes Marie Leeson,* a match that his parents disapproved of – perhaps the reason that he decided to practise about as far away from his Borders home as was possible without going abroad. Once he had established himself in Camborne he set about finding a suitable house, somewhere smart enough to reassure his clients of his success, and with enough space downstairs for a suite of consulting rooms.

In a 1918 photograph he is dressed in the uniform of the Royal Army Medical Corps. At the outbreak of hostilities, he had taken a troop of miners from Camborne and Redruth to serve in the 25th Field Ambulance, headquartered at Estaires in French Flanders. He kept up the morale of his men by organising rugby matches against soldiers from Devon. Enemy shells damaging the pitch were often a problem, as one soldier, Jack Solomon, told the *West Briton* in 1915: 'Before we could start, we had to fill up a hole in the ground, and there was chance of a few more holes being made during the match. The Germans however left us alone, as perhaps they did not want to spoil our game.'

Lieutenant Colonel Blackwood, as he eventually became, commander of 2/1st Wessex Field Ambulance, was a brave and efficient soldier, receiving the DSO with bar for 'conspicuous gallantry and devotion to duty while in charge of the evacuation of casualties from the Divisional front during an enemy attack'.

---

*The Blackwoods seemed to like their weddings in smart London churches. Agnes and Fred had married at All Souls, Langham Place; Agnes and William wed a short walk away at St George's Hanover Square, the church where Handel had worshipped.

His distinguished military record undoubtedly helped swell his client base back in Camborne after the war – but he was already highly respected for his work campaigning for better medical care for miners. In January 1908 he had argued that the town should have its own ambulance unit, shocking fellow guests at a Masonic hall dinner with the story of an incident at Dolcoath when an injured man had to lie in a filthy outhouse for two and a half hours before he could be removed to hospital. His address led to the founding of a local division of the St John Ambulance; subsequently he served for two decades as County Ambulance Commissioner, spending much of his time lobbying for the provision of proper first-aid facilities for injured miners.

William Blackwood died in 1960. 'A much-loved figure – his duty done' reads the epitaph on his gravestone at Camborne Church. His career lasted for fifty-six years, an obituary in the *British Medical Journal* reflecting the varied workload of a Cornish doctor in the first half of the 20th century. As well as general practice he was a respected obstetrician ('to watch the dexterity, speed and skill with which he applied forceps was both a privilege and an education', noted 'E.T.' in the *BMJ*) and as a surgeon frequently operated on patients at the West Cornwall Miners' and Women's Hospital in Redruth. He was also chairman of the National Service Medical Board, a police surgeon and a factory medical officer, a job that would have taken him often to Holman Brothers.

* * *

When I started at Helston School, careers master Howard Curnow had three proposals for those not destined to enter further or higher education – join the Royal Navy, the merchant navy, or apply for an apprenticeship at Holman Brothers. In the early 1980s the firm was still recruiting bright young people, and promising a career that could take them around the world. Holmans' very existence offered proof that Camborne was still a place of industry.

In 1801 Nicholas Holman opened a foundry and blacksmith shop at Pool to supply boilers for mine engines – thus starting a business that would grow and thrive alongside Cornish tin and copper production. The firm's 1879 catalogue offered 'steam engines, air compressors, pulverisers . . . and mining machinery of every description'. The company sold its drills internationally, its advertisements assuring potential purchasers that its equipment was efficient and modern.

Profits quickly grew – in 1890 John Holman showed his gratitude to the people of Camborne when he presented the town with a fountain that still stands in the market square. In the 1920s the company announced itself as the 'The British House for Pneumatic Tools', its telegraphic address 'Airdrill-Camborne'. During World War Two it used its expertise to develop the Holman Projector, a maritime anti-aircraft gun powered by compressed air or steam. In the 1950s Holmans merged with Climax, another local company – 'For Dogged Reliability choose Climax Pneumatic and Electric Tools'.

Camborne was a company town. Holman Brothers was by far the biggest employer, with over 3,000 staff. Most were based at the No. 1, No. 2, and No. 3 Works, where there were pattern and machine shops, a foundry, assembly lines, an apprentice school and a research and development department. Rosewarne House, an early-Georgian pile in the centre of town, became the corporate headquarters. In the 1960s a five-storey administration block was built on the road leading to Pool; three miles away in the village of Troon, Holmans had its own experimental mine, where new inventions were tested.

Don Gardner's father worked as foreman; Don joined himself in 1962, as a trainee electrician, one of 144 apprentices taken on that year alone. The firm underpinned Camborne's economy, and provided it with entertainment as well. Don recalls the annual Holman Week that coincided with Camborne Feast: 'there were window-dressing competitions in local shops, a mannequin parade, talent show and grand firework display at the end'.*

The firm was an old-fashioned employer. 'The company electricians looked after the bosses' homes as well as the factories,' says Don. He installed Cornwall's first sauna at the Carbis Bay house of director James Holman and his wife, the actor Linden Travers. 'Afterwards, as it was hot we decided to take a dip in their pool. Of course they came back early and caught us. Jim was not amused. I was told to report to head office on the Monday and was then sent to spend a few days cleaning the glass lanterns deep down the mine at Troon.'

Holmans designed and built its products in Camborne, but sold them to the world. A 1940 advertisement boasts of offices, showrooms and engineers in Johannesburg, Ndola, Salisbury (now Harare), Bulawayo, Melbourne, Sydney, Kalgoorlie, Christchurch, Montreal and Vancouver.

Twenty years later the company still had a global presence, but business was beginning to slow. Another apprentice, John Osborne, had a grandfather and great-uncle who worked as

*Holmans had the largest workforce in 1960/70s Camborne, but it was not the town's only significant employer. Lastonet made its celebrated self-ventilating tights in a factory at Pool. Next door was the Heathcoat textile plant where Don Gardner's late wife Jen worked. He recalls her pride when the firm made the tracksuits for the British team at the 1972 Munich Olympics.

managers. 'On the shop floor we knew nothing about any problems, but my grandfather intimated things were not going as well
as they should be, and he stayed well beyond retirement age as
the company tried desperately to maintain the sense that it was
still flourishing.'

In 1968 Harold Wilson's Labour government launched the
Industrial Reorganisation Corporation, which aimed to encourage
British companies to merge and thus become more efficient.
The Corporation's civil-service matchmakers brought Holman
Brothers together with Broom & Wade, a compressor manu-
facturer based at High Wycombe in Buckinghamshire. The new
entity was called the International Compressed Air Corporation,
shortened six years later to CompAir.

Holman Brothers tried to maintain its separate identity – as
late as 1979 it was continuing its tradition of commissioning
portraits of company partners. No one used the new name in
Camborne, but a further series of takeovers and mergers steered
the company away from its Cornish roots. Don Gardner was
on a training course in Milwaukee in 1987 when he was made
redundant – 500 workers were laid off on the same day. By the
end of the 1990s the factory employed just 180. A £5 million
government grant was pledged to ensure that the firm remained
in the town, but it wasn't enough. In 2003, two centuries after
Nicholas Holman had launched his foundry, the business closed
down.

By the time I got to the sixth form at Helston School, there
was little chance of starting a career in technology or manufacturing and staying in Cornwall. Howard Curnow's response was to
organise a school trip to the West Midlands so that we could
see what a career in heavy industry might look like. We spent
a week staying in a Birmingham youth hostel, at night washing
down plates of pie and chips with pints of Bass bitter. Eleven of

us went, eight boys and three girls, with just Howard to look after our welfare and drive the school minibus. He arranged visits to reflect our particular interests – I went to BBC Pebble Mill and the commercial radio station BRMB. We would listen to presentations held in company boardrooms and visit the shop floors of car plants, high-precision engineering firms and even a rivet factory. Coventry Round Table hosted us for dinner – Mr Curnow alluding to Cornwall's rich industrial past in his thank-you speech.

In Camborne the Holman name has not been erased completely. The Holman-Climax Male Voice Choir survives, and so does the old company sports and social club on Boundervean Lane. A sign, topped with Holman Brothers' distinctive trade-mark (an H framed with laurel leaves), offers bowling, cricket, darts, football, pigeons, rugby and shooting. There is little sign of No. 1 and No. 2 Works, knocked down to make space for a Tesco superstore and car-park. But a street in a new development is named Rotair Road, after Holmans' highly successful brand of portable air compressor, and next door to the railway station deep-green capital letters are fixed to the front of a building – 'Holman Bros, Rock Drill Department'. These were the No. 3 Works, which included the school for company trainees. All that is left now is the façade, the site filled with a block of flats called Apprentice Court. Once an apprenticeship at Holmans' represented the first step of a steady, respectably remunerated career. Today in what was once Cornwall's industrial heartland, the few jobs that are available to young people are in the retail or hospitality sectors, are poorly paid, and come with little security. Don Gardner spends his retirement running a food bank based out of a warehouse at Pool. His list of clients grows larger every month.

* * *

In the 1980s the last gasps of industrial Cornwall provided a steady stream of material for the local television news programmes, *BBC Spotlight* and *Today South West*. Every few months brought grim news from Holmans and other smaller specialist engineering firms. The miners were working their final shifts too. Increased use of aluminium and plastic in packaging, and the start of recycling had pushed tin consumption into a deep trough. The market was flooded, as America sold off metal it had stockpiled before World War Two and Brazil doubled its tin exports.

The International Tin Council tried to fix the commodity's price by buying vast amounts of it on the London Metal Exchange. The move failed and the ITC became insolvent, suspending its operations in October 1985. The tin price collapsed by a third and it quickly became clear that Cornwall's remaining mines, with their high extraction costs, were unviable. In February 1990 miners at Geevor, at Pendeen in the far west, worked their last shift. The following year Wheal Jane, the last mine in the Carnon Valley south-west of Truro, closed. After the pumps used to drain its tunnels were switched off, nearly 50 million litres of highly acidic metal-laden water leaked out, staining Restronguet Creek and Carrick Roads with a chemical plume the same red-orange colour that once gave Redruth its name. Camborne's South Crofty was the longest-surviving Cornish mine, but it shut down in March 1998.

A residual embarrassment about the collapse of our mining industry seemed to hang in the air during my childhood. Statistics that reminded us how Cornwall had once led the market for tin and mined two-thirds of the world's copper seemed only to hammer home the sense of what we had lost. We understood that mining was dirty and dangerous, and knew that the workers saw little of the money that funded grand estates for the gentry and substantial town houses for the managers. But nothing had replaced the wealth and leverage it gave. The days of remittances from abroad were long gone, and fishing and farming appeared to be under threat too. It seemed that tourism was the only earner left. It all felt a bit humiliating. No wonder in 1987 our teachers didn't feel like making the link between Cornwall and the Industrial Revolution.

* * *

In the quarter of a century since mining stopped there have been frequent newspaper stories about the industry making a comeback. So far each one has proved a false dawn, generating a flurry of headlines and then silence. Now the tin price has risen. Could workers descend the shaft at South Crofty again? The mine's headgear still stands proud, a metal frame looming over Camborne like a dystopian Eiffel Tower.

There may be another metal to harvest too – lithium. Millions of pounds of government grants and private capital have been invested in businesses seeking ways to extract what is an essential component to the rechargeable batteries used in phones, laptops and electric cars. One company plans to remove lithium compounds from water sitting in geothermal hot springs deep under the earth; another hopes to extract it from the granite upon which the county is built. There have been promises of enough lithium for the batteries of up to 400,000 cars each year. Along with China, the top five lithium-producing countries are Australia, Chile, Argentina and Brazil – all places where emigrant Cornish miners worked in the 19th and early 20th centuries. Perhaps this is the moment for Cornwall to proudly reclaim its industrial past.

In 2006 a site covering 20,000 hectares of land marked by centuries of mining was inscribed on UNESCO's World

Heritage List. Roadside signs across the county mark specific sites: the engine houses that cling to the cliffs at St Agnes and Cape Cornwall, Harvey's and Copperhouse; the rival foundries at Hayle; the late-18th-century china clay port at Charleston near St Austell; all now to be considered in the same breath as Egypt's Pyramids, India's Taj Mahal and the Galápagos Islands.

CHAPTER 12

Educating Cornwall

Howard Curnow's sister also taught at Helston School. French was Beatrice Kerno's first subject, and Cornish her second. She was a highly charismatic woman who would not suffer fools gladly; I was never brave enough to enquire why she and her brother spelt their surnames differently. Her partner, Neil Plummer, was a county councillor for the Cornish nationalist party Mebyon Kernow, and every summer Beatrice would recruit candidates to be part of the Cornish delegation at the Festival Interceltique, a gathering of musicians, dancers and artists drawn from across the Celtic diaspora, held each year at Lorient in Brittany.

The school leadership seemed at best lukewarm towards the idea of Cornish classes, refusing to include them in the official lesson plan, forcing Beatrice to teach the language in her own time, during lunch breaks and after school. She was proud when one of the exam boards launched a syllabus for CSE Cornish, but I am not sure she ever managed to shepherd a student through it; more mainstream subjects, along with sport and extra-curricular activities, took up all the time. I started the course, learning numbers – *onan, dew, tri, peswar, pymp*; days of the week – *Dy'Lun* (Monday), *Dy'Yow* (Thursday); essential phrases – *Myttin da* (Good morning), *Fatla genes* (How is it going?) – but my teenage lack of focus, combined with frustration at the idea of how long it would be before I could have even the most basic of conversations, meant that I soon dropped out of the class. Miss Kernow made her disappointment clear, shaking her head as she admonished me: 'If someone with a name like Petroc Trelawny can't be bothered with Kernewek, what hope do we have?'

Once the Cornish language was dominant here. In amid the thick grass of a municipal park in Penryn, lines of stones mark out the ancient floorplan of Glasney College. A remnant of an east wall survives, a tiny fragment of a grand ecclesiastical building. Bishop Walter Bronescombe founded the college in 1265 as the western outpost of his sprawling Exeter diocese. It became one of the most important religious centres in late medieval Cornwall. At its heart was a collegiate church, two thirds the size of Exeter Cathedral, with a central tower topped with a spire. A close of houses for the provost, canons and vicars choral were surrounded by twelve acres of parkland protected by walls, towers, dykes and lockable gates. There was a purpose to this vastness – it was designed to impress locals and remind them of their place in the Catholic hierarchy. But Glasney was also an institution that helped Cornwall establish a sense of otherness, a belief that it was not merely another English county. Though services were conducted in Latin, one of the key roles of the college was to promote the Cornish language. Bishop Bronescombe and his successors saw the evangelical benefits of priests being able to speak in the vernacular tongue. A series of dramas created at Glasney helped the process, most famously the late-14th-century Ordinalia, a trilogy of plays that told the story of The Creation, The Passion and The Resurrection, with Cornish text and Latin stage directions.

Decline set in at the end of the fifteenth century as the Tudor regime attempted to suffocate any sense of Cornish semi-independence. Glasney closed in 1549, one of the institutions destroyed by Henry VIII's religious revolution. The wood, glass and stone of the magnificent church were sold to Giles Keylwaye, a local scrap merchant, who paid £149 for the lot. Much of the stone he collected ended up in the walls of houses built in Penryn over the following centuries.

The demise of Glasney, and the subsequent ban on the use of Cornish as part of the liturgy, marked the beginning of the end of the language. By 1700 it was only commonly heard west of Truro, and was already widely shunned by young people. Before the end of the century, it had probably ceased to be anyone's mother tongue. But remarkably, it didn't completely disappear. Some words found a place in Cornish dialect, and were thus spoken daily; others were kept alive due to their inclusion in local place names. And thankfully, a handful of forward-thinking philologists saved and translated proverbs, poems and plays, including the Ordinalia. Welshman Edward Lhuyd published a Cornish grammar in 1707. William Borlase added a vocabulary in 1759.

The language's faltering revival got underway at the very start of the 20th century, led by Henry Jenner – a librarian and manuscript expert born at St Columb Major in 1848. Returning home at the age of nineteen, on holiday from his first job as a school-teacher, Jenner made a trip to the churchyard at St Pol-de-Leon, or Paul, near Penzance, where he saw the grave of Dolly Pentreath. A fish seller who had died in 1777, Pentreath was said to have spoken nothing but Cornish until she turned twenty. According to legend she was the last fluent speaker, her story set out on postcards and souvenir tea towels to this day. Her memorial prompted Jenner to start studying and promoting the language himself.

'There has never been a time when there were not some Cornishmen who knew some Cornish,' Jenner wrote in a paper

he presented to the 1904 Pan-Celtic Congress. Cornish was, he argued, with the possible exception of Manx, the least cultivated of the Celtic languages, with the smallest vocabulary, 'but one may fairly say that most of what there was of it has been preserved.'

That year also saw the release of Jenner's *A Handbook of the Cornish Language* – an occasion often cited as the starting point for Cornwall's reclamation of its old tongue. His book was published by David Nutt, the address of the firm's London office listed on the title page as being ' "At the Sign of the Phoenix", 57–59 Long Acre'. Jenner was delighted at the symbolism of this, the idea that the language might rise from the ashes and take flight once again.

He was happy to admit that Cornish had little practical purpose, that there were few great texts for the fluent speaker to read, that it really couldn't bring much more than sentimental pleasure.

But surely that was enough. As he wrote in his *Handbook*'s preface, his comments reflecting the age in which he was living: 'every Cornishman knows well enough, proud as he may be of belonging to the British Empire, that he is no more an Englishman than a Caithness man is, that he has as much right to a separate local patriotism to his little Motherland... Why should Cornishmen learn Cornish?... The question is a fair one, the answer is simple. Because they are Cornishmen.'

In 1934, the year Jenner died, his protégé, Morton Nance, published the first English–Cornish dictionary; five years earlier he had written a textbook, *Cornish for All*. But in the century that has elapsed since Jenner's and Nance's pioneering work, the progress of the Cornish language has been a slow one.

A series of rival methods of spelling and pronunciation did not help. Academics were unable to agree on whether medieval or late Cornish should take precedence as a source, or decide if loan words from Welsh, Breton and even English were acceptable. In 2003 the UK government ratified the inclusion of Cornish in the European Charter for Regional or Minority Languages. This led to the adoption of a standardised orthography known as Single Written Form, *Furv Skrifys Savonek*. It has been seized upon by public bodies, relieved that they can burnish their Cornish credentials with no risk of getting it wrong. *Galwewgh orth 101 rag apoyntyans mar pleg* reads the sign outside Truro police station, translated as 'For an appointment please call 101'.

But while there are contemporary plays, comics and children's books in Cornish, progress is hampered by a lack of skilled teachers, a distinct shortage of contemporary Beatrice Kernos. Today it is estimated there are between 300 and 500 fluent speakers, and 10,000 who know something of the language, or are learning it. Ubiquitous bilingual place and street signs help remind locals and visitors of Cornwall's uniqueness. When the former Duke of

Cornwall was proclaimed King Charles III in September 2022, in Truro the announcement was delivered in Cornish by Pol Hodge, the Grand Bard, and broadcast on radio and television. But there is no Cornish language channel, no equivalent of Wales's S4C, Scotland's BBC Alba, Ireland's TG4 – the number of speakers would simply not support a dedicated service. On air the language is limited to a short summary of the news *yn Kernewek* once a week on Radio Cornwall. If I am pragmatic, I wonder about the point of a more extensive revival – surely Cornwall has much bigger issues to address first. But when in a sentimental mood, I delight at the idea of a return of the old tongue. Encouraging young people to learn the basics would be an effective way of promoting a stronger sense of Cornishness, no matter if the students' roots were in Penzance or Newquay, Manchester or Birmingham, Ukraine or West Africa. The language was once a key part of Cornwall's identity – perhaps it is time to dip into those dictionaries, phrase books and grammars once again.

* * *

In the 19th century many members of the working class in Cornwall were hungry to learn. Despite labouring long hours, a significant number strove to dedicate what little spare time they had to study. The Cornish language was not considered a subject of consequence, but science, mathematics, history and literature were. Self-improvement and the concomitant chances that education offered for a better existence were considered something highly desirable.

Camborne's Literary Institute was founded in 1829 by a group of men that included a schoolmaster, a surgeon, a mine captain and a safety fuse manufacturer. They raised funds for a permanent building which opened in the town centre in 1842, a Greek Revival-style lodge with a substantial Doric portico. It is one of

Camborne's most attractive buildings, today used as a community centre. When it opened there was a full programme of public lectures, a library of 1,100 books and a collection of 400 specimens of minerals and curiosities. It became an outpost of the Society for the Diffusion of Useful Knowledge, a national organisation that encouraged workers to improve themselves intellectually.

Such establishments were found in mining towns and villages across the county. A thick mist hangs low as I drive across the Penwith moorland to St Just. Old mine workings beside the road make brief appearances through the murk. With its tightly packed terraces of workers' dwellings radiating out from the Market Square, St Just feels more like a mining community of the midlands or north, rather than Cornwall. A thousand-seat chapel has a granite façade that is only a few shades greyer than the sky above. Further down Chapel Street, squeezed in between two cottages, another Greek Revival building – St Just's Literary Institute, built the same year as Camborne's.

Francis Oats came to St Just from Fowey with his family when he was six. As a boy miner he came to this hall of learning whenever he could, listening to visiting lecturers and taking exams offered by the Mining Association of Cornwall and Devon. He won a scholarship to the Royal School of Mines in London, but could not afford to go. Instead he became underground superintendent at the local Botallack Mine. In his mid twenties Oats emigrated to South Africa and learnt about diamonds. Cecil Rhodes appointed him to the board of the De Beers Company in 1887; nearly two decades later he became chairman, and thus, for a while, one of the world's most powerful mining magnates.

There are many other stories of Cornishmen from relatively modest backgrounds who later enjoyed glittering success. Three are celebrated with statues in their home towns: the scientist and inventor Humphry Davy, whose father was a Penzance woodcarver; Camborne's Richard Trevithick, a miner's son who invented the first steam engines to move on road and rail; and the Truro-born African explorer Richard Lander, son of an innkeeper.

John Passmore Edwards's father was variously a carpenter, nurseryman and brewer. Born in Blackwater, his only formal education came from the village school. A contemporary described it as being a place 'where the pupils, of all ages, were packed like herrings in a box'.

The inadequacies of the place did not dampen his desire to learn. At twelve his schooldays reached their end, and he went to work alongside his father. The pennies he earned were spent in a second-hand bookshop in Truro, a six-mile walk away. At night he would set out to hear visiting speakers. At sixteen he became a Sunday school teacher, and launched himself, initially unsuccessfully, as a public speaker, addressing audiences at the Carharrack Literary Institute and the Young Men's Association in St Agnes.

In 1843, at the age of twenty, Passmore Edwards became clerk to a Truro lawyer. The following year he met a representative of the radical London newspaper *The Sentinel*, who encouraged him to become its agent in Manchester. With the railway yet to reach Cornwall, he travelled most of the way to his new job by sea – a steamer from Falmouth to Dublin, the mailboat across to Liverpool, and finally the train to Manchester. The position did not work out, but he used his time in the north to find his voice as an orator, speaking about the evils of alcohol and the benefits of abstinence, and encouraging his audiences to sign the temperance pledge.

Passmore Edwards moved to London in 1845, where he stayed for the rest of his life, dedicating much of his energy to campaigning. He was appointed a delegate of the London Peace Society, attending international conferences in Brussels, Paris and Frankfurt; he fought for new legislation to prevent gambling and

the sale of opium, highlighted the plight of indigenous popula-
tions in lands colonised by Britain, and rallied against the slave
trade, telling consumers it would be better to 'not to know the
taste of sugar than be responsible for the broad black iniquity
of slavery'. An end to capital punishment was another of his
demands, a position he had first taken as a seventeen-year-old
after witnessing the hanging of two men at Bodmin Gaol in 1840,
an occasion that drew crowds of more than 20,000.

Soon the tax on newspapers was in his sights – a tax against
knowledge, as he saw it, and an encumbrance to the small
weekly newspaper, the *Public Good*, that he had launched in
1850. Passmore Edwards wrote much of its content himself, in
particular frequent attacks on *The Times*, which he saw as a paper
in hock to its shareholders, 'a huge intellectual machine without
conscience or heart'. The *Public Good* was a modest success, and
his media empire soon expanded to include a series of other
newspapers, magazines, almanacs, partworks and publications for
children. Unfortunately, his ambitions as a proprietor were let
down by his skills as a businessman; a failure to settle creditors'
bills led to bankruptcy, time in a debtor's prison, and a temporary
disappearance from public life.

It took him more than a decade to pay off his debts, something that he was determined to do. Then he relaunched himself
as a publisher, acquiring two specialist journals, *Building News*
and *Mechanics' Magazine*, and then, in 1876, a daily London
newspaper – *The Echo*. Two decades later he recalled that it was
the realisation of a 'long-cherished dream ... producing a paper
devoted to the public good'.

Passmore Edwards was now wealthy enough to become a
philanthropist, funding a series of buildings that would better
the lives of the working classes, an echo of the encouragement
he had received six decades earlier. He concentrated his works

on two geographical areas – deprived parts of London including West and East Ham, Southwark, Edmonton, Whitechapel and Limehouse, and Cornwall.

His first gesture here was to build a small Literary Institute at Blackwater, his birthplace. Elegantly restored, it is still in use today as the local village hall. In September 1893 he laid the foundation stones for two more institutes, one in Chacewater, where he had spent much of his childhood, and another, on an altogether grander scale at Hayle. When finished it contained a reading room and library, a lecture hall, a science laboratory, a sailor's rest room, a gymnasium and a skittle alley. He funded the Miners and Mechanics Institute in St Agnes, the Newlyn Art Gallery, schools in Helston and Truro, convalescent homes and hospitals in Perranporth, Liskeard and Redruth.

Passmore Edwards wanted every town in Cornwall to have a library – and offered £2,000 – a sum that would cover construction costs – to any borough that was prepared to support one.

Camborne, Redruth, St Ives, Liskeard, Launceston, Bodmin, Falmouth and Truro accepted his largesse.

In 1896 the first books were stamped out of the Truro Free Library, and three years later an extension opened, built to house the Central Technical Schools for Cornwall, which offered classes in science, art and agriculture. A frieze over the central first-floor windows alludes to the education provided – a finely carved row of craftsmen that includes masons, draughtsmen and carpenters.

The building was the work of architect and former Truro mayor Silvanus Trevail, who announced that a thousand students would be educated, 'all without the ratepayers of Truro having to put their hands in their pockets for a single sixpence'. Passmore Edwards was a lucrative client for Trevail, who was determined to remain in his patron's good books, making sure the philanthropist's name was carved prominently into the stone frontage of the buildings he paid for.

By 1900 Passmore Edwards had become disillusioned at the development of his Cornish libraries and institutes. He had provided the buildings, and in return he expected local councillors to sanction the purchase of books to fill them. But in St Ives the library was allocated just two rooms, the others used as municipal offices and as a rehearsal space for the local band. Councillors in Liskeard let the ground floor of their library to the Post Office; in Bodmin staff had to beg for donations of books as there was no municipal cash to buy any.

Gradually the shelves did fill up, and the spaces that Passmore Edwards had created became thriving centres of learning, places where generations of autodidacts would study. Five of his libraries still serve their original purpose, and his buildings in Bodmin, Hayle, Blackwater, Helston and St Agnes remain places where the local community gather for everything from talks and film screenings to keep-fit sessions and art classes. His former Redruth library is being reimagined as a theatre, called The Ladder, the name inspired by the philanthropist's statement of intent: 'If I can fund the Ladder, the Poor might climb it.'

* * *

Passmore Edwards opened his new Falmouth Library in May 1896. He was presented with a silver key with which to open the front door, and after inspecting the premises, appeared on the balcony to loud cheers from the gathered crowds.

This building was not the work of Trevail, but rather Falmouth's Borough Surveyor, W. H. Tresidder, who seemed uncertain as to which architectural style he should follow. In the end he settled on an eclectic mix that contains elements of Italianate, Renaissance, neoclassical and Flemish design. The materials were sourced locally, with granite from nearby Mabe, sand from Kergilliack, and ground-floor joists of old ships' oak, presumably sourced from the town docks. As with Truro, there were rooms set aside for the teaching of science and art.

Passmore Edwards had sown the seeds for the Falmouth School of Art, which opened in 1902, its remit gradually expanding to include courses in weaving, block printing and bookbinding, alongside drawing and painting. It was to become an internationally respected institution, which would win the support of leading Cornish artists including Peter Lanyon, Terry Frost, Barbara Hepworth, Bernard Leach and Patrick Heron. Places like St Ives, Newlyn, Lamorna and Penzance had long been famous for their communities of painters, sculptors, print-makers and the like; now there was finally a place where aspirant Cornish artists could receive a decent education.

Not that London civil servants always saw it that way – in the 1980s the Advisory Body for Public Sector Higher Education announced that they found Falmouth School of Art 'academically and geographically isolated', and proposed its closure. It survived, and today is part of Falmouth University, whose crest features a chough, Cornwall's national bird, clutching an artist's brush, pencil and quill.

* * *

As we started the second year of sixth form at Helston School, my friends and I would sit on the threadbare, torn, ink-stained sofas in the student common room and discuss our higher education prospects. In one corner a shelf was piled high with prospectuses, but they were almost all for institutions across the Tamar. Other than the arts courses at Falmouth, or undergraduate studies in mining and metallurgy at the Camborne School of Mines, our options were all outside Cornwall.

As we prepared to fill in our UCCA and PCAS forms, we studied railway and bus timetables and debated the merits of distant northern cities. In the end I put off thoughts of university and got a job, but the other members of my friendship group fanned out between Portsmouth, London, Liverpool, York and Oxford.

Today an eighteen-year-old can leave Helston School and study for a degree a mere ten-mile bus journey away. Falmouth and Exeter universities share a campus at Tremough in Penryn, once a country house and small estate that later became a convent and school. The range of courses on offer is broad – Exeter staff teach subjects including geology, geography, politics and history; Falmouth offers courses including fashion, photography, creative writing, animation, fine art and architecture.

Falmouth's Vice-Chancellor and Chief Executive, Professor Emma Hunt, walks me around the campus. Natural light pours into the fashion and textiles block, its hangar-like space occupied by a hundred students, some leaning over cutting tables, others working at looms and sewing machines, every available bit of wall space hung with items of clothing in different stages of development. A rail of sportswear takes its lead from Cornwall's surfing heritage. On a table are samples of fabrics coloured by natural dyes made with plants from one of the campus's well-stocked gardens.

We walk out into a copse of monkey puzzle trees, and pass banks of daffodils and mature rhododendron bushes on the way to the Academy of Music and Theatre Arts. Its site, on a slope, means the upper-floor entrance is low-key and unobtrusive. The grand scale of the building is only revealed at ground level, where two projecting wings, clad in Delabole slate, accommodate the main performance spaces. Technicians are setting the lights for a concert in one studio; in the other dancers are warming up before class, the windows thrown wide open onto the lawn and mature shrubbery outside.

On an adjacent industrial estate the air is heavy with the smell of hops from a craft brewery that is one of the tenants. A unit the size of a large barn houses the Games Academy. Inside dozens of students are gathered in small groups around banks of computers, working together to develop new apps, produce spectacular animations, learn about computer and data science, and explore AI and immersive computing. It is now the biggest department in the university, but it didn't exist a decade ago. The hope is that some of the ideas being developed here can become viable businesses. The Launchpad Scheme, based on the campus, helps realise the commercial possibilities of work developed by students, or by other Cornish-based entrepreneurs, offering advice, mentoring and funding to start-ups. In return for investment the new companies have to remain headquartered in Cornwall for at least five years.

'The European Union and UK government funded Falmouth because they wanted it to have a major impact on the local economy,' says Professor Hunt. 'We want to give young people from Cornwall the chance to study at the highest level without leaving the area, and we want to get the best students from around the world to come here and stay. Graduate retention is key to what we are doing. We intend to keep a good percentage of the people we have taught – and their skills, energy and ideas – here in Cornwall. We want our students to join us in making the case that Cornwall's remoteness should not stop it being a leader in the modern creative industries.'

Between them, Falmouth and Exeter have commissioned a series of striking buildings that offer spaces for traditional and vocational teaching. The low-level structures sit well in their landscape: balconies offer views down to Penryn, Falmouth and the Carrick Roads; broad windows look out over the farmland behind. The latest Cornwall edition of the architecture-lover's bible, *Pevsner's Buildings of England*, is enthusiastic: 'This may be the last of the great campus universities... arresting in its architectural ambition and responsiveness to its dramatic site.'

Exeter University's Institute of Cornish Studies is located here. It conducts and publishes research into history, language and heritage, and considers issues including politics and devolution, health provision, the natural environment and the challenges facing Cornish society, from hidden homelessness to food banks. From its building on the campus it is barely a ten-minute walk down to the Penryn park where stones mark the outline of what was Glasney College. After a gap of nearly 500 years, Cornwall once again has an institution that champions and celebrates its unique identity.

CHAPTER 13

Hireth

Hireth is one of the most romantic words in the Cornish language. We share the noun with speakers of Welsh and Breton, but there is no direct equivalent in English. It suggests a melancholic homesickness, a nostalgic, wistful yearning for something that seems out of reach. When I am away from Cornwall certain memories will trigger the sensation of *hireth* – walking with my mother on Kennack beach; having a pint with my father at the Railway Inn in St Agnes; the woods by Helford River in autumn; St Michael's Mount seen early on a summer morning; being a passenger on a train crossing the River Tamar.

Music can inspire *hireth* too. Occasionally, when a sympathetic producer is on duty, I try and squeeze a recording of the singer Brenda Wootton into my morning radio show. She was the voice of Cornwall, cherished at home, treated as a star in France but, except in the folk world, pretty much unknown east of the Tamar. Her breakthrough album, *Pasties and Cream*, was released in 1971, the year I was born. It became part of the soundtrack of my childhood. Wootton planned the photograph on the LP's cover with great care. Shot in the kitchen of a Mrs Hitchens of Trewarveneth Street in Newlyn, a black Cornish range provides the backdrop. A table in the foreground is set with a blue-and-white chequered cloth, a brown teapot and pink cosy, two cups on saucers, a cut-glass dish of clotted cream, a pasty sliced in half, and a copy of *The Cornishman*, the Penzance newspaper. The songs on the record quickly became Cornish standards – 'Lamorna', 'Little Eyes', 'Camborne Hill', 'Something about a Pasty' and the spiritual 'Old Time Religion'.

Wootton made more than twenty albums, but she was happiest appearing live on stage, dressed in a capacious, kaftan-like dress, each of her fingers bearing a ring, home-made strings of beads and bright silk scarves tied around her neck – period hippy-chic with strong Cornish overtones. I saw her fill large chapels and school halls, sharing the space with male voice choirs and brass bands, her untrained soprano voice confidently belting the words out over the noise made by her fellow musicians. Seeing her in full flow was never short of thrilling, but she was at her best in more intimate spaces, a village hall or folk club, singing a cappella or performing with white-bearded guitarist John the Fish, her longest-serving duo partner.

John Langford was a Londoner who came to Cornwall in the 1950s with dreams of being a fisherman. When they didn't work out, he started gigging, appearing regularly at the new Count House Folk Club, opened in 1964 in a building on the cliffs at Botallack near St Just. Brenda (also born in London, where her Cornish parents had briefly moved to, to find work) grew up singing in chapel choirs in Newlyn and Penzance. Later she became an amateur actor, a member of the Sennen Drama Group and the Madron Players, a regular in productions at the Minack and the Playgoers Little Theatre in Penzance. After reading an article about the new folk club in *The Cornishman*, she took her daughter along one night to check it out. She soon became a regular, initially joining in sessions from the floor. When John the Fish spotted her natural talent, he invited her to join him on stage, where together they performed 'Lamorna'. At the age of thirty-six, Brenda Wootton had launched her musical career.

Her partnership with John the Fish saw the two of them drive up and down the country performing at folk clubs for a few pounds a gig. In 1967 she opened her own Cornish venue, Pipers Folk. The opening night saw 280 pack into St Buryan Village Hall; Raph McTell, soon to enjoy fame with his song 'Streets of London', was the compère. Wootton relished the response she got from the audience, who often had to be told to go home at the end of the night. But however satisfying she found performing, it was not a living – that came from her day job, running the Penzance outlet of Tremaen Pottery, the family business.

Wootton finally handed the shop over to her daughter and went professional in 1975. Her first foreign booking had come four years earlier, from the Festival Interceltique de Lorient in Brittany, where she shared a bill with harpist Alan Stivell and

The Dubliners. The connections between Brittany and Cornwall meant she immediately felt at home – here was another place that was remote, reliant on fishing, farming and tourism, proudly independent with a distinct language that shared its Brythonic roots with Cornish, and above all proudly Celtic. Inevitably Breton audiences immediately fell in love with the woman they called *La Grande Cornouaillaise*.

Her popularity in France quickly spread beyond Brittany. She started appearing regularly on national radio and television and in Paris was booked to sing at major venues – the Théâtre de la Ville, L'Olympia and the Palais des Glaces. For a 1983 engagement at Théâtre Bobino, once the long-term home of Josephine Baker, she brought Camborne Town Band along to share the stage.

I met Brenda Wootton half a dozen times when I was sixteen and helping out at the weekends at Radio Cornwall, answering phone calls from listeners. When it launched in January 1983 the station signed her up to present *Sunday Best*, a weekly request show aired live at noon. Wootton would arrive at the Phoenix Wharf studios with her husband John, and a wicker basket full of food – pasties, sausage rolls, hard-boiled eggs, heavy cake and sandwiches – to be shared as the music played. The engagement was a labour of love – her weekly fee was never more than £30, but the response she got from the audience seemed to make up for the paucity of the remuneration – at the height of the programme's popularity her postbag exceeded 600 letters every week.

Many listeners requested Wootton's own recordings – but she limited her appearances, and would only occasionally allude to her travels and her career abroad. To most Cornish listeners she remained the woman from Newlyn who loved to sing. Yet in between her weekly visits to the BBC's Truro studios, she shared stages with artists including Stéphane Grappelli, Jacques Loussier,

Yves Montand and Mercedes Sosa. Huge poster-photographs advertising her concerts were displayed on the tiled walls of Paris metro stations. She sang for the French President François Mitterrand, and, in an echo of Johnny Cash at Folsom and San Quentin, performed for criminals serving life sentences at the Île de Ré prison. In Cornwall Wootton recorded for Sentinel Records, a tiny company based in a former school at Paul, near Newlyn. In France, her discs were released by the international mega-label RCA. 'It is difficult to compare Brenda with any other singer', wrote the critic in *France-Soir* after the first night of a week of performances at Théâtre de la Ville. 'With her Cornish origins, she carries on stage a kind of soufflé of sea and air ... this large lady with eyes wide with expression, a fringe of little laughs like champagne corks, with rings on every finger, her uncertain French ... she is all of the grandmothers in fairy tales, warm and friendly as in children's dreams.'

Wherever in the world she sang, Wootton would include a Cornish song in her programme. In 1972 she began a collaboration that became even more important to her than her relationship with John the Fish. Richard Gendall was another language teacher at Helston School with a passion for Cornish. He dedicated much of his life to the academic study of modern or late Cornish, a version of the language he considered far superior to the more popular *Kernewek Kemmyn* or Common Cornish.* He was also a talented composer and poet, and when he first met the singer at the Pan Celtic Festival at Killarney, he offered to write a song for her.

While Cornish dialect had often featured in her lyrics, she did

---

* When Single Written Form (*Furv Skrifys Savonek*) became the official version of the language in 2008, Gendall was scathing, describing it as 'Celtic Esperanto'.

not know the language at all. Undeterred, Gendall established a process that served the two of them well. After he had created a song, he would send her the handwritten lyrics, a note about the meaning of the text, and a cassette recording of him singing and playing the tune. Wootton would learn the words phonetically, work up an arrangement for her guitarist, and then rehearse, with Gendall on hand to offer advice. He wrote as many as 460 songs for her, of which she performed at least 90, including 'Mordonnow', a paean to the oceans, 'Kemer Ow Ro' (Take My Gift), a celebration of Cornwall's virtues, 'Cala Me', marking the start of spring, and 'Onen, Deu, Try', a song to teach children Cornish numbers.

Brenda Wootton was deeply proud of her Cornishness, sometimes appearing clad in green, yellow and black tartan, or with the black-and-white flag tied like a cape over her shoulders. She was not a nationalist; according to her daughter Sue Ellery-Hill, she wanted 'little to do with the politicisation of Cornwall and the too-ardent nationalism of some Cornish'. But she was determined that her foreign audiences – and she found success in Germany, Canada and Australia as well as France – would leave her concerts fully aware that Cornwall had an identity that went far beyond its geographical position at the western tip of the island of Britain.

At home she gave us new confidence. There was something comforting in her lyrics, retelling familiar legends, praising the beauty of the landscape, reflecting the pain of departure and celebrating great figures of Cornish history. At a time when national homogeneity was seen as the desirable direction of travel, she encouraged us to enjoy and rejoice in our heritage.*

---

*Brenda Wootton died on 11 March 1994, five years after suffering a stroke while recording her final album, *Sailing Gulls*, at a studio on the Lizard.

* * *

These days I feel the sensation of *hireth* when I am away from Cornwall, but when I was growing up here as a teenager, it was dreams of London that prompted a yearning melancholy. Having been removed from the capital's suburbs at the age of five when the family returned to Cornwall, I retained clear memories of the bustle of Waterloo and Paddington Stations, the strings of lights lining the Embankment, the illuminated signs of theatreland, the densely packed crowds of people, drawn from around the world. Picture books of the capital were favourite presents when I was ten and eleven. As I got older, I began to feel I was missing out on something, particularly when it came to culture. When I got home from school, I would make myself tea and buttered toast, and then spread Dad's *Times* (still a broadsheet newspaper then) out across the kitchen table, poring over the reviews of plays and concerts and marking up West End shows that I dreamt of seeing. There was little professional theatre in Cornwall then, no dance, and limited classical music. The Bournemouth Sinfonietta made sporadic visits, the Three Spires Festival in Truro burned brightly for a few years, and then folded. There was at least occasional world-class chamber music, thanks to the International Musicians Seminar at Prussia Cove, a series of masterclasses and workshops held twice annually in a sprawling house on the coast near Marazion. The participants – students and celebrated virtuosi – would give concerts in local churches, and in the tiny chapel of Trelowarren House, which my mother would take me to. Jointly founded by the four-masted-barque sailor and violinist Hilary Tunstall-Behrens and the great Transylvanian-born violinist Sándor Végh, there was always a strong Hungarian flavour to the choice of works, which meant I heard string quartets by Béla Bartók and piano pieces by György Kurtág before I turned ten. I did not know that this was considered difficult, tricky repertoire; to me it was just music. Alas, the concerts were few and far between, only happening when maestri and students gathered to work together for three weeks in April and three weeks in September, but these performances were my first exposure to live classical music, and I devoured them hungrily.

We had regular access to the movies. The Electric was the first name given to the cinema on Wendron Street in Helston when it opened in 1914. It subsequently became The Empire, before being renamed The Flora during the Second World War. In the 1950s a 26ft-wide Cinemascope screen was installed, and the façade was modernised, with a new foyer beneath the central rose window, a reminder of the building's origins as a Baptist chapel.

Patrons entered from the street through a metal gate and then ascended a flight of broad steps, dressed to look as if they were marble. Rows of arches on either side were filled with up-lit ruched crimson silk. Inside the auditorium there were red velvet tip-up seats for 500. A small premium was charged for balcony tickets – up there, cinemagoers could smoke, the beam of the projector cutting a sharp line of light through the haze.

Mum strictly controlled the films I was allowed to see. *Chariots of Fire* was a bit slow for a nine-year-old, but two years later I was well ready for the three hours of Richard Attenborough's *Gandhi*, so long an intermission was inserted halfway through. *Raiders of the Lost Ark* and James Bond in *For Your Eyes Only* were more obviously thrilling. Sometimes my mother and I would go alone to a matinee, *Annie* and *E.T. the Extra-Terrestrial* among the last films we were to see together.

I would check the screening times in the *West Briton*, telling my parents the film started ten minutes earlier than it actually did. I was determined we would be seated in plenty of time to enjoy the whole event: the soaring strings of a recorded light orchestra playing over the speakers, the slow dim of the auditorium lights and then the roll of percussion, rich brass and session singers pa-pa-pa-pa-ing the Pearl & Dean theme tune. The first adverts were always for Lyons Maid Neapolitan ice cream, Butterkist popcorn and Kia-Ora soft drinks, all available from the kiosk in the foyer. More sophisticated ads for Babycham and Beefeater Gin followed – products that were not on sale at The Flora. A century and a half after the building began its life as a church, the deeds of the place still stipulated no alcohol was to be sold in the premises, and no films shown on a Sunday.

* * *

Forty years on, I am in Newlyn in another cinema, this one housed in what was once a fish warehouse. Every seat is taken for the Tuesday evening screening of Mark Jenkin's new film *Enys Men*. Newlyn is his home town, and the picture will run here twice daily for several weeks, playing to capacity houses, as it does in cinemas across the county.

Jenkin is the leading chronicler of modern Cornwall, a brilliant, critical observer of the way we are now. His films are immediately recognisable. He shoots on 16mm stock, with a hand-cranked camera. Over-exposed frames, jumps, scratches and gate hairs along the edges of the picture have become trademarks of this sophisticated film-maker's work. Dialogue is kept to a minimum, and post-synced, meaning each uttered sentence is a clearly delivered, unequivocal statement. There are no superfluous lines in a Jenkin script; words matter less than the pictures and the carefully created Foley sounds. There are moments of high energy – for example, when he cuts together a series of different conversations at breakneck speed – but for the main part his narratives unfold slowly with little sense of urgency: shots of seagulls, boiling kettles, crackling fires and pints of beer being poured give the viewer time to consider the steady evolution of the story. His films are full of views of 'beautiful Cornwall' – pretty harbours, dramatic cliffscapes, thatched cottages – but they will not sell the county to tourists in the way that *Poldark* and *Doc Martin* did. These are uncompromising and provocative works, raising vital questions about what it means to live in contemporary Cornwall.

His 2015 film *Bronco's House* considers rural homelessness. Shot in Mousehole, Paul and Newlyn, the forty-four-minute feature starts when Bronco and his unnamed pregnant partner are thrown out of the home they have been living in after their landlord decides to cash in and sell to an outsider. In one particularly painful scene, Bronco returns to the cottage to redecorate it before it is put on the market. He needs the work badly, but later the landlord refuses to pay him for his efforts. Bronco's sister encourages him to squat in an empty second home, and helps change the lock on the front door. 'Can't just be a free-for-all,' the landlord tells Bronco's sister, who replies: 'Open your eyes, man, it is a free-for-all.'

The themes of *Bronco's House* are developed further in Jenkin's first full-length feature, *Bait*, released in 2019. Martin and Steven are brothers and fishermen, though Martin doesn't own a boat, and Steven reckons he can make more money by taking visitors on pleasure trips. Martin considers his brother has sold out, his anger compounded by the fact that they have had to sell their parents' cottage to Sandra and Tim, who use it as a second home.

Sandra stocks her fridge full of expensive food and wine, but none of it was bought locally; she stopped en route at an up-country supermarket. She has decorated her cottage with buoys, nets and portholes that seem to Martin and Steven to mock its past as a simple fisherman's home. The children of holidaymakers seem unaware of the privilege of their lives compared to those of their Cornish contemporaries. Sandra and Tim have converted a net loft into a rental flat, whose occupant appears furious at the gate one morning, complaining of being woken early by the engine of a departing fishing boat. 'He's got to go to work – what do you want him to do?' shouts Martin. 'You shouldn't be making this kind of noise until at least eight o' clock – I think it's actually illegal,' argues the boxer-shorts-clad tourist. 'You going to change the tides for them?' comes Martin's retort.

At the end of the credit roll comes the inevitable disclaimer: 'Any resemblance to actual events or locales or persons, living or dead, is completely coincidental.' Jenkin creates dramas, but they are close to being documentaries, the issues they raise commonplace, witnessed in Coverack and Helford and other villages up and down the Cornish coast, where life has changed due to an influx of new money, and where rage fuelled by insensitivity and jealousy lies just beneath the surface.

Jenkin's company of actors live in Cornwall and include his partner Mary Woodvine and Edward Rowe, who in his alter ego performs on stage as the comedian Kernow King. Bronco was played by Henry Darke, himself an acclaimed writer and director of work that explores the modern Cornish story; other players are drawn from local companies including Wildworks and the much-missed Kneehigh, once Cornwall's de facto national theatre. This casting helps ensure Jenkin's films play well with Cornish audiences, relieved at last to see themselves presented on screen in a straightforward, honest way, as real people, not stock characters dressed in smocks and fishermen's jumpers, speaking with generic, often rather ropey West Country accents.

His work has found a national and international audience as well as a Cornish one. At the 2020 BAFTAs, *Bait* won the award for Outstanding Debut by a British Writer, Director or Producer; it was also a contender for the prize for Outstanding British Film, nominated alongside *Rocketman* and Sam Mendes's *1917*, the eventual winner. The critic Mark Kermode, who has done much to champion Jenkin's work, described *Bait* as 'one of the defining British films of the year, perhaps the decade'.

The sense of anxious foreboding that pervades *Bait* is taken further in *Enys Men*, which saw Jenkin introduce rich, saturated colour to his Cornish palette. Released in 2023, the film is set half a century earlier. On Stone Island (the English translation of the film's Cornish title) a character called 'The Volunteer' (Mary Woodvine) monitors the life of a rare wildflower. Each day she takes the temperature of the earth it grows from and enters it into a logbook kept in her lonely cottage. Over and over we see her routine play out: visiting the plant, throwing a stone down an old mine shaft, firing up the generator, making tea, tuning in the radio, and eventually retiring to bed to read Edward Goldsmith's 1972 manifesto for environmental change, *A Blueprint for Survival*.

At first the film feels like an art installation, something to be watched in a gallery rather than from the comfortable recline of a cinema seat. But though its narrative is less linear than *Bait* or *Bronco's House*, the viewer is soon drawn into the story, as the routine subtly varies, and other characters appear, including a boatman played by Edward Rowe.

Enys Men was shot over twenty-one days during the Covid pandemic in 2021. Its outdoor locations and the small number of actors involved meant it was straightforward to enforce lockdown protocols. Jenkin had processed his previous films himself, making use of an environmentally friendly coffee-based developing agent for *Bronco's House*. The colour stock of *Enys Men* had to be sent away, the lab team at Pinewood Studios instructed not to clean it up, so the scratches, bright bursts and occasionally flickering, unstable images remain.

I have watched each of Jenkin's films several times – they are a vital part of this journey. There is no better chronicler of modern Cornwall. In the past few years every television channel seems to have had a returning series that paints an easy, fantasy vision of Cornwall-the-beautiful, more often than not reflecting lifestyles that would need the support of a generous London salary or trust fund to maintain. *Bait* and *Bronco's House* show how life really is for those trying to exist year-round in pretty seaside villages, the absolute opposite of familiar picture-postcard images. *Enys Men* takes what might at first seem like Cornish clichés and turns them on their heads, helping remind us of all that lost industry and abandoned tradition. Jenkin uses familiar, reassuring iconography but makes it appear alarming, troubling, even sinister; the scenes he creates remain in the mind for a long time. Miners look up from the bottom of a shaft, their eyes full of desperate hope; a Methodist preacher speaks from the pulpit, but there may be no faithful left to hear him; a boat on the ocean delivers both essential fuel and death; The Volunteer sees bal maidens and is serenaded by children singing songs; the outcrops of granite contain a myriad shades of grey, the sunsets and springy underlay of heather are rendered in shockingly brilliant colour.

* * *

Enys Men contains a series of scenes that fire up that feeling of *hireth*, not least the moment when The Volunteer switches on her transistor radio to hear Brenda Wootton singing 'The Bristol Christ' with Four Lanes Male Voice Choir. Not long after watching the film I experience the sensation again, as I play a recording of Malcolm Arnold's *Cornish Dances* on Radio 3.

Arnold was a Midlander, born in Northampton in 1921. By the time he reached his early forties, he had written five of his eventual nine symphonies, but was best known for his film scores – *Hobson's Choice*, *Whistle Down the Wind*, *The Bridge on the River*

Kwai and the *St Trinian's* franchise among his many credits. In 1964, when he met his second wife Isobel Gray, he was a wealthy man, but he was also an alcoholic and prone to bouts of severe depression and psychosis. His work as a composer was suffering; it was hard to extricate him from the restaurants of Soho or the bar of the Three Horseshoes, the pub in Thursley, the Surrey village where he lived. Knowing that he had spent many happy holidays on the north coast of Cornwall, Isobel suggested they should come and live here, and at the start of 1965, husband, wife and their infant son Edward moved into Primrose Cottage in St Merryn, two miles west of Padstow.

Arnold embraced his new homeland with open arms, supporting local music festivals and amateur orchestras, and writing his brass-band piece 'The Padstow Lifeboat' for the opening of a new RNLI boathouse and slipway at Trevose Head. Key to the four-minute work is a perfectly tuned, fart-like sound that represents the Trevose foghorn, a cry that penetrated deep inside Primrose Cottage.

Any hopes that the composer might find sobriety in Cornwall were soon dashed. He quickly became a regular in pubs up and down the north coast. He was often recognised thanks to his regular appearances on television, and seemed to feel he had to play up to his avuncular image, pushing wads of cash into the publican's hand, and announcing 'drinks for all'. Drink-driving regulations were only just being introduced. After a heavy session Arnold would get into his car and attempt to navigate his way home, rarely getting out of first gear. Local farmers got used to calls begging them to bring their tractor to tow his Fiat Cinquecento out of a ditch. His Cornish sojourn lasted seven years before money problems put paid to it; in the spring of 1972 he moved to Dublin, where his accountant advised he would benefit from a more sympathetic tax regime.

His time here saw him become increasingly interested in Cornish nationalism and identity. Arnold was delighted when he was asked to become a Bard of the Cornish Gorsedd, an old order that had found new purpose during the Celtic revival of the 1920s. In September 1969, he was one of thirteen new bards initiated in a ceremony at Castle Park in Liskeard. Dressed in the order's blue hooded robes, he took the Bardic name of *Trompour* or trumpeter. The following month he told the *Western Morning News*: 'I am now aggressively, chauvinistically Cornish'.

This passion for Cornwall had clearly come on quickly – he had been here for just a year when wrote the *Cornish Dances*. He conducted the premiere, given by the London Philharmonic Orchestra, at the 1966 BBC Proms. The programme note he provided lays out the influences behind the piece – the music of male voice choirs, brass bands, Methodism, May Days and the hymns written by the American gospel composer Ira Sankey and his friend, the evangelist D. L. Moody. Arnold aimed to capture the landscape as well, the 'sad and strange beauty' of the deserted engine houses of the tin and copper mines – proof, as he saw it, of how the Cornish had been 'ruthlessly exploited'.

The first dance is robust and driven, with great brass chords pushing the music forward. High strings seem to portray angry gulls, the clanging percussion represents the energy and heat of the foundry. In the second dance we might be in an abandoned industrial landscape; a crying bassoon seems to mourn all that has been lost. Visibility is low – it is easy to imagine the mist blowing in from the sea and obscuring the shapes of old mining infrastructure. One of Arnold's biographers, Piers Burton-Page, links the mood to a line in a letter from the composer: 'Sometimes you climb down the cliff and you have a feeling of mystery, of all those people who have suffered, and yet who are still walking out there'.

We are in chapel for the third dance. The brass seems to suggest a pipe organ playing the introduction to a hymn that a congregation, squeezed into well-polished pews, will sing with gusto and love. As the tune builds, evangelic passion seizes the Sunday-best dressed worshippers, who lustily sing, Amen, to the last chords. Marching musicians come into view at the start of the finale; it feels as if the sun is rising over a great pageant, perhaps May Day in Padstow; later the two Obby Osses will swing and gyrate their way through the streets. Locals and visitors will cheer, but there is an element of danger here – this is a celebration with a hard edge. Arnold suggested the conclusion of the dance might be titled 'Bruckner's Day Trip to Cornwall'.

He had already composed two sets of *English Dances* and one of *Scottish Dances* when he wrote this work; in the 1980s he would go on to add *Irish Dances* and *Welsh Dances* to his catalogue. But the *Cornish Dances* are the finest, together a deeply felt work with moments of painful beauty placed alongside hints of his anger and frustration at the oppression the Cornish have faced. This set of miniature tone poems is one of Arnold's finest creations. Alone, it justifies his Cornish sojourn.

* * *

A century and a half before Malcolm Arnold, the Black violinist Joseph Emidy was the unrivalled star of the Cornish music scene. He was a virtuoso soloist, provider of musical ensembles for society balls, and director of the Truro Philharmonic Orchestra. Though his gravestone lists him as being 'a native of Portugal', he was born at Guinea in West Africa where Portuguese traders enslaved him, taking him first to Brazil and then to Lisbon. It was there that his musicianship was first noted, leading to lessons and in time a job in the orchestra of the Lisbon Opera House.

In May 1795 the British frigate *Indefatigable* called at Lisbon for repairs. When it set sail again, Emidy was on board, press-ganged into service as ship's musician, and forced to entertain the crew with jigs, hornpipes and reels rather than the Gluck, Haydn and Mozart that he loved. There are several accounts of his kidnap. In one, the ship's master, the Penzance-raised Sir Edward Pellew, heard Emidy perform at the opera house and immediately arranged for a group of his sailors to accost him as he left the theatre. Another version has him coming on board voluntarily to play at a ball, after which members of the crew get him drunk and he wakes to find the ship at sea. Emidy spent four years in enforced naval service, finally freed when his ship reached Falmouth in March 1799. There he set himself up as a teacher and performer, marrying the daughter of a local mariner, with whom he moved to Truro in 1815.

There was talk of him going to London to make his name;

the German-born impresario Johann Salomon, who had master-minded Haydn's lucrative and hugely successful visits to the capital, might have been his promoter. But perhaps put off by his traumatic earlier journeys, or maybe all too aware of the racism he could face in the course of launching a career in the capital, he stayed put in his house on Charles Street in Truro, convenient for the town's burgeoning music scene, and a relatively straight-forward journey by coach to Helston, Falmouth, Camborne, Lostwithiel and Bodmin, where he also performed.

Emidy was a composer as well as a player – contemporary accounts of his life reference a string quartet and quintet, two symphonies, a horn concerto, and one or more violin concertos. None of them have been heard since Emidy himself played them, the scores long lost. But perhaps they are merely forgotten, in the midst of a sheaf of old papers, fallen down behind books on a back shelf, neatly tied up in a dusty attic of a house that once belonged to one of Truro's first families. Lost violin sonatas written

by Vivaldi in the 1720s were discovered in a Manchester library 250 years later; perhaps Emidy's scores are out there, waiting to be placed on a music stand once again, performed, and celebrated for their part in Cornwall's musical heritage.

Hireth has a direct equivalent in Portuguese, Emidy's first language – *saudade*. Homesickness, yearning and melancholy must have been sensations he came to understand as his remarkable life played out across three continents. Emidy died in 1835 when he was reportedly aged sixty, though he may have been a little older. He is buried at Kenwyn Church, where a beautifully carved gravestone describes his 'talent sear'd and genius mark'd . . . in harmony he lived in peace with all'.

CHAPTER 14

Cathedral City

Truro sits in a great bowl with Kenwyn Church perched on the rim to the north-west. Today the view of the city below is largely blocked by houses. An engraving made in 1806 shows an open vista, as it was in Georgian times. The spire of St Mary's Church is the tallest building, the harbour is out of sight, but the broad valley of the Truro River stretches out into the distance. Clearly visible are the houses of William Lemon and Thomas Daniell, two more men made rich by tin who used their new wealth to improve Truro's fortunes.

Lemon was born in Breage in 1696 and started out as an office boy, rising to become manager of a smelting house. In his late twenties, using his wife's capital, he took control of the well-named Wheal Fortune mine near Helston. It made him a profit of £10,000 (more than £2.3 million today). He had received scant education as a child, so he paid the master of the grammar school in Truro to teach him. Elected mayor in 1737, he set about building himself a majestic town house, one that would not look out of place in London or Edinburgh. The front door of Princes House is approached by an imposing flight of nine steps; a quay at the rear gave direct access to the River Kenwyn. His architect was Thomas Edwards, who he subsequently engaged again when he bought Carclew, a mansion six miles outside Truro overlooking

Restronguet Creek. The London-based architect turned it into a magnificent Palladian residence widely considered to be one of Cornwall's finest houses, now a ruin after a devastating fire in 1934. Edwards was to earn more money in Truro when Daniell, who had started as Lemon's clerk, and become a formidable mining speculator in his own right, commissioned him to design his town house, Mansion House. Built in the late 1750s of Bath stone, it was just down the street from Lemon's residence, and just as grand.

The view shown in the engraving is surely a romanticised vision of a town where it was said, 'one was more likely to find a shod horse than a shod child'; it unashamedly focuses on its grand dwellings and ignores the inevitable rows of rough workers' cottages. But it presents a helpful image of a place that was rapidly becoming a social and business centre, nicknamed 'Little London' by the contemporary press.

In the 1780s the new Assembly Rooms became the gathering point for fashionable Truro. Evidence of a busy schedule of recitals and concerts reflects the cultural interests of the wealthier members of the town's population. Joseph Emidy would often perform here, but there were other equally important figures in what was a well-developed cultural community.

For nearly a century, from 1764 to 1857, Truro's musical leaders were three successive organists at St Marys, the church next door to the Assembly Rooms – Charles Bennett, then Charles William Hempel and finally his son Charles Frederick Hempel. Bennett, who had been born in Bodmin, lost his sight as the result of a childhood accident. That did not stop him spending seven years in London as a student of John Stanley, the blind violinist, organist and composer. A friend of Handel, Stanley was Master of the King's Music from 1779 until his death seven years later. Hempel Sr was born in Chelsea, and studied first in London with his uncle, Augustus F. C. Kollman, the Hanover-born organist of the Royal German Chapel at St James's Palace. Hempel completed his musical education in Leipzig and Dresden before winning the Truro job. He taught his son, who succeeded him 1844.

Few other distant provincial towns could boast of having the services of such distinguished musical figures, and their presence encouraged others. Ann White was the daughter of a Truro cordwainer. Mrs White, as she was billed, did not embark on a career as a singer until after she had married – more often the time that women of the day were forced to say farewell to the stage. She would sing in concerts promoted by Hempel Sr, performing arias, duets, songs and religious numbers. On 23 April 1816, 'Under the Patronage of the Ladies of Truro', she mounted a gala that featured two works each by Haydn and Mozart, songs by the popular London glee composer John Callcott, and a *Grand Sinfonia* written by one of the Rombergs, either Andreas Jakob or Bernhard Heinrich, German musicians and cousins who sometimes passed themselves off as brothers. Both were still alive in 1816, as was Callcott. Haydn had been dead less than a decade, Mozart had died just a quarter of a century earlier. By today's standards this would have been considered a concert of contemporary music.

Truro was also a stopping-off point for international stars. The Italian soprano Angelica Catalani had sung at La Fenice in Venice and the Teatro alla Scala in Milan before she came to England to join the company at the King's Theatre on Haymarket. In 1812 she sang Susanna in the first London production of Mozart's *Le nozze di Figaro*, and the following year appeared for three nights at the Truro Music Festival. There was palpable excitement before her arrival: 'Madame Catalani . . . has completely charmed the good people at Exeter, and we doubt not will have equal success here', noted the *West Briton*.

Complete operas were staged in Truro too. Weber's *Der Freischütz* reached Cornwall in 1825, just four years after its Berlin premiere. It disappointed the critic of the *Royal Cornwall Gazette* who declared that 'it has nothing to recommend it to the chaste and moral conception of a British audience ... we have listened to English music which in our unscientific ears has sounded more pleasing, however unfashionable it may be to say so.'

Not everything at the Assembly Rooms was so highbrow. The 'fire proof phenomena' of Monsieur and Mademoiselle Chabert visited in 1819 – though local audiences were not treated to their most famous illusion, in which they spent an hour sharing an oven with a leg of mutton. At the conclusion of the trick the meat was roasted, but they were unscathed. In Truro they limited themselves to consuming boiling oil and hot charcoal, and 'eating a lighted torch with a fork as if it were sallad [*sic*]'.

Today all that remains of the Assembly Rooms is its façade. Medallions of William Shakespeare, David Garrick and Minerva, the Roman goddess of wisdom and art, indicate its former use. The building, also historically referred to as the Theatre Royal, welcomed performers for nearly ninety years, before closing in 1869. By the mid 20th century the space where audiences had once cheered on singers, actors, dancers and comedians had become the Cathedral Garage, the central Venetian window removed to allow motorcars access. A clothes shop, Leonard Modes, sold the latest fashions on the first floor, once the salon where gossip had been exchanged and matches made. Now there are offices upstairs; at street level what was once the ticket office had a recent turn as a pasty shop; on my last visit it was available to rent.

David Garrick never played the theatre; he died in 1779, just as it was being built. It would have been more appropriate if the architects had included an image of his contemporary Samuel Foote, Truro's greatest theatrical son. Born in Boscawen Street and christened at St Mary's, he was twenty-three when he enjoyed his London breakthrough, taking the title role in a 1744 production of *Othello*. Later, as owner of the Haymarket Theatre, he became one of London's three Theatre Royal patent holders.

Foote lived extravagantly and flamboyantly. His wardrobe included one outfit of bright orange lined with pea-green satin, and another of 'striped strawberry coloured corded silk with spangl'd buttons'. His expensive tastes meant that he was often in debt, thrown out of Worcester College, Oxford for idleness and unpaid bills, the latter leading to a spell in a debtors' prison. He relished high-risk sexual encounters, lost his leg in a riding accident that followed an ill-advised bet, and enjoyed multiple theatrical feuds with often unfortunate consequences. All this provided rich meat to the writer Ian Kelly, whose 2015 stage comedy *Mr Foote's Other Leg* saw Simon Russell Beale portray this child of Truro, who became a gay, wild, dangerous and brilliant man of the theatre.

* * *

Today Truro is firmly established as Cornwall's capital, but it only gained that status relatively recently. Launceston, on the edge of the border with Devon, was the first place to lay claim to the title of county town. Assizes were established there at the end of the 12th century, and there they remained for more than 650 years. By the early 19th century the County Jail had been built at Bodmin; close by was the Cornwall Lunatic Asylum, its six-wing panopticon ensuring minimal staffing was required to supervise the inmates. It seemed logical that the courts should be nearby, and they moved to Bodmin in the late 1830s, with the Shire Hall on Mount Folly Square built to accommodate them.

Later that century Truro began to assert its power. It gained city status in 1877, the year after it had been chosen as the place where Cornwall's new Anglican diocese should have its headquarters. A cathedral and a county hall followed – though Truro had to wait more than a century before it became the legal capital. The crown and county courts finally moved west in 1988, accommodated in a postmodern-style complex built on the site of Truro's cattle market, where its medieval castle once stood. The courtrooms sit around a central atrium, in a building that feels open and approachable, yet also has the stern formality demanded of a place where justice is delivered and lives are forever changed. It won its architects, Eldred Evans and David Shalev, the 1998 RIBA building of the year award.*

---

* Eldred Evans and David Shalev made another major contribution to Cornish architecture – Tate St Ives, opened in 1993, the gallery fitted into a tight site by Porthmeor beach. After Eldred Evans's death in 2023

The drive from St Martin takes just over an hour, around the Helford's winding creeks, along the narrow lane to Rame, through Longdowns, Perranarworthal and Playing Place. At the round-about at the top of the city there is a choice to be made – which road to take down the hill into the city centre: a steady descent on Lemon Street, the old grand entrance route, or the gently curving dual carriageway of Morlaix Avenue?

The mile-long stretch of bypass is named in honour of the Breton town that Truro is twinned with. It was officially opened in May 1983, with a visiting delegation of Morlaisiens on hand to help cut the ribbon. A year later a group of Truronians made the return journey, taking the Plymouth–Roscoff ferry as they went to help open Avenue de Truro.

Descending Morlaix Avenue, there is a clear view across the city to the buildings of Truro School, the local boarding school that my four brothers went to. By the time we came back to Cornwall, three had already left, but Christopher, a decade older than me, was still there. I would have been seven or eight when we went to speech day, with a lavish buffet lunch afterwards. There was another family outing to see him on the stage of the Epworth Hall in a production of *Oh! What a Lovely War*. His tales of tuck boxes, science trips and dorm life sounded fun, and I suppose I just assumed I would be following in his footsteps. But there was a problem. When my father was in the army, the government paid the lion's share of the school fees, part of a scheme to ensure military children could complete their educa-tion in one place. Now he was a civilian, with a lower salary and no access to service benefits.

---

an obituary in *The Times* noted, 'Sitting intensely in a plume of Dunhill cigarette smoke, Evans agonised over every curve in a wall to maximise the light that dropped deep into the space'.

A conversation happened in the kitchen at St Martin. I must have had dandruff, as Mum had just finished rubbing cod liver oil into my hair. I was sitting on the floor in front of the Rayburn, playing with the dog. Dad did not dance around the subject: 'Of course your mother and I, we want you to go there ... we just can't really afford it.' I didn't want to make their task any harder, and tried to console them, saying that I hated the idea of boarding school, and was quite happy with all that Helston had to offer. That wasn't the end of the matter, however. A few months later I was back in the Epworth Hall taking the entrance exam. I had agreed to do it just in case my marks were so remarkable that I qualified for a scholarship. I didn't. Truro was never mentioned again, and I started preparing for Helston. For a few years after, each time Dad drove us down Morlaix Avenue I would feel awkward, embarrassed for both of us. I'd feel my cheeks heating up, and would turn to look out of the side window, determined there would be no chance of our eyes meeting.

Perhaps that's why I preferred it when we drove straight across the roundabout and descended Lemon Street. Ornate Victoriana at the top soon gives way to simple Georgian elegance. The wealthy Lemons started developing the street – then the main road to Falmouth – in the late 18th century. They issued leases for the sites of shop-houses at the lower, town end, and sold plots for the simple two- and three-storey dwellings that accompany the road as it gently rises. As the buildings were constructed piecemeal, there is little uniformity to the architecture, yet the different houses together form a street that brings me pleasure every time I walk it. It has changed little since it was first laid out – there are no jarring shopfronts, even the façade of the 1930s Plaza Cinema sits comfortably in between its elderly siblings. It is not hard to imagine a well dressed pair setting out from their Lemon Street home to hear Mr Emidy and Mrs White performing together at the Assembly Rooms.

Halfway down is Strangways Terrace, five pairs of three-storey-over-basement town houses. My orthodontist had his surgery in a ground-floor room here; lying back on his chair, I'd focus my eyes on the yellowing ceiling mouldings as he gently tightened the screws of my teenage brace or measured me for a new dental plate. Afterwards I'd walk back to the car where Dad would be waiting, stopping for a moment in the shade of the Richard Lander statue – a memorial that dominates Lemon Street in the same way Nelson's Column commands Trafalgar Square.

Richard Lander was born in Truro in 1804, and started travelling at the age of thirteen when he went to the West Indies. As an explorer his greatest achievement was proving that the River Niger flowed into the Atlantic Ocean rather than running inland to Lake Chad, a discovery that opened up the interior of Central Africa to colonial exploitation. He died two days before his thirtieth birthday, on the West African island of Fernando Po, now Bioko, part of Equatorial Guinea. A year after his death a memorial column was built on Lemon Street. It fell down almost immediately, but was quickly rebuilt, a statue of Lander placed on top in 1852.

The Lander memorial was the work of Philip Sambell, a deaf, non-verbal architect born in Devonport who was to make a generous contribution to Truro's 19th-century townscape. St John's Church on Lemon Street was his work, a delicately resting cupola taking the place of a traditional tower, and graceful interior balconies supported on painted columns, under a carved wooden ceiling. As soon as that project was complete he moved on to the 1,500-seat Methodist chapel on Union Place, which opened in 1830.

Sambell may also have been responsible for Walsingham Place, an elegant crescent of small town houses. Corbels like lions' heads top each doorframe; some of the properties have maintained their original stucco, others have been stripped to reveal rough stone underneath. Today the houses are all used for commercial purposes, but their beauty demands that one day they should be cherished again as domestic dwellings.

Nearby on River Street are two of Sambell's later buildings – the former Truro Savings Bank, and an adjacent Baptist chapel, which together now accommodate the Royal Institution of Cornwall. The former banking hall is filled with vitrines displaying its treasures. An upstairs room contains cases of Cornish minerals. The walls hold a rich art collection: portraits of William Borlase, Billy Bray and Humphry Davy; work by John Opie, Henry Scott Tuke, Harold Harvey and Brian Pearce; paintings of mines and ships.

Truro is a port, a fact that not all visitors immediately grasp. The concrete and tarmac of Morlaix Avenue has created a barrier between the city centre and the docks. Until a century ago ships could unload at the bottom of Lemon Street. Back Quay was central to Truro's boat-building and pilchard trades in the 18th century; when more space was needed Lemon Quay was developed to unload cargoes of wood, wine, and fruit and vegetables. The back doors of Truro City Hall opened directly onto the water, allowing supplies to be delivered easily to the traders working its indoor market.

In the 1990s the market hall was turned into a theatre. A long silence, lasting a century and a quarter, had passed between the closing of the Assembly Rooms and the opening of this new space – a time when the city had no proper venue for music, drama or dance. I have spoken at and, after a fashion, sung on the Hall for Cornwall stage, introduced live broadcasts there, and sat in the audience to listen to choirs and brass bands, operas by Wagner and Verdi, plays by Alan Bennett and Agatha Christie, music by Richard Strauss, Beethoven and Schubert. Now the building has been reinvented once again. A £20-million-pound refurbishment coincided with the pandemic. A new auditorium, the Cornwall Playhouse, has space for 1,354 patrons, a broad proscenium stage, an orchestra pit and fly tower, all neatly fitted within the walls of the original mid-19th-century building.

Walking out of the theatre onto Back Quay after a night of entertainment, sometimes one still hears the sound of water. The old quays were covered over in the 1920s. The Truro River had started to clog up with silt and Falmouth had managed to pick off much of the remaining trade. The quays were covered and turned into a large open square, a useful space when filled by fairs or food markets; a windswept, desolate place when not. The Kenwyn, a tributary of the Truro River, still runs below; on occasion its gentle flushing sound can be heard through the grilles of the rainwater drains.

The theatre's other entrance is on Boscawen Street, a broad cobbled mall, Truro's main shopping throughfare. The buildings are a mix of Victorian commercial premises and Georgian town houses, with the occasional example of mid-20th-century infill. An ugly, triple-gabled Co-op supermarket occupies the space where the Foote house once stood, where Samuel Foote was most likely born in January 1720. Half a century later it became the Red Lion Hotel, with a 73ft-long cedar-panelled dining room, guest lodgings and chambers to accommodate servants. By the 19th century it was the principal site for gala dinners, auctions and public events, and a place where the gentry and professional classes would eat, drink, gamble and rest. By the late 1880s business was so good that the owners commissioned Silvanus Trevail to extend the building. He added two new floors in mock Tudor style, and a substantial restaurant with gable windows offering views over the city.

Pictures from a 1960s brochure show tables set for dinner, with bright-red chairs and white damask tablecloths; in the principal lounge little groups of seats are laid out, neatly accessorised with orange cushions. My eldest brother William recalled being taken there by our grandparents for high tea after school. He saw it in its final days. In June 1967 a fire destroyed a third of its rooms and the following month a lorry, the brakes of which had failed, ploughed into the front of the building. The coincidence of the Red Lion suffering two accidents so close together did not go uncommented on. The building was condemned, and though campaigners fought to save it, it was demolished soon after.

The biggest change to the Truro skyline had come in the second half of the 19th century. The arrival of the railway saw I. K. Brunel lay out two long viaducts over the valleys of the Kenwyn and Allen rivers, stone-and-wood bridges that carried their first trains in 1859. They were replaced in 1904 with stronger brick-arched, granite piers, twenty-nine spans in total, forming an elegant line that rises above the north of the city, and frames Truro's greatest piece of architecture, its cathedral.

* * *

Henry Phillpotts began his near four decades of service as spiritual leader of England's most sprawling Anglican diocese in 1830. The new Bishop of Exeter started by making a grand tour of his realm. The threat posed by the growth of Methodism, particularly in Cornwall, was immediately clear. He responded by ordering the construction of a library in Truro and thirty-six new parish churches. At the same time he pushed for the establishment of more church schools and parish guilds.

In 1840 Phillpotts started to campaign for Cornwall to become an independent diocese. But where should its cathedral be located? Bodmin, as county town, made a strong case, but voices in Truro were pitched louder, arguing that they were closer to the populous mining districts of the west, enjoyed a main-line railway connection and had multiple churches to ensure the continuation of parochial Anglican life. The decision was delayed by an unexpected third proposal – St Columb Major, a town six miles inland from Newquay. Its proponents suggested the parish church could become the new cathedral, the rectory turned into the bishoprical residence. Truro eventually won – but by the time the new diocese was confirmed, in December 1876, Phillpotts had been dead for seven years.

The Truro diocese needed a bishop – a job Prime Minister Benjamin Disraeli offered to Edward White Benson. After some deliberation he accepted and was consecrated at St Paul's Cathedral in April 1877.

Benson was a complex character, puritanical in outlook and prone to periods of depression. His first big job had been as

headmaster of Wellington College. He left colleagues in no doubt
as to his strong work ethic and was proud of his ability to get
by on a maximum of six hours' sleep a night. According to a
biography written by his son, A. C. Benson,* he had a 'suspi-
cion of all irresponsible enjoyment, as tending to relax the moral
fibre. He had a horror of all waste, a mistrust of all by-paths,
and comfortable halts, and arbours of refreshment.' But he was
the ideal choice as Cornwall's first bishop in modern times, a
straightforward and earnest preacher, excited by the challenge of
addressing the numerical supremacy of Cornish Methodism. He
was also sensitive to history and tradition, naming his palace, the
old rectory at Kenwyn, Lis Escop – Cornish for Bishop's Court.

His priority was the creation of a cathedral – and from the
outset he was determined Truro should get a brand-new building – the first English cathedral to be built on a new site since
the Reformation.† At first the Bishop, who also held the office
of dean, established a temporary cathedral in St Mary's Church.
Many in the diocese would have been happy with that arrangement continuing, with the addition of a modest extension if more
space was needed.

Benson disagreed. He wanted to sweep away all traces of the

---

* Bishop Benson and his wife Mary Sidgwick raised five children while
living at Lis Escop. All became prolific writers. His daughters were educated at Truro Girls' High School. As well as his father's biography, Arthur
Christopher also wrote the words to 'Land of Hope and Glory'. Edward
Frederic was author of over ninety books including the *Mapp and Lucia*
series; Mary Eleanor, known as Nelly, was a social worker who helped
establish the Women's University Settlement in Southwark; Margaret was
an Egyptologist who excavated the Temple of Mut at Luxor; Robert Hugh
was the author of the early dystopian novel *The Lord of the World*.

† Christopher Wren's St Paul's stood on the site of another cathedral,
destroyed in the Great Fire of London.

early 16th-century church. Seven architects were invited to submit plans, and the winner of the competition was John Loughborough Pearson. More diplomatic than Benson, he realised that retaining the ornate Gothic aisle of the old church as the cathedral's south chancel would be a useful investment to ensure public support for the more ambitious elements of his new building. A final service of holy communion took place in the church on Monday, 11 October 1880; no sooner had the altar been cleared than the demolition team started work.

The project had begun five months earlier. In May 1880 the Duke of Cornwall laid the cathedral's foundation stone. Dressed in the full Masonic rig of a grand master, he used an ebony-handled silver trowel to apply mortar to the stone. The Mayor of Truro then passed him a plumb line to ensure it was level. The ritual continued with the Duke scattering corn, then wine, then oil onto the stone, before handing the drawings of the building to Pearson and commanding him to 'proceed without loss of time to the completion of the work'.

Pearson turned sixty in the year that he won the Truro commission. He had already built over forty new churches, including the magnificent St Augustine's Kilburn, the 'cathedral of North London'. Built for the Anglo-Catholic Tractarian movement, its design embraced Gothic forms borrowed from across Europe, with a long, wide nave, a chancel and sanctuary lined with rich carvings, and a magnificent spire visible for miles around. His work on cathedrals, including Lincoln, Bristol, Canterbury, Chichester, Peterborough and Exeter, had helped him establish a reputation as a sensitive restorer of the old. Pearson was already known in Cornwall, having designed a new church at Devoran – St John and St Petroc, with a lofty interior, a steeply sloped roof and a confident spire, standing in sharp contrast to the Cornish tradition of churches that lie low in their landscape.

He had a tight plot on which to build. The nave would run over the graveyard of St Mary's; the west door would nearly touch the entrance to the old Assembly Rooms. To the east, the rectory, a row of cottages and a public house, the Bear Inn, all had to be knocked down. The limited space meant that the nave had to be built at a slight angle to the choir and chancel. Pearson relished the challenge, deciding to increase the impact of the building with twin west towers and a more substantial tower over the main crossing.

The size of the plot meant there was never any chance of a cathedral green to provide space to separate the sacred from the profane. Pearson chose to emulate the great baroque churches of Normandy, their buttressed bases sitting hugger-mugger with shops and houses, their towers soaring high above the banal realities of street life.

Once building got properly underway, Pearson and his assistants received a steady stream of criticism – the design and choice of stone were not Cornish enough; there were complaints that, at a time when the tin industry was failing and emigration was rife, the project was simply too expensive. James Bubb, Clerk of the Works, who lived in a red-brick house in the shadow of his building site, was on occasion abused when he stopped the traffic outside to take theodolite readings.

It was thirty years before the cathedral was finished. Pearson oversaw construction of the eastern part of the building, the choir, the chancel, the great crossing and the first two arches of the nave. Then work stopped. There was real concern the building might never be completed. The Duke of Cornwall had laid two foundation stones on his visit, the second at the base of a pillar at the west end of the nave. For two decades it remained a stump, six feet or so high, standing alone in the open air in the midst of the stonemasons' yard. It is easy to find inside the cathedral today – the pillar is thinner than those that surround it, its weathered stone a darker colour.

The Duke had become King Edward VII by the time the next stage of the cathedral was ready. The death of his mother provided the impetus needed to get the project done, with James Hawke Dennis, a rich metal broker originally from Redruth, offering to meet the cost of the central tower, subsequently named the Victoria Tower.

A benediction service on 15 July 1903 was attended by two dozen bishops and the new Duke of Cornwall, who had accompanied his parents at the stone-laying ceremony thirty years earlier. 'Then you were a youthful Naval midshipman, now you are a Vice-Admiral,' joked Lord Mount Edgcumbe, the Lord Lieutenant, as 700 guests sat down to a celebratory lunch in the Market Hall.

Neither of the men responsible for the cathedral saw it finished. Benson left Truro in 1883, appointed Archbishop of Canterbury by William Gladstone. He was still in post when he died in October 1896. On his way back from Ireland he had broken his journey to stay the night with Gladstone at Hawarden Castle in North Wales. The next day, while attending morning prayers, he suffered a fatal heart attack. Pearson died at his home on Mansfield Street in London the following year, aged eighty. He was buried at Westminster Abbey, another of the churches he had helped to restore. His son Frank oversaw the final works, the twin west towers which were completed in 1910.

In the time it took for the building to go up, Birmingham, Newcastle, St Albans, Southwark and Wakefield also became cathedral cities, but none of them got new buildings, instead adapting existing parish churches. Liverpool got its first bishop just three years after Truro, but did not appoint Giles Gilbert Scott as architect of its cathedral until 1903. Even though Edward VII laid the foundation stone the following year, work was not completed until 1978.

The low buildings that surround Truro Cathedral ensure it can be seen from afar. Its towers and spires appear unexpectedly over roofs or at the end of narrow lanes. They draw the eye of passengers on trains arriving at Truro from the east, and drivers descending any of the city's approach roads – Pydar Street, Tregolls Road, Lemon Street or Morlaix Avenue. They are a beacon, a symbol of homecoming. The breathtaking height of the vaulted interiors and the scale of the rose windows might once have seemed impossibly extravagant for such a small community. Perhaps Pearson realised this, including images of fishermen and Dolcoath miners in the stained glass, assurance that we are deserving of this grand space, that this is a building for Cornwall, one and all.

* * *

The choristers – since 2015 girls as well as boys and men – sing evensong each weekday at 5.30 p.m., continuing a tradition that stretches back to the earliest days of the cathedral. William Mitchell was the first organist, succeeded in 1881 by the seventeen-year-old George Robertson Sinclair, who was later to move to Hereford Cathedral, where Elgar immortalised him as the subject of the eleventh of his *Enigma Variations*. It was Sinclair who commissioned Truro's organ, built by the London maker Henry Willis & Sons. Today it is considered one of the country's best cathedral instruments.

Christopher Gray, the former director of music, says that the quality of sound the instrument makes is as much due to its location as it is to the machine itself. 'In most cases late-Victorian organs were squeezed into the tight corners of medieval churches,' he tells me. 'Here Pearson built a vaulted chamber for the instrument, giving it the space it needs for its glorious sound to properly fill the building.'

On one autumn afternoon, after he had conducted choral evensong, Christopher took me to the organ loft to demonstrate. Discarding the score of an arrangement of the Queen song 'Bohemian Rhapsody', performed at a recent concert, he picked up the music to Bach's *Toccata and Fugue in D Minor*.

The twilight had turned the great stained windows black. A verger, keen to be off home, shuffled around the cathedral floor, locking doors and turning off lights. Christopher started to play, his fingers caressing the keys as his feet danced on the pedals. The 2,700 or so pipes range from 32ft-long wooden boxes ('broad enough for a small child to hide in', says Christopher) to tiny metal tubes the size of pencils. Once the organist sat directly under the pipes, but in the 1960s an electric console was installed across the nave.

Bach's notes pour out, sometimes compressing the air to an extent that I feel the vibrations running through my body, sometimes delicately caressing the ear. Finally the swell organ thunders out the last chords, which seem to take forever to drift around the building before eventually dying. After a few moments of respectful silence Christopher speaks again: 'There is no compromise here – organ and building are as one. And that means you get this wonderful, visceral effect that few other cathedral instruments can produce.'

* * *

Sinclair introduced the Willis organ to worshippers in 1887 when the first part of the new building was finished. Before that Truro Cathedral had briefly been accommodated in a wooden shed, purchased by the diocese for £430.

Fitted out with altar, font, pulpit, brass lectern and organ from the old church, it was used for seven years before being taken down and rebuilt at Redruth. There it became the home of Smith's Cathedral Boot Works, its cobblers and bootmakers working in what had been the nave, arched windows above a reminder of the building's former purpose. Remarkably, the timber structure survived for a century on Drump Road in Redruth, until it was finally destroyed by fire in 1981. As a cathedral it had proved less than perfect. A correspondent wrote to *The Times* in 1884, reporting: 'it is somewhat hard to have a small wooden building, stifling in summer and bitterly cold in winter, as our only substitute for a holy and beautiful house.'

A shed it may have been, but it least it gave the new diocese a focal point. And it was where, at Christmas 1880, Bishop Benson introduced a service that was to become a staple part of Anglican Christmas celebrations.

The first ever Nine Lessons and Carols took place at 10 p.m. on Christmas Eve. Though Methodists and other nonconformists had long included communal singing in their acts of worship, it was still a relatively new concept for the Anglican Church – the first edition of *Hymns Ancient and Modern* had been published less than two decades earlier. The Cornish carol tradition had been kept alive by the mathematician and MP for Helston and Bodmin, Davies Gilbert,* and his friend, the musicologist William Sandys. In the first half of the 19th century they had collected, notated and published local versions of carols, including 'I Saw Three Ships', 'God Rest Ye Merry Gentlemen' and 'Tomorrow Shall Be My Dancing Day', ballads that were generally performed domestically or in taverns and inns rather than at church.

In an effort to provide 'counteraction to the public houses and as a right prelude to Christmas', the cathedral's first succentor, Somerset Walpole (later Bishop of Edinburgh), introduced Christmas Eve carol services to St Mary's in 1878 and 1879. The next year he and Benson devised a more formal order of service that included two hymns, a selection of carols, three movements from Handel's *Messiah*, and a sequence of Bible readings that would explain the Christmas story, from the fall of Adam in the Book of Genesis, to Isaiah's prophecy of a saviour, to Luke's account of the shepherds travelling to Bethlehem. The readers would reflect the cathedral hierarchy, starting with a boy chorister, and ending with the Bishop.

'Benson was an entrepreneur who saw this as a good way of getting people over the threshold of his cathedral,' says

---

* Born Davies Giddy, he changed his surname in order to ensure the survival of his wife's family name, and thus inherit her family estates.

Christopher Gray. The 400 worshippers that the shed could accommodate were presented with what was as much a show as a service: midway through the now-forgotten carol 'Once Again O Blessed Time', at the line 'on our knees confessing', he commanded the congregation to kneel. They had to stand as the choir sang 'Glory to God in the highest' in *Messiah*, and leap up again for the Hallelujah Chorus. 'It was shallow and superficial in some ways,' says Gray, 'but Benson knew people liked a bit of theatre. The story in Truro is that he put on Nine Lessons and Carols in order to ensure the congregation was sober for midnight mass. That's a myth – we didn't have a midnight service here until 1952. But he certainly saw it as a way of diversifying the range of people who came into the building.'

Benson took the service with him when he left Truro for Canterbury and gradually it was picked up elsewhere, most notably by Eric Milner White when he was appointed Dean of King's College Cambridge in 1918. Rather than starting with the Lord's Prayer, as was the Cornish tradition, he chose to open the service with 'Once in Royal David's City', used as a processional carol, the first verse sung as a solo by a boy chorister. The BBC broadcast the ceremony for the first time in 1928 and was soon sharing it with an international audience, dramatically extending the reach of a service first given in Cornwall nearly half a century earlier.

* * *

When Truro Cathedral celebrated its centenary in 1980 the artist John Miller painted his picture *Cornubia – Land of the Saints*, a view of the Cornish peninsula, the ground lined with tiny Celtic crosses, each representing a parish church. Born in London, Miller first crossed the Tamar in 1958 to work as an architect, the author John le Carré among his early clients. Slowly he started his career as an artist, rich blues becoming his trademark – the sea off Tresco in the Isles of Scilly, or the sky as seen from his studio, the Beach House at Lelant with its views out over the Hayle Estuary to Godrevy Lighthouse.

But there is barely any blue in *Cornubia* – the clouds are coloured gold by the sun, the land and the sea are serpentine red. Displayed in a corner of the cathedral's great crossing, it is popular with visitors wanting to locate their local or favourite church.

The gazetteer below the picture offers a rich list of saints, men and women who were often travellers across several Celtic lands, their names found in Brittany, Wales and Ireland as well as Cornwall. Spellings may have changed over the centuries, but these ancient figures are now inexorably linked with the county. Their names form a beautiful lexicon, which I sometimes murmur softly to myself while looking at Miller's picture: St Austell (St Austol), Breage (Breaca), St Budock (Budoc), St Buryan (Buriana), Cury (Corentin), St Euny, Germoe (Germocus), St Ives (Ia), St Keverne (Akeveranus), St Levan (Selevan), St Maybn, St Mewan, St Petroc, St Ruan (Rumonus), Sennen (Senan), St Tudy (Tudius), St Veep.

Altogether 248 hamlets, villages and towns are listed, and it is easy to imagine that number of granite church towers, every one of them dwarfed by the spires of the mother church, Benson's and Pearson's cathedral that gave Cornwall a civic stamp of authority as well as an ecclesiastical one.

CHAPTER 15

Three Poets, Four Churches

John Miller's ecclesiastical picture-map forces me to think about the big swathes of Cornwall that I have never properly explored. Helston, Penzance and Falmouth were where we did most of our family business. Truro was for special occasions, the orthodontist, or a visit to Treliske Hospital for an X-ray of a twisted ankle. There was no need to go any further up-county. St Austell, Lostwithiel and Liskeard were places only familiar through a railway carriage window, Bodmin and Launceston were represented by signs on the A30, the Atlantic coast around Bude seemed unimaginably far away, the drive from far south to far north taking more than two hours.

Morwenstow sits in the top right-hand corner of *Cornubia*, a parish bordered by Devon to the north and east, and the sea to the west. St Morwenna was a Welsh-born, Irish-educated missionary who settled in Cornwall in the 6th century. Thirteen hundred years after her arrival, the church that took her name came under the pastoral care of Cornwall's great Victorian poet-priest, R(obert) S(tephen) Hawker.

Hawker first made his mark on the local community while still in his early twenties. Under a full moon, he sat on a rock just off the shore at Bude and impersonated a mermaid. According to his first biographer, the Devon priest and hymn writer Sabine

Baring-Gould, he 'plaited seaweed into a wig, which he threw over his head, so that it hung in lank streamers halfway down his back, enveloped his legs in an oilskin wrap, and, otherwise naked, sat on the rock, flashing the moonbeams about from a hand-mirror, and sang and screamed till attention was arrested.' He repeated his performance over several nights, attracting crowds of locals, some of whom brought their telescopes to better inspect this strange creature.

In 1834, when Hawker was thirty-one, Bishop Phillpotts of Exeter appointed him to the living at Morwenstow. He was to stay there until his death more than forty years later, an eccentric figure who hated clerical black and grey, and would instead wear brown vestments with red buttons, augmented variously with a long purple coat, a pair of scarlet gloves, a fez or a blue fisherman's jersey. Long before blessing pets became fashionable, he would include his extensive menagerie of cats and dogs as worshippers in his services, which he would conduct twice daily, even when his wife, Charlotte, was the only human member of his congregation.

He was a man who believed passionately in the social responsibilities of the church. His appointment coincided with new poor laws, aimed at taking beggars off the streets and accommodating them in workhouses, which he considered were little more than 'prisons for the poor'. He instituted church collections for the indigent of the parish, and published a verse pamphlet called 'The Poor Man and His Parish Church', the words of which are still prescient today:

The poor have hands, and feet, and eyes,
Flesh, and a feeling mind:
They breathe the breath of mortal sighs,
They are of human kind.

He believed that no workhouse would ever replace a proper house:

They should have roofs to call their own,
When they grow old and bent:
Meek houses built of dark grey stone.
Worn labour's monument.
There should they dwell, beneath the thatch,
With threshold calm and free:
No stranger's hand should lift the latch,
To mark their poverty.

Hawker's other great concern was the fate of drowned sailors. Dead bodies, or body parts were occasionally discovered washed up on rocks at the foot of the cliffs below his church. Historically corpses from shipwrecks had been buried where they landed, or left for the waves to wash them back out to sea. Hawker's parishioners were interested in the cargo of stricken ships, not the crew. They cared about luxuries – barrels of wine, boxes of coffee and rolls of silk and indigo cloth; he believed the drowned deserved a proper Christian burial.

When the *Caledonia* sank in September 1842, Hawker decided it was the moment to take action. The 200-ton brig had been carrying wheat from Odessa to Gloucestershire. After a stop at Falmouth it had rounded Land's End, and was near the mouth of the Bristol Channel when, according to the one surviving crew member, Edward Le Dain, 'the wind went mad, our canvas burst into bits... at last there came on a dreadful wave, mast-top high and away went the mast with the board and we with it into the sea.' *Caledonia* was driven onto the rocks at Sharpnose Point. Seven or eight crew members lost their lives that night.

Hawker buried them in his churchyard and later placed the ship's figurehead over the captain's grave.

In time he buried more than forty sailors at Morwenstow, a duty that triggered a period of depression. His mental health went into steep decline, exacerbated by the death of Charlotte, twenty-two years his senior, in 1863. The following year he married again. This time his wife was forty years his junior – Pauline Kuczynski, a governess by profession. They had three daughters, and christened the first Morwenna, after the saint.

On his deathbed Hawker was baptised a Roman Catholic; afterwards his second wife wrote that he had been 'at heart a Catholic' all the time she had known him. But his outlook and behaviour did not easily fit into a box, and he kept many of his thoughts to himself. A tourist who once asked him about his views and opinions was taken to one of the rectory windows for a brief lecture. 'There is Hennacliff, the highest cliff on this coast, on the right; the church on the left; the Atlantic Ocean in the middle. There are my views. My opinions I keep to myself.'

* * *

The sea is calm and flat as I drop down into Morwenstow, the road opening to reveal a fine view of the great lozenge of rock that is Lundy Island. The rectory that Hawker designed for himself is visible through the trees. Its chimneys stand out, each one different, modelled on churches where he had previously served or worshipped – Stratton, Whitstone and North Tamerton in Cornwall, and two towers he remembered from his days at Oxford. The kitchen chimney was inspired by his mother's tomb, represented, he claimed, 'in its exact shape and dimensions'.

After a pot of tea and a sandwich in the café in the garden of Rectory Farm, I walk down to the Norman church that was once Hawker's domain. The words, 'This was made in the year of our Lord 1575' are carved into the side of a pew, the same year that the rood screen was first constructed, reinstalled by Hawker in 1845. A stone on the floor marks the death of Charlotte: 'for nearly forty years the wife of one of the vicars of this church'. On a stand behind the back pew is a simple polished oak casket, the words, 'Hawker's Alms Box' carved into the lid. Dried-out Sellotape holds a faded handwritten message in place, instructing generous visitors that, 'Due to vandalism, the box is out of use. Donations should be left in the wall safe.'

The *Caledonia* figurehead has been moved inside the church, slowly and painstakingly restored after a survey in 2004 found that it had become rotten and decayed. A replica sits over the captain's grave; nearby is a granite Cornish cross that forms a memorial to the other seamen Hawker buried. It is inscribed with lines from II Corinthians: 'unknown yet well known'.

A stile leads out of the churchyard and into a field full of sheep. As I follow the curve of the land down, I start to hear the sound of the waves carried on the breeze. I cross a couple of fields, and eventually spot a narrow path leading towards a tiny wooden cabin that Hawker built himself on the cliffs. Perhaps he began to feel there was something sanitised about the view of the sea from the windows of his comfortable rectory. His hut perches above the water, its basic structure offering protection from the elements. It seems remarkable that such a simple hideaway, built more than a century and a half ago, should have survived. Its hatched doors, made from the timber of a wrecked ship, can be locked shut against the wind with heavy wooden bolts. It is no bigger than a cupboard; inside are a pair of pew-like benches.Hawker would come here carrying a basket full of short, large-bowled clay pipes already filled with his favourite Syrian *Latakia* tobacco, and pens and paper to write. He would watch for wrecks, com- pose poems, worry about his finances and contemplate his faith

as he looked over the waters 'with no land between us... and the coast of Labrador.'

Gradually, as his mood darkened, he took to smoking opium rather than tobacco. As his son-in-law and biographer C. E. Byles wrote: 'He took opium, at first as a medicine, afterwards from habit, and there can be little doubt that this explained a great deal in his character and mental attitude. Under its influence perhaps much of his finest work in poetry was written; but it had its inevitable reaction, in irritability and moods of profound depression.'

Today Hawker's Hut is the smallest property owned by the National Trust. More than a century of graffiti scrawled on its doors and walls provides evidence of those who have followed in the clergyman's footsteps, smoking, drinking, and staring out at the Atlantic, soaking up the power and spirit of the sea as daylight turns to twilight and then darkness.

* * *

'The Song of the Western Men', its words used in the anthem 'Trelawny', is the only one of Hawker's poems that is widely remembered today. In contrast, Charles Causley's poetry is very much alive. At a school concert one Christmas, three of us shared out the verses of 'Ballad of the Bread Man', in which Causley brings a farmer's club, a corrupt dictator and the television news into a contemporary telling of the birth, life and death of Christ. Mr Nankivell had us reading 'Timothy Winters' in English class, his room of eleven-year-olds relishing the subversiveness of a poem whose scruffy, dirty hero has a mum who has run off with a soldier and a grandmother high on gin. Collections of his poems are still in print, and there is an annual Causley Festival in his home town, Launceston. A twenty-five-mile drive inland from Morwenstow, there is no town in Cornwall that is further from the sea than this one. Causley was born, lived and died here.

It is easy to spot the poet's memorial in the graveyard of St Thomas's Church. It is one of the few slate stones amid serried rows of polished granite. The River Kensey, a tributary of the Tamar, runs along the side of the road. It takes me less than a minute to walk from Causley's grave to his birthplace, a low cottage in the midst of a tiny terrace. A Launceston Civic Society blue plaque marks his front door. Once a grey gasometer stood nearby, where he remembered mothers bringing their young babies and holding them over the wall in the belief that coal gas was a remedy for whooping cough.

Causley was born in 1917, when the remnants of Launceston's industrial heartland were still to be found along the river, with tanneries, a serge factory and wash-houses. His mother Laura earned her living laundering clothes and bedlinen. When he was seven his father, another Charles, died of tuberculosis, the result

of a gas attack during his time as an Army Service Corps driver
in the First World War. Subsequently the poet and his mother
grew ever closer, living together until she died in 1971. Her grave
is immediately adjacent to his.

Laura had a strong faith, and would attend church every
Sunday, her son often joining her at what he considered 'their'
pew, just in front of the Norman font where he was baptised. The
largest of its kind in Cornwall, it feels out of scale in this small
church. Benign-looking, hirsute faces decorate each corner with
six-petal daisy wheels between; an elaborate iron bolt holds the
wooden cover in place. The pews, exposed beams, tiles and light
fittings are evidence of a Victorian restoration that Causley did
not entirely approve of: 'The church itself was tiny, shiny, had
been gruesomely over-restored in the 1870s, varnished pitch-pine,
lion-coloured walls, brass gas brackets, our only incense the smell
of the coke boiler.' But he found perfection at the start of each
service, as the tower captain instructed the ringers of the six St

Thomas bells. 'For years I thought all church services began like this: a splendid cacophony of cries, bells, the dry whistle of ropes rising and falling, the organ gasping out a voluntary.'

Today the only mention of Causley inside the church is a tiny brass plaque on the organ, just beneath the pipes, noting that the instrument was cleaned to mark the centenary of his birth in 2017. Standing by the pulpit, I wonder about the sermons, gospel readings and prayers that he must have heard spoken here. The building is almost silent, the only noise comes from the river outside.

The Kensey was omnipresent in Causley's boyhood. In a BBC talk in 1977 called *Childhood Landscapes* he recalled that in the summer it sometimes 'stank like a dead whale'. In autumn and spring, when the 'granite sponge' of Bodmin Moor was filled by rain, the Kensey would 'suddenly turn a rich caramel, rise, cross the road, and invade us'. He went on to note its noise: 'chattering over its slim sandwich of mud and stones it never stopped its gabbling day or night. At Riverside, after dusk, you could never tell if it was raining, you had to go outside to find out.'

Causley turned left out the front door when he wanted to go to church. He would head right if he had a train to catch. Two separate stations stood a four-minute walk up St Thomas Road, the terminus of the GWR route to Plymouth and an intermediate stop on the LSWR line to Padstow. The railway was a pressure valve for Causley when small-town life became too much. As a teenager he would escape to Plymouth, an hour and forty minutes away. In 1939 he took the train at the start of his naval service as a coder. Despite suffering acute seasickness, this Cornishman, who before had never as much as crossed the Channel, saw the world, from West Africa to Sydney, from Scapa Flow to New Guinea.

He had left school at fifteen to work in a builder's office,

and after the war seized the opportunity to continue his education, training as a teacher in Peterborough, before returning to
Cornwall. He would supervise and inspire his primary school
pupils by day, write at night and at the weekend, and travel
in the long summer holidays. Later, after he had established
himself as a man of letters, there were invitations to lecture in
Dublin, Warsaw, Moscow, Naples and Berlin, East and West.
After his mother's death he was able to accept opportunities
that took him away from Cornwall for longer, taking writer-
in-residence positions at universities in Perth, Melbourne and
Banff in Canada.

But he always returned, unpacking memories of his journeys
once he was home, and revisiting them in verse. Events and
experiences witnessed in bright sunshine, relived on grey Cornish
days. In one poem he recalls the sight of Sydney harbour, as seen
from the deck of the aircraft carrier HMS *Glory*. Schooners of
beer await in a circular bar on Castlereagh Street; these events
noted in pencil in his correspondence and diaries, and brought
to life once again in Launceston:

> *O Sydney, how can I celebrate you*
> *Sitting here in Cornwall like an old maid*
> *With a bookful of notes and old letters?*

Before Ted Hughes became poet laureate in 1984, he was asked
who he would recommend for the post. His response was
unequivocal: 'Without hesitation I named Charles Causley – this
marvellously resourceful, original poet, yet among all known poets
the only one who could be called a man of the people, in the old,
best sense. A poet for whom the title might have been invented
afresh.' After Hughes' death in 1998, Causley was in the running
again, though he was past eighty. The bookmaker William Hill

offered odds of 10–1 on him getting the job, well ahead of Simon Armitage (16–1), Derek Walcott (20–1) and Pam Ayres (33–1). In the end the post went to the favourite, Andrew Motion.

* * *

To get back to Race Hill at the top of the town, where I parked, I have to ascend a steep path called the Zig Zag. It has rained a little, and it is slippery under foot. As I climb, I start to get a clear view of the route the railway once took, the land where its stations once were now accommodating a car dealer and a builder's merchant. St Thomas is out of sight now, but the church of St Stephen can be seen across the valley.

I am out of breath by the time I reach St Mary Magdalene, rated four-star by the great collector of ecclesiastical buildings, Simon Jenkins. Built in the early 16th century, its exterior is dressed with richly carved granite panels filled with shields and fleurs-de-lis topped with roses, thistles and pomegranates. Outside Mary Magdelene reclines under the east window, her sculpture the subject of another popular Causley poem, 'Mary, Mary Magdalene'. According to old Launceston lore, anyone who manages to lodge a stone on her figure will be rewarded with a new suit of clothes. I throw a pebble, but it fails to find a resting place; as it falls to the ground I spot a previously unnoticed moth bite on the sleeve of my jersey.

I leave the old town through the Southgate Arch, the last remaining medieval town gate. Just before it is a red-brick town house, its ground floor turned into business premises. Three of the windows display the wares of Country Chic, purveyors of 'home/gifts/interiors', and the fourth provides an entrance for the Panda House Chinese and Thai Restaurant & Bar.

Two plaques proclaim the building as the birthplace of Philip Gidley King. A draper's son, he was also christened in St Thomas's

Church. He joined the Navy as a servant before receiving an officer's commission and eventually becoming the third Governor of New South Wales in 1800. After his death eight years later, Tasmania's second city was named Launceston in his honour. I realise that I made it to the Australian Launceston five years before I reached its Cornish namesake. Tasmanians squeeze three syllables into its name – *Lorn-cess-ton*. The more economic Cornish are happy with two – *Lorn-stun*, or *Lan-son* as a few older people still say.

Causley never lost his Cornish accent and he never tired of Launceston, listing 'the rediscovery of his native town' as a recreation in *Who's Who*. He rejoiced in the evidence of its grander past – the ruins of an ancient castle, mentioned in the Domesday Book; the 'weed and soft grey stones' that he played in as a child, remnants of an Augustinian priory founded in 1136 near where St Thomas now stands; the 500-year-old packhorse bridge that linked the church with Newport; the quality of some of the older houses in the town centre that reflect Launceston's former mercantile wealth.

The year Causley turned eighty he reflected on younger days when he had first dreamt of travelling the world, exploring his interest in poetry and left-wing politics in 'distant, romantic metropolises: London, Paris, New York. Launceston seemed closed and local, not the kind of place for a writer.' Then he realised he had got it wrong. 'I used to think you had to travel to find a subject. But my subject was right under my nose all the time. It took me so long to realise this.'

Causley's gravestone is simple. It carries his name, his dates, and his occupation – poet, all set out in a matter-of-fact font. Above the writing is a relief carving of a hand clutching a pen. It is sober and simple, very different to the sprawling curlicues that dress the stone of Cornwall's other great resident poet, John

Betjeman. He is buried at St Enodoc, an hour west, back towards the coast. Local flowers and heavy Gothic type embellish his stone. If Causley's memorial was intended to be unobtrusive, Betjeman's seems to be waving and shouting out to the visitor: 'Over here!'

They were near contemporaries, both found a broad audience for their popular, highly accessible poetry, and both capitalised on the exposure offered by the still young medium of broadcasting.

If a medal for the promotion of Cornwall existed, Betjeman would certainly have been a justified recipient. He never missed an opportunity to praise the county, starting with the *Shell Guide* that he wrote in his late twenties, which included, alongside photographs and architectural details, a pasty recipe and an essay on fishing. He dedicated the guide to his father, who he said 'taught him to love Cornwall'.

Causley's relationship with his homeland was absolute and unceasing. Apart from his time away in the war, Launceston always provided his postal address. Betjeman's Cornish existence, at least until his last decades, was more transient, a love affair that could be packed up and put away at the end of a holiday or extended stay. The writer Patrick Gale, whose 2022 novel *Mother's Boy* explores Causley's young life, argues that of the two men it was Causley who offered the county its true poetic voice: 'John Betjeman was the incomer's idea of a Cornish poet', he suggests, 'but Causley has always been the locals' laureate.'

* * *

I start my journey to St Enodoc in Rock. In terms of architecture, it is not one of Cornwall's prettiest villages. The houses that line Rock Road seem at times bulky and cumbersome, built in the interests of comfort rather than elegance; some explicitly designed to signal the wealth of their owners. The television chef Gordon Ramsay spent £4.4 million on a waterfront, five-bedroom house here in 2015, before knocking the property down and building a new one. Location is what has turned Rock into the apogee of Cornish holiday-home desire – it sits on the east side of the Camel Estuary, with Padstow opposite and the golden sands of Daymer Bay just a short stroll away.

On a late weekday morning in early June there are already queues for tables outside the Rock Inn and The Mariners, and it looks like a twenty-minute wait for coffee from the Blue Tomato Café. Porsche, BMW and Tesla SUVs line the pavements. In a garden a man shouts as he conducts a Zoom meeting on his iPad, oblivious to who might hear his business. A woman collects her order of hot chocolate, mint tea and almond-milk flat white from the coffee stand by the water-ski school, balancing a cardboard tray in one hand as she holds onto her young child with the other.

In the years around the millennium the national press feasted on tales of bad behaviour by rich teenagers at Rock, with accounts of rowdy school-holiday beach parties lasting all night, discarded cans, bottles and condoms providing evidence at sunrise. The *Daily Mail's* correspondent witnessed visible displays of privilege, noting that: 'at the local Costcutter store, the bottles of champagne fly off the shelf with teenagers offering to pay with gold credit cards'; the *Independent* reported Rock had been nicknamed 'Knightsbridge-sur-Mer'. In 2001 Channel 4 made an eight-part fly-on-the-wall documentary series called *Posh Rock* – capturing 'life in a village that descends into chaos every summer' thanks to an 'influx of public-school teenagers'.

An increased police presence on summer nights and stern warnings from headteachers may have calmed these displays of youthful hedonism a bit, but the wealth of Rock's part-time residents is no less conspicuous in its display. The money spent here does drip down, providing a good income for the caterers, builders, vendors and cleaners who service the second-home owners, holiday renters and other summer crowds. But it feels like a community where the reality of contemporary Cornwall is kept firmly at bay, a place whose *raison d'être* is to provide untrammelled pleasure to its visitors.

I had thought about taking the pedestrian ferry across to Padstow for my lunch, but give up on the idea when I see the queue of several boatloads of passengers lining up around the pier. Instead I walk through the Quarry car-park to join the coast path along the dunes to St Enodoc Church. Just before Brea Hill I head inland, the public footpath crossing the greens of the golf club. Passive-aggressive notices tell non-members where they can and can't go. Signs warn of fast-moving golf balls, though it's not clear what one should do to avoid the hazard.

Details of the genealogy of St Enodoc are vague, their gender unknown. She or he may have been a cave-dwelling hermit who baptised converts at a local well. The name survives in this medieval church, with its kinked 13th-century spire, the building and its graveyard sitting in a space that seems cut out of the dunes, a hedge, thick with tamarisk, holding back the encroaching sands.

For years the church was almost lost. The Doom Bar is a sandbank that lies where the Camel estuary meets the Atlantic. According to legend, in ancient times the bar was clearly visible through the water, and sailors could plot a safe channel across it. But one day a fisherman spotted a mermaid sunning herself on the sandbank and decided to shoot her, for sport. As she lay dying, she cursed him and all fishermen, saying that, henceforth, any ship that foundered on the bar would be a total wreck. That night there was a terrible gale, which blew the top of the sandbank away, leaving the bar submerged and invisible. The wind carried the sand across the water, and dumped it on St Enodoc Church.

By the 19th century only the spire and the apex of the roof were visible, the rest of the building buried by the dunes. In order to continue claiming a living from the church, the local vicar had to perform divine service inside at least once a year. To do so he and a few hardy congregants were lowered in through a hatch in the roof. 'The high pews were mouldy green and worm eaten and bats flew about', recounted one contemporary witness. It became known as the 'Sinkininney Church'. In the 1860s a new parish priest arrived, the Revd W. Hart Smith, who decided that the situation needed to be sorted, and saw to it that the church was dug out and restored.

A little over half a century later, a young boy fell in love with St Enodoc Church. Trebetherick, less than a mile away, was John Betjeman's home in Cornwall. He came first when his father Ernest took lodgings for the family in a boarding house called The Haven. The village was already popular with outsiders – in particular teachers and colonial civil servants who had retired there after careers in China and India. But it was a place of acute social rivalries. Ernest, a furniture manufacturer, was considered to be 'in trade', meaning, as Bevis Hillier wrote in the first volume of his biography of the poet, 'many of the Raj families and old China hands of the bungalows... looked down on the Betjeman family.'

Whatever social discomfort Betjeman Sr may have felt, it was not enough to stop him building a house in Trebetherick. Undertown was a late example of the Arts and Crafts style, the work of Robert Atkinson, pioneer of British cinema design. At first the building did not appeal to John Betjeman, who in 1929 wrote to the author and journalist Patrick Balfour, complaining about 'the old world floor and older world grate and the crazy paving of bits of brass and pewter... I wish to heaven it were more comfortable'. Eventually he warmed to Undertown, but when his widowed mother Bess sold it in 1938, Betjeman decided his Cornish days were over. Concerned by the creep of mass tourism, he felt he might be able to find a more convivial base to escape to in Ireland.

His peripatetic visits to Cornwall recommenced in 1943. At first he accepted the hospitality of others, but soon started yearning for his own place. He was living in Berkshire in 1951 when he told his friend Anne Channel: 'I do want to buy a house in Trebetherick. Nowhere else. Not even Rock or Polzeath... somewhere to escape when life here is too much... somewhere to retire to with old friends and old hills around.'

He finally found the right property in 1959 – Treen, a modest house on Daymer Lane. What was at first a second home became more and more central to his life. In January 1969 he wrote to Mary Wilson, the Prime Minister's wife: 'It rains here without stopping. Trevose Head foghorn moans, the sea mist is down, the silence is profound. I feel fairly secure.' In another letter to her, sent from his home at Cloth Fair in the City of London, and dated 19 June 1970, he anticipated his return to Treen eight days later: 'Isn't it a relief that the waves still break, estuaries fill up and flowers bloom and the steady friends who are inanimate remain.'

Betjeman was at Treen in October 1972 when he received a call from Buckingham Palace appointing him poet laureate; the next day he briefed the press, clad in his dressing gown. He was at Treen when he died on 19 May 1984, after suffering a series of strokes.

Three days later he was buried at St Enodoc. The hymns 'The Church's One Foundation' and 'Dear Lord and Father of Mankind' were sung by the congregation of just over 100 mourners, numbers limited by the capacity of the tiny church. The bearer party had struggled against torrential rain and near-gale-force Atlantic winds as they carried the poet's coffin the 250 yards from hearse to church door. At least there was no risk of low-flying golf balls (*goff balls*, as Betjeman would have called them); the club was closed for the day as a mark of respect.

CHAPTER 16

Maria Asumpta

My neck is starting to redden in the bright, midday sun, and I am relieved to find that the door of St Enodoc is unlocked. Inside every surface is covered in expensive-looking displays of pink and yellow roses. There must have been a wedding at the weekend.

Once my eyes have adjusted to the relative gloom, I spot an oval-shaped memorial to John Betjeman's father Ernest. The surname is spelt with a double 'n', as it was on the poet's birth certificate – at the start of World War One the family decided it would be prudent to anglicise their Teutonic-sounding moniker.

There is another tablet on the wall of the church's south aisle, commemorating three victims of a shipwreck. The finely carved memorial shows the two square-rigged masts of the brig *Maria Asumpta*, lost on The Rumps, the double-headed promontory that juts out into the Atlantic a few miles north of the church.

I make a mental note to do an internet search for the ship's name when I get home – another 18th- or 19th-century maritime calamity to read about. But as I study the stone more closely, I realise this is not a story from the past, but a tragedy that happened in my own lifetime. The names of the dead seem timeless – Emily Macfarlane, John Shannon and Anne Taylor. But the date of the disaster was not even three decades ago – 30 May 1995. On the side of the stone the man who made the

IN MEMORY OF
EMILY MACFARLANE   JOHN SHANNON   ANNE TAYLOR
WHO PERISHED ON 30ᵀᴴ MAY 1995 WHEN THE BRIG
MARIA ASUMPTA WAS WRECKED ON THE RUMPS
TWO AND A HALF MILES NORTH OF THIS CHURCH

memorial has carved his name, and two other words: 'Philip Chatfield – sculptor-survivor'.

He sounds familiar, but I can't immediately think why. Back at Broadcasting House the following week I mention on Radio 3 that I had visited St Enodoc, and Philip immediately emails the programme to ask if I had spotted his carving. I realise straight away why I know his name – the respected sculptor and stonemason, who lives partly in Swansea and partly in a restored Pullman sleeping carriage on the Severn Valley Railway, gets in touch from time to time with well-considered musical ideas for the show.

We finally get to meet more than a year later, in Bodmin, where Philip is spending a month installing an altarpiece at St Mary's Catholic Church. The delicate structure was created a century ago for the chapel of St John's Seminary at Wonersh near Guildford. Made of black Belgian marble and Italian alabaster, it is a shrine to three of the Catholic martyrs, John Fisher, Thomas

Becket and Thomas More. The seminary closed in 2021 due to a lack of trainee priests, and so the three-ton, twelve and a half-foot-high altar was brought from Surrey to Cornwall, packed up in twenty-two plywood crates and accompanied by a few photographs to help Philip as he put it back together.

He has turned the area around the altar into a temporary mason's yard, with scaffolding, pulleys and hoists, and bags full of chisels, rasps, rifflers and mallets. Earlier a practising organist provided some company; when I arrive the music of Hildegard of Bingen is playing through the PA system. Philip's father was a Royal Marine commando, fit and strong, and his son has the build of a rugby player, easily able to gently lift heavy pieces of marble into place. Amidst his tools, he pulls out what he calls his logbook, its pages filled with simple, elegant drawings and clearly written text setting out his life's adventures.

He was in Swansea working on the redevelopment of the maritime quarter when the *Maria Asumpta* visited the port for a sea shanty festival in 1990. When the ship sailed for Mousehole a week later, he had joined its crew, having become 'captivated, even obsessed' with the vessel. He stayed on board for three months, sailing around Europe. 'After that I was with her on and off for five years. She would not let me go.'

Maria Asumpta was launched at Barcelona in 1858, named in honour of the eighteen apparitions of the Virgin Mary seen at Lourdes that same year. On its maiden voyage it carried textiles to Buenos Aires, sailed on to Havana with a cargo of salted beef and then returned to Europe with rum, spices and gold. Bullet holes were testament to its role trading around the Balearic Islands during the Spanish Civil War. By the late 1980s it was the oldest square rigger still sailing, popular with film-makers looking for a ship to add period authenticity to their productions. In 1995 it starred alongside Anjelica Huston in *Buffalo Girls*, an American television movie about the sharpshooting entertainer Calamity Jane and 'Buffalo Bill's Wild West Show'. The scenes were filmed at Gloucester Docks and the production fee covered the cost of a major refit.

Maria Asumpta set sail again in late May 1995. Philip was on board with his woodworking tools and a sheaf of plans for future commissions, including the drawings for his Merchant Navy Monument at Barry in South Wales. His duties included serving as ship's carpenter, navigator, rigger and gunner, firing his own pair of ceremonial cannons each time a port was reached. Following in the wake of a severe storm, the ship crept down the Bristol Channel, sheltering off the north Devon coast in the lee of great gusts of wind coming off Exmoor. When conditions calmed, it crossed to the Welsh coast, mooring off the Mumbles, where a group of yachtsmen from the Mariners International Sailing Club disembarked, leaving the permanent crew to sail on. 'It was a good crew of very experienced sailors,' Philip says.

On the morning of 30 May *Maria Asumpta* weighed anchor for Padstow. Though the winds were still heavy, they were not a cause for major concern. But perhaps the strength of the tide had been misread. Philip had gone below deck to do some woodwork, when suddenly the vessel was swept in towards land by a strong current. The skipper decided to start the engines, and the ship began to chug out to sea. Then, suddenly, the engines failed. 'I remember the engineer trying and failing to fire them up again. The atmosphere became very tense.' The ship was in a position of no return, the swell was heavy, the sea state had a rise and fall of fourteen feet. Travelling at four knots an hour, *Maria Asumpta* hit the Seven Sisters Rock, the point where the tail of The Rumps meets the sea.

A Mayday call was issued at 4.20 p.m. Philip recalls the ship bouncing off the rock. He had got back up to the deck, and was near the prow: 'The whole ship tilted over on its starboard side, the deck becoming near vertical. My fingernails scratched the surface as I slid down, crashing into the starboard pin rail. Then the sea came back and levelled us out again. I legged it to the port side and jumped off.'

The sea was full of spume and bubbles, with little weight of water to provide buoyancy, so he sank down and down until he hit the base of the granite rock. 'I thought I was going to get crushed by the ship, but thankfully it rolled the other way.' He clambered over pinnacles and leapt across gullies, forming himself into a ball and holding his breath each time a wave came in. Slowly he managed to get himself higher, until finally he was safe. Philip describes a rush of adrenaline that seemed to give him the 'super-strength' he needed to get through the experience. Once he was clear of danger, his body started shutting down. 'For a while I couldn't see or hear or feel anything.'

When his vision came back, he found he was looking directly at his ship, its hull broken in two. The galley was open to the sea, a kettle he had filled a few moments earlier still sat on the hob of the coal-fired Aga. For a second he saw Anne Taylor, the ship's chef, then she disappeared under the waves. Emily Macfarlane, the bosun's mate, was just nineteen but had been on and off the ship for five years. 'I saw her briefly in the water and then lost sight of her too. She was already dead. All I could think of at that moment was John Everett Millais' portrait of Ophelia.' John Shannon, an experienced Australian sailor, managed to get off the ship and made it to the rocks, but was dragged under the water and drowned.

There were eleven survivors. Hundreds of people witnessed the tragedy, visitors who had come to see a splendid sailing ship enter the harbour. A helicopter from RNAS Culdrose airlifted Philip and two others from the top of the cliffs to hospital in Truro; he had broken bones, a bashed-in right shoulder and multiple cuts, yet somehow his sailor's cap was still on his head.

'*Maria Asumpta* was beautiful, the loveliest of all sailing ships,' he tells me. 'For me she had been a home, an adventure and a community. I knew every inch of her. I loved her and she would draw me back again and again.'

A few days later he went to sea again, on Port Isaac's inshore lifeboat, to rescue one of his cannons that had been spotted floating amid the wreckage. The other was returned to him, having been stolen from the wreck site. Two people were arrested at the time, with local police officers expressing their disgust that bounty hunters, some armed with chainsaws, were trying to salvage artefacts. Later Philip's wooden mallet was washed ashore twenty miles up the coast at Bude. He had bought it in Plymouth years before, and carved *Maria Asumpta*'s name into its head. Today it sits on his mantelpiece in Swansea.

Emily Macfarlane and John Shannon were initially listed as missing. It was nearly a month before their bodies were found at sea by one of the lifeboatmen. Remarkably, the pair were discovered in the water just yards apart. 'I met that lifeboatman sometime later,' Philip says. 'He was drinking alone in the pub by the quay in Port Isaac. I was at a table with a journalist from the *Cornish Guardian*, who told me he was the person who had found Emily and John. I looked over and caught his eye. I nodded, he nodded. It was all that was needed; we both knew there was nothing more to say. Centuries of old Cornish tradition were manifest in that man and his outlook – respect the sea and respect those who live with it and those who die with it.'

Philip quickly decided he wanted to create a physical tribute to the ship and her dead, in part thinking it would be a cathartic process that might help heal some of the trauma he had suffered. It was not easy; an ever-changing stream of priests and disagreements within the local parochial church council meant it was more than half a decade before he got permission to install a memorial. He carved it in a boatyard at Golant on the River Fowey belonging to the Luck family, friends and fellow sailors. It is held in place by corbels made of granite from the Grand-Île Chausey, the archipelago between Jersey and the French coast, cut from a block found at the home of Graham Maclachlan, the ship's bosun and a fellow survivor.

In the years since the shipwreck Philip has found himself drawn to create a series of Marian works. He has carved statues for Tintern Abbey and St Mary's Church in Monmouth; his latest project is a life-sized sculpture of the Virgin Mary carrying a model of *Maria Asumpta* for a church in Barcelona, her original home port. 'I often find myself asking: Why was I spared when others were not?' When the St Enodoc memorial was dedicated, the archdeacon, the Ven. Clive Cohen, marked out the sign of the cross on it with holy water. 'When he reached the last corner I felt a huge burden lift.'

CHAPTER 17

The Slow Train: Three Cornish Branch Lines

No one departs, no one arrives
From Selby to Goole, from St Erth to St Ives
Flanders & Swann

John Betjeman liked to travel by train when visiting his Cornish home. He had a choice of two routes. Before the railway system was nationalised in 1948, he could take the Great Western from Paddington to Bodmin Road,* where he would change onto the Padstow branch line. Or he could catch the Southern Railway service from Waterloo. The *Atlantic Coast Express* called at Salisbury, Yeovil, Honiton, Exeter and Okehampton before the train split at Halwill Junction. From there, one line led to Barnstaple, another to Bude, and a third crossed the Cornish border just east of Launceston.

It is easy to imagine an excited Betjeman mentally ticking off the stations that followed – Egloskerry, Tresmeer, Otterham, Camelford, Delabole (adjacent to the rich slate quarry), Port Isaac Road (a good three miles from the village itself) and finally Wadebridge, where his bags would be removed from the luggage

---

* Renamed Bodmin Parkway in 1983.

van and loaded into a waiting car. As the train continued on the last stage of its journey towards Padstow, crossing the three-span bridge at Little Petherick Creek, and then following the west side of the Camel estuary, Betjeman was being driven home along the opposite bank, to Trebetherick and journey's end.

He had fallen in love with Wadebridge station as a boy and his infatuation continued into adulthood. In his mid thirties he recalled 'the oil lights, the smell of seaweed floating up the estuary, the rain-washed platform and the sparkling granite, and the hedges along the valleys around, soon to be heavy with blackberries.'

My mother and I would take the Waterloo service when we came to Cornwall to visit my grandparents in the 1970s. A suburban electric train would take us on the five-minute journey between West Byfleet, where our army quarter was, and Woking, where we would pick up the express, by then part of British Rail's Southern Region operations. The last vestiges of the line's former grandeur were still present – in the dining car white-jacketed stewards flamboyantly poured hot drinks out of silver pots held high; high-tea meant egg and cress sandwiches, slices of fruit cake and toasted teacakes served with tiny pats of butter and miniature pots of jam. But the line terminated at Exeter – from there we had to join a Western Region train to take us on to Redruth or Camborne.

'The withered arm' was the unkind nickname for the Southern Railway lines that ran north and west of Exeter to the north-coast seaside towns of Cornwall and Devon. Richard Beeching's 1963 report *The Reshaping of British Railways* saw the arm finally amputated. Betjeman turned sixty the year that the trains to Wadebridge stopped running. The last service to Okehampton and beyond departed on 1 October 1966; passenger trains to Bodmin stopped less than six months later. Today the former station buildings at Wadebridge house the John Betjeman Centre, a community hub offering exercise classes and support groups, and hiring out mobility scooters and wheelchairs.

Betjeman died the week before I turned thirteen. His death felt like a personal loss. His very public passion had helped make railway enthusiasm polite – a man of letters who relished a journey in a gently rocking, half-empty carriage on a sleepy Cornish branch line, who spearheaded the campaign to save St Pancras, London's grandest station, who shared his love of suburbia-beside-the-tracks in his and Edward Mirzoeff's BBC film *Metroland*.

Richard Beeching died less than a year later. In hindsight his radical scheme, which saw track mileage slashed by a third and 4,000 stations closed, ensured the preservation of the rest of what remains an extensive national railway network. But at the time it was hard to mourn a man who had helped close down so many of the lines on the Cornwall pages of my well-thumbed railway atlas.

The one that hurt the most was the Helston branch line. The last passenger services ran the year before Beeching's report was published – but I considered him complicit in the closure – signing the papers that confirmed the decision was one of his early duties upon becoming chairman of the British Transport Commission in 1961. While the tracks had been lifted soon after traffic had stopped, plenty of evidence of the railway's former presence remained – buildings, bridges, cuttings and embankments, each one a cruel reminder that trains had once come to my local town.

* * *

On a sunny Sunday afternoon, I am shimmying down the side of a granite bridge just up from Lowertown, hoping that the grooves on the soles of my boots will provide enough grip to keep me upright. Thick vegetation has taken control of the cutting below, the mud squelches underfoot and discarded beer bottles and cans provide evidence that I am not the first person to explore here in recent times. I miss an overhanging bough and get a scratch on my face, then have to gingerly clamber over a clutch of slippery moss-covered tree trunks.

To the left a waterfall pours in, making a deep puddle that comes close to the top of my wellingtons. A little further on are the roofless remains of a track workers' hut, a rudimentary fireplace in one corner. Then suddenly the surface underfoot is dry, and light floods in. What was a railway cutting becomes first an embankment and then a viaduct built to carry trains high above the narrow River Cober. Any residue of steam-engine soot has long been washed off the thick granite walls; a haze of yellow flowering gorse spreads out where the track once lay.

In the second half of the 19th century a railway connection was the prize that every town wanted. On Wednesday, 22 March 1882, a grand parade celebrated the cutting of the first sod of the Helston Railway. Volunteers, Freemasons, the mayor and corporation, railway directors and shareholders lined up on the bowling green for a one o'clock start. Later there was a free tea for 'the children and aged people of the town' and a spectacular firework display followed in the evening. The main thoroughfares were dressed with decorated arches bearing portentous slogans: 'Perseverance Insures Success' claimed one on Church Street; 'Prosperity to the Trade of Helston' and 'Union Is Strength' read the banners above Coinagehall Street.

It had taken a long time for Helston to get its link to the permanent way. In the first outbreak of Cornish railway fever in the late 1830s, Bodmin, Launceston, St Austell, Liskeard, Penzance and Falmouth appeared on sketches of route maps, but Helston was left out. In 1846 a Falmouth, Helston and Penzance Railway

Company was wound up soon after it had reassured investors of its potential: 'the mineral, granite and passenger traffic upon this line will be very great'.

The failure of the potato crop – which caused famine in Cornwall as well as Ireland – and the repeal of the Corn Laws led to a sudden rise in inflation, which in turn pricked the over-inflated bubble of railway investment. Other schemes around this time proved more durable – the West Cornwall Railway ran its first trains between Penzance and Redruth in March 1852, reaching the outskirts of Truro five months later. Seven years on, it linked to the Cornwall Railway which provided services to Plymouth. A steel spine of track now ran down through Cornwall, and once both companies had adopted the same gauge, through trains became possible, the first Penzance–London service running in March 1867. But it was to be another two decades before Helston was connected to the Great Western Railway.

Gwinear Road, a junction in remote countryside between Camborne and Hayle, was where the branch broke away from the main line. From there eight and three quarter miles of track ran to Helston. To begin with there were two intermediate stations, Nancegollan and Praze (a truncated version of Praze-an-Beeble). The village name comes from the Cornish word for 'meadow' and has nothing to do with faith – not that that stopped generations of guards hollering, 'Next stop Praze, Praze, Allelujiah!'

The inaugural train left Helston at 0940 on 9 May 1887. Once again the town was *en fête*, with scores of dignitaries invited to a gala luncheon at the Angel Hotel.

* * *

The Helston route was part of a network of Cornish railway lines that opened the county to mass tourism. The *Atlantic Coast Express*, launched in 1926, made much of its through coaches to Padstow and Bude. The train departed London at eleven o'clock in the morning, though on busy summer Saturdays up to five trains carrying the name would set out from Waterloo. In the 1890s *The Cornishman* was the fastest of the named Paddington expresses – but it was the *Cornish Riviera* that was to become the most romantic way of starting a holiday in the far west.

It first ran in 1904, its name chosen after a competition in the *Railway Magazine*. Originally it covered the 225 miles from Paddington to Plymouth non-stop, shaving half an hour off previous timings. The flagship of the Great Western Railway, it sometimes ran to fourteen carriages, with dining cars and kitchens to ensure its passengers were well looked after. In the years immediately before World War Two its daily run was a major operation, involving dozens of guards, marshallers and shunters. Slip coaches served Westbury, Taunton and Exeter. At a particular point on the route, at a location determined by gradient, distance and speed, the guard would uncouple his carriage from the main train, and freewheel the final part of the journey, using his brake to ensure a smooth halt at the platform. One of the carriages slipped at Taunton went to Ilfracombe, another to Minehead. A Kingsbridge carriage formed part of the Exeter slip. Slipping required special rolling stock that combined all three classes of travel in one coach – but passengers had to bring their own food, as there was no way to walk through to the restaurant car. There were further through carriages for Newquay, Falmouth and St Ives, meaning that the train that eventually arrived at Penzance was less than half the length of the one that had left Paddington.

Getting to other seaside destinations generally required a change of trains, but that did not stop Fowey and Looe becoming popular resorts after the railway reached the towns in the 1870s. A line between Truro and Newquay was built in part to meet the demands of hoteliers and guest house owners in St Agnes and Perranporth who feared they were losing their tourists to better-connected parts of the county. It was one of the last of the Cornish railways to be built, opening to passengers in 1905. In 1931 it gained an extra station – Perranporth Beach Halt, just ten minutes' walk from the start of the town's two miles of sandy beaches.

Having created this tourist network, the companies were determined to exploit their assets. The London and South Western Railway* introduced a special *King Arthur* Class of locomotive to operate its Cornish expresses, the engines bearing romantic names including *Merlin*, *Pendragon*, *Excalibur* and *Iseult*. The Southern Railway and the Great Western both ran long-running advertising campaigns that sold a Cornwall where the sun always shone,

---

* The London and South Western Railway reached Bude in 1898 and Padstow the year after. The 1923 amalgamation of Britain's private railway operators into four big companies saw it absorbed into the new Southern Railway.

commissioning pictures of surf breaking in front of Pentire Point, the saltwater swimming pool on Perranporth beach, the lido at Penzance, St Michael's Mount, the golden sands of Newquay and more generic images of rustic cottages tumbling down to the sea or harbours crammed with fishing boats. The original artwork was printed on posters, and displayed on station hoardings across the country.

My favourite is one produced by the Great Western that juxtaposes wildly out-of-scale maps of Cornwall and Italy alongside images of fruit trees and two women, each wearing national dress. The copywriter had a field day: 'There is a great similarity between Cornwall and Italy in shape, climate and natural beauties.' Smaller type tells observers that 'The Western Land' was how the Romans described Cornwall and the Greeks Italy. 'See your own country first', it commands potential visitors.

The poster clearly shows a solid red line of railway running out

to Helston, and then dots onwards to the Lizard. The original plan was that the line would eventually run on to the coast. Helston station was constructed on an embankment so that the railway could cross a bridge over Godolphin Road and then continue south. But by the time the line from Gwinear Road to Helston was finished, railway mania was on the wane and it had become clear that many routes built at great expense were attracting desultory numbers of passengers.

In order to spark further development, the government tabled the Light Railways Act 1896 to simplify the process of building a new line. Previously any would-be railway baron needed an individual act of Parliament to be passed before work could commence. The new legislation enormously simplified matters. The Light Railway Commissioners, a panel of three people appointed by the president of the Board of Trade, would consider the case for each new project, taking evidence locally. While 'the safety of the public' had to be ensured, there were few specific rules and regulations.

The act made particular reference to encouraging agriculture and fisheries. On the Lizard Peninsula it was clear to farmers that vegetables grown in its rich soil could fetch a far higher price if they could be transported to the major cities, as could the fish landed from boats based at Cadgwith, Mullion, Porthallow and Coverack. One Mr Bolitho, a fisherman from Cadgwith, told the inquiry how he and his colleagues were using turbot, cod, plaice and sole as bait for their crab pots – fish that would sell for good money up-country.

The Lizard line quickly gained support and a route was mapped out. The line would curve around the top of the town and cross what is now RNAS Culdrose. A halt at Griglow Green, near Double Lodges, would serve St Martin, Mawgan and St Keverne. The line would cross Goonhilly Downs, with a station for Mullion, before reaching its terminus near the Free Methodist Chapel in Lizard village. The cost for the eleven-mile line was estimated at just over £60,000. The engineers were well aware of the need to keep costs low as they plotted their course – level crossings were to be avoided, as they required staff to operate them, so too were costly tunnels and viaducts.

The plans were popular – farmers, workers and the local gentry were all in favour. At the end of the inquiry in Helston in October 1897, the Commissioners announced it was 'quite evident that there was considerable support for the railway' and gave their assent. But that turned out to be the Lizard Railway's finest hour. The line was never built and the Great Western Railway set up a bus service to take passengers from the peninsula's villages to the railhead at Helston.

* * *

Tourism was one part of the Helston Railway's income, but the goods traffic was more important. Fishermen sent cases of seafood packed on ice to Billingsgate in London and farmers dispatched vegetables for Covent Garden. Though the line came too late to be of benefit to the mining trade, it did carry heavy loads of stone from the quarries of St Keverne, and in 1944 extra sidings were built at Nancegollan to unload supplies for the new airbase at Culdrose. But by then the line was firmly in decline. In the summer of 1928, there were sixteen daily passenger services; twenty years later that number had halved; 10,306 passenger tickets were issued at Praze in 1913, but just 4,821 were sold in 1933. This was one of Cornwall's quietest lines – in 1937 its passenger revenue was £5,751, compared to £19,025 on the Newquay branch and £32,162 between Truro and Falmouth. The amount of general goods handled slumped from 694 to 118 tons. It was a familiar tale; road freight, and increasing car ownership were slowly killing the line.

When it became clear in the 1950s that some sort of rationalisation was needed, economy measures were introduced on many underused lines in an attempt to make them appear more viable. Staff were removed from stations and cheap-to-run diesel railcars were introduced. But not on the Helston line. A set of pictures from the middle of that decade show the station at Nancegollan, a place that is barely a village. It boasts two platforms and three sidings. There is no sign of life but the door to the stationmaster's office is wide open, a porter's trolley sitting outside. At the north end of the up platform is a signal box, a chair placed on the outside balcony for the signaller to sit in the sun in the gaps between the infrequent services. There was clearly time to tend the roses too; another picture identifies the staff – Signalman W. H. Dale, Porter E. A. Bone, Leading Porter-Signalman W. A. Stephens and Stationmaster S. J. Jeffery. They are posing proudly by the station's flower beds, having won the Plymouth Section of the South West Region of the 1956 British Railways Garden Competition.

Steam had gone – and the old locomotives had been replaced with new heavy diesel stock, a class of engine nicknamed 'Baby Warships'. The Helston Railway was burying its head in the sand. In September 1962 a British Transport Commission notice appeared at stations announcing that from Monday, 5 November that year, 'the local passenger train service between Gwinear Road and Helston will be discontinued'. As there were no Sunday services on the line, engine D6312 hauled the final train at 8.45 p.m. on Saturday, 3 November. For once it was full, but the passengers were dressed as mourners at a funeral, and sang 'Auld Lang Syne' as they reached the end of the line.

* * *

A year or so after Mum died, Dad relented on his hard-line no-television policy, and purchased a set. Inevitably his strict rules about when it might be on or off were soon abandoned. Its flickering presence much reduced the amount of time we spent talking to each other; the people on screen did that for us. This was great for an adolescent, awkward teenager who found almost everything his father said irritating or embarrassing. After a few months he agreed I could have a black-and-white portable set in my bedroom. The consequence of this was that we spoke even less.

The time we did talk was in the car. On the morning school run I would inevitably be in a silent, surly mood, but by lunch-time I would have become more loquacious. Every few weeks we would drive somewhere, park up and eat lunch together. We would visit Bourdeaux's Bakery at Praze and buy cheese and chutney or ham and egg rolls, with cans of brightly coloured fizzy drink, and sweet, greasy almond slices to eat after. One of our favourite places to consume this feast was by a remote old railway bridge a couple of miles north-west of Helston. Parked hard against the wall, with just enough space for another car to edge past, we would sit and chat. I would talk about my ambitions to explore and travel, to see famous places and witness great events. Desperate to keep the memory of Mum alive, sometimes I would try to get him to talk about her, how they met, what her passions where, whether she was happy, how she dealt with her cancer. I would not get very far. He would never actually close the conversation down, but he was a adept at steering it quickly into safer, easier waters. I was happy enough to hear tales from his army career anyway, exciting vignettes of life lived in the Far East and Europe, observations on watching an empire unravel. The other subject I never tired of were his stories of railway travel. He could talk of the Berlin Military Express, sleepers in Thailand, or Continental boat trains, but what interested me most were his memories of our local branch line. It felt galling that, had I been only ten years older I could have ridden the train to Helston myself. At least I had Dad's memories of travelling the line.

The gully underneath the bridge where we parked was filled with thick weeds and decades of dumped waste. But once there was a station here – Truthall Halt. Dad showed me a photograph of it in Helston Museum, taken soon after it opened in 1905. It looks spick and span – two silver milk churns sit on the wooden platform, the edges of which are painted bright white, with slats to prevent passengers slipping on wet or icy days. But it is the tiny waiting room that catches the eye, a fine example of the GWR pagoda shelter, its corrugated-iron roof delicately curving upwards, all four sides eventually meeting to form an elegant crest. Installed at many rural halts, it would be delivered by train in kit form and could be erected in less than a day.

Lunch done, as Dad drank bitter black coffee from his flask, I would get out of the car and lean across the thick wall of the bridge, balancing my body on my stomach as I peered down, gazing intently into the thick undergrowth and wondering if it hid the rusting walls of the shelter or perhaps even the old cast-iron station sign.

* * *

My father died in 2013. A decade on, my niece Clemmie and I park by the bridge. The rubble and weeds have gone. A crisp white line runs along the edge of the platform. Steel tracks glint in the late morning sun. A Ruston and Hornsby shunting engine ticks over, in front of it a wooden brake van with a hand-painted sign proclaiming its name – *Daisy*. A silver-grey-haired man wearing a black waistcoat with a watch chain and a peaked cap with a British Railways badge on the brim stands smiling in front of the Pagoda shelter. Truthall Halt is open once again. It is now a terminus itself, Britain's most southerly railway station, the end of the line for the 21st-century Helston Railway, which currently runs over a mile or so of the original route.

Whistles blow, a green flag is raised. When the railway is busy they run a compartment carriage drawn by a steam engine borrowed from the Somerset and Dorset Railway. But the brake van's open platform is much more fun. The track passes through a landscape of green fields with clusters of trees gathered around solid hedges. We slow and then halt at the point where a farm is split in two by the tracks, moving on again once it's clear there are no cows to be led between fields. There's a puff of black diesel exhaust as we build up speed, ten miles an hour, fifteen at most. Past the sidings at Trevarno, where a station stood when the gardens were open to the public. The estate's current owners are more interested in their privacy than trains; a heavy-duty security fence runs behind the closed platform. On to Prospidnick Halt, for now the end of the journey, where a Park Royal Class railcar built in the 1950s serves as a café with steaming pots of tea and home-made flapjacks.

Today, with two drivers, a guard operating the brake van, three platform staff, one person in the shop and two in the café, there are twice as many volunteers as passengers – which number Clemmie and myself, and another family – mother, father and toddler. But it's nearly the end of the season; in the summer holidays this is a popular attraction. And there are big dreams for the future. Reopening all the way to the old Helston Station is impossible – an industrial estate, housing and the school sports pitches where I once sulked my way through rugby and football games, cover where the track bed lay. 'That's a never-going-to-happen scenario,' a chatty volunteer tells me. 'But we could get over the viaduct, and built a new station on the edge of town.' Maybe the flower beds of Nancegollan will sprout prize-winning blooms again too – that is the ambition the other way – three miles of track in total. But the man in the brake van thinks it could even be possible to reach the main line at Gwinear Road, with deals to be done with farmers – and the owners of the house that sits where the platforms were at Praze-an-Beeble.

* * *

I was eleven when I made my first unaccompanied railway journey – the ten-minute ride between Falmouth and Penryn. I sprang the plan on my parents at the end of a morning's shopping. On the way back to the car the words came tumbling out: 'There is a train . . . twenty minutes from now . . . I could get it to Penryn . . . you could collect me there.' My father was not one for spontaneity and immediately dismissed the idea. 'Another time,' he said. 'We'll plan it properly and do the whole line to Truro.

We can all go.' That was the last thing I wanted. I saw myself as a solo traveller, an adventurer – not an accompanied minor. Then Mum smiled at me and turned to him. 'Come on, why not?' she said. 'It will only hold us up a little.' Dad shrugged his shoulders. My heart started beating faster. The journey was going to happen.

The train was already waiting under the barrel canopy of Falmouth Docks Station. A Class 118 Diesel Multiple Unit, then the workhorse of branch-line Cornwall. Three carriages, with doors between every set of seats that slammed shut, making a sound as evocative of railway history as a stationmaster's whistle.

Once passengers would have gathered under an airy, glazed roof, their catering needs met by refreshment rooms operated by the Falmouth Hotel, the mighty Victorian edifice looking over the town beach. Now there was not even a solitary member of staff to sell me a half-single to Penryn. Crumbling walls and weed-strewn former track beds helped me plot out where goods and engine sheds and sidings once stood.

Mum stayed in the car. After checking the train was running, Dad too left me alone. 'Don't forget where to get off!' he shouted, planting a tiny seed of anxiety in the back of my mind.

There was an immediate dilemma. Where to sit? The end carriages of the Class 118s were known as 'Bubble Cars' because a window allowed passengers to see into the cab. Secure the front seat and you could have a direct view of the track – while at the same time watching and learning how to drive the train. On a later trip I must have overplayed my enthusiasm; the driver turned round, scowled, and snapped down a previously unnoticed black blind on his side of the glass. But today this was not where I wanted to be.

Cornish branch lines were entirely second class, however this train had once served commuters in the south-east, who clearly demanded higher standards. Most passengers seemed wary of sitting in one of the old first-class seats. An eleven-year-old I may have been, but I knew the fare rules well: 'All accommodation to be treated as second class.' No one could evict me from the big, soft chair, with clips that had once held an antimacassar in place, and rusty elongated springs pushing up through the worn-down leather. Next to the seat was a chrome ashtray with a hinged lid that could be opened and closed with a satisfying clunk, leaving my fingers covered in the residue left by decades of smokers. After checking no one was looking I surreptitiously rubbed the ash onto the underside of the cushion.

The last door slammed shut, and we departed, rolling slowly past overgrown sidings that once ran right up to ships moored in the docks. Two minutes later the first stop – The Dell – a fine example of British Rail parsimony. When in 1970 it was decided Falmouth needed an extra station, BR planners looked in their stores, and found they had a mothballed platform ready for use – the one that had once served day trippers alighting at Perranporth Beach Halt.

We continued for four minutes, running behind residential streets to Penmere, a simple platform, the paint on its tiny shelter chipped and faded. No evidence of the sidings where once rested freight trains from Liverpool, carrying fuel for Second World War flying boats based in the harbour.

Across the eleven spans of the Collegewood Viaduct. To save the cash-strapped Cornwall Railway money, I. K. Brunel built wooden bridges, perfectly safe but flimsy-looking constructs towering over rivers and valleys. Collegewood was the longest lasting, not replaced by a sturdier, granite bridge until 1934. I don't think I appreciated what an engineering feat the viaduct was – I was getting anxious about missing my stop and being conveyed on to Truro where inconceivable uncertainties might present themselves. Relief swept through me as we slowed for Penryn and I saw my mother walking down the platform, ready to help me with the fiddly lock on the carriage door.

* * *

My Falmouth adventure was in 1982, the year that saw the lowest usage of the network in the second half of the 20th century – a statistic that encouraged Margaret Thatcher's Conservative government to question whether such an extensive national railway system should be maintained. Sir David Serpell was commissioned to write a report that would consider all options. Two decades earlier, as a civil servant at the Ministry of Transport, he had been one of those responsible for Richard Beeching's appointment. But some of the proposals in Serpell's *Review of Railway Finances* made Dr Beeching's ideas seem almost benevolent. One plan would have made Bristol the railhead for the south-west, another proposed the end of all railways in Devon and Cornwall, save for the main line as far as Exeter.

The seventy-one-year-old mandarin had done what was asked of him, imagining a series of potential money-saving scenarios, but soon he found himself under personal attack. The British Rail chairman, the respected Sir Peter Parker, described him as being 'cosy as a razorblade'; on one journey to his home in Dartmouth in Devon, Serpell was harangued by the guard, presumably worried that he would soon be unemployed. 'A really rotten report' was how a leader in *The Guardian* summed up his work.

Serpell's suggestions were quietly forgotten ahead of the 1983 general election and trains continued to run between Penzance to Plymouth, and on branch lines to Calstock and Gunnislake, from Liskeard to Looe, Par to Newquay, Truro to Falmouth and St Erth to St Ives.

* * *

St Erth is a pleasing country station, virtually unaltered since it was first built by the West Cornwall Railway in the early 1850s. An elegant footbridge crosses over the track between the main-line platforms. Four chimneystacks sit on top of the squat granite station building, two – sadly, now sealed – fireplaces taking pride of place in the refurbished waiting room. In the Branch Line Tea Room home made cakes are on sale and hot drinks are served in china cups. Next door is a new wood-and-stone mess room for railway employees, a discreet plaque by the door acknowledging the support of the European Union in maintaining Cornwall's transport provision. The village the station is named after is three-quarters of a mile away, and has fewer than 1,500 residents, yet as many as nine trains a day arrive here direct from London. Most of the disgorged passengers don't exit the station, but simply walk across to Platform Three to catch the train to St Ives.

Even on a wet November morning there are more than forty fellow travellers on board the 1148 departure. The village of Lelant is the first stop. With no sun in the sky, the mudflats of the Hayle Estuary are painted in shades of grey-green, a sense of continuous movement provided by curlews, oystercatchers and flocks of wigeon. On through a tunnel of foliage, and when the view is restored, estuarine mud turns into bright-yellow sands flecked with white sea spume. The octagonal tower of Godrevy Lighthouse, made famous by Virginia Woolf, sits on its island in the bay, warning mariners of the peril posed by the Stones Reef.

The train clanks across the jointed track, climbing what feels like a steep gradient. Carbis Bay Station is a request halt; this morning no one on board has asked the guard to stop, no one hails the service from the platform.

A viaduct soars above the Carbis Bay Hotel, where then British Prime Minister Boris Johnson hosted Presidents Biden and Macron, Chancellor Merkel and Prime Ministers Trudeau, Draghi and Suga at the 2021 G7 Conference. Air Force One and a fleet of smaller government jets landed at Newquay Airport, press and protestors were corralled at Falmouth, missile batteries and snipers offered VIP protection, and world leaders sat around firepits on the beach eating seared moorland beef, Carbis Bay lobster, salted baked beetroot and St Just purple-sprouting broccoli. The lanes linking a millionaire's row of cliffside houses, gardens tumbling down to the beach, were sealed off by police and this train stopped running for the three days that the great global circus was in town.

A first glimpse of St Ives harbour comes as we reach the end of the ten-minute journey. Seen through the rain-stained carriage window and cast at an odd angle by the track's camber, it looks unreal, as if it is a painting by the fisherman-artist Alfred Wallis, a self-taught master who died in the Penzance workhouse in 1942, and whose pictures now create art-world excitement when they come up for sale.

There is only a single platform at St Ives Station today, and no staff to check tickets or offer advice. That can be got from the travel agent in the building behind the buffers, who sells singles to Truro alongside coach trips to the Highlands and all-inclusive holidays to Mauritius. Old black-and-white photographs are pinned on a board, one showing the station at its busiest. A three-carriage local train rests at the platform closest to the sea. On the adjacent track stands a ten-coach express, engine belching steam at it prepares for departure. The carriage doors are shut, dozens stand on the platform waving off loved ones. The picture is not dated but the cars parked along the platform suggest the late 1920s or 1930s – a summer service direct to London.

A vast park-and-ride car-park at St Erth protects St Ives from an influx of vehicles that would otherwise cause summer suffocation. But Richard Beeching had no interest in the nuances of narrow streets. He simply looked at the passenger numbers, and decided that the line should close. The publication of his report marked the start of a three-year campaign to save it. Disparate forces including the St Ives Hotel and Boarding House Association, the local Ratepayers Association, the Townswomen's Guild and the Labour Party united in their campaign against the closure, highlighting the potentially calamitous impact of the decision.

All seemed lost when on Friday, 8 October 1965 the British Railways Board placed a notice in the *St Ives Times and Echo* announcing that all passenger services would cease a year later. It seemed as if Flanders and Swann, the hugely popular satirists and entertainers of the day, had been right – St Erth to St Ives was on the list of soon-to-be-closed routes that they included in the lyrics of their 1963 hit 'The Slow Train'.

But St Ives fought back. Those attending a town meeting on 15 March 1966 were shown colour film of weekend congestion on the road between Lelant and St Ives. Statistics were produced, including a suggestion that as many as forty extra buses would be needed to convey passengers on busy summer Saturdays. Delegates were well aware of a report that showed the resort of Perranporth, twenty miles up the coast, had lost a third of its visitors the year after its railway had closed. As the town clerk W. Rainey-Edwards admitted, St Ives was entirely dependent on tourism for its living.

Barbara Castle, who had been appointed Minister of Transport a few months earlier, was no great train enthusiast, and signed off many of Beeching's proposed closures. But she did listen to the arguments presented by the people of St Ives, and just two weeks before the line was due to shut, she cancelled its closure.

The Liskeard–Looe branch was also saved, but there were limits to the minister's largesse – there was no last-minute reprieve of a reprieve for the north Cornwall railway lines so beloved of John Betjeman.

CHAPTER 18

Plymouth Approaches: The Most Beautiful City in the World

The railway never got as far as Millbrook, the largest village on the Rame Peninsula. The community is barely four miles from Plymouth city centre, as the crow flies, but the journey between the two places takes a good forty-five minutes via the car ferry at Torpoint, or is a twenty-six-mile drive on the road that slowly meanders its way around the Tiddy and Lynher rivers. This outcrop of land backs onto Devon and has a broad swathe of the south Cornish coast in its sights, yet seems cut off from both.

Military Road takes visitors towards the tip of the peninsula. The route links a series of Victorian forts known as 'Palmerston's Follies'. In 1859, with increased concern about French militarisation, in particular the new iron battleships the country was building, the Prime Minister established a Royal Commission to consider the safety of Britain's maritime approaches. Dozens of batteries, keeps and forts followed, twenty around Plymouth alone. The Whitsand Bay battery was designed to house three long-range guns to stop enemy attacks on Devonport Dockyard; Polhawn and Tregantle forts both had moats with drawbridges that could be raised in the event of a land attack. Tregantle is still in military use – a red flag flies this morning to indicate that the Royal Marines are busy honing their shooting skills.

I park up on the side of the road by the hamlet of Freathy, and lean against the car, luxuriating in the sunshine, the fresh salty air, and the view which seems to stetch almost as far as Looe, its harbour pier lost in the haze. There is no perceptible line of division between the deep blues of sky and sea. Another car pulls in behind me, and an elderly couple get out. We say polite hellos and talk about the weather. He moves slowly, the result, he says, of osteoporosis. She clutches a pair of secateurs and waves them in the direction of a path that leads down from the road to their chalet, one of dozens perched on the cliffs along the edge of Whitsand Bay.

'We have had it for twenty-five years,' she tells me proudly, pointing out the steeply sloping garden they have made together. The accommodation is pretty basic, she says: 'just a wooden hut with no mod cons – no electricity, no flushing loo.' They have a lease on the property; Plymouth City Council are the freeholders. 'We paid £7,500 for ours, but another sold recently for £450,000. One is owned by a professional footballer.' Her husband tells me that most people, as soon as they have completed their purchase, knock down the old hut and build a much smarter new house in its place. 'Then they rent them out for a week at a time,' his wife chips in, 'so you never know who your neighbours are.'

Later I search online and find a dozen chalets available as holiday lets, with photographs of dramatic sunsets, alfresco dining arrangements and the sea reflected on picture windows. My new friends say that their poor health means they make the journey from their flat in Torpoint much less often these days. 'These were just fishing huts when we came here first,' she says, 'for poor people from Torpoint, Devonport and Plymouth. All you used to hear were local accents. Now the whole feeling of the community has changed.'

I leave them as they start a slow descent towards the sea and their wooden hideaway, and drive on towards Rame Head, passing St Germanus Church, with its softly shaped, dormer-windowed 14th-century spire. As the peninsula thins out, the land tumbles down towards the water, before rallying at the last minute and rising to form a tip of rocky headland, embellished with a small rectangular chapel. It has been used as much as a look out post as it has been a place of prayer, first put into military service at the time of the Armada. A flat concrete plinth abuts the building, with two iron rings in the centre, the seemingly indestructible remains of a World War Two radar station intended to provide the people of Plymouth with an advance warning of incoming attack.

Through the chapel's ancient window surrounds I watch a wooden yacht making good speed, its sails gloriously puffed up by the wind. A modern cruiser runs parallel – dazzling new white fibreglass offsetting tirelessly polished old mahogany. To the east I can see the Great Mew Stone, a rocky island where one Samuel Wakeham and his wife Ann lived in the early 19th century.

Wakeham had been sentenced to transportation to Australia, but managed to win permission to see out his punishment on the island. There are no humans there now; it is owned by the National Trust and is home to a community of shags, cormorants and other seabirds.

From here Plymouth is out of sight and what I can see of Devon is entirely rural – fields, woodland, and a few small villages and hamlets. There is no evidence of a city of 300,000 people, no sense of the myriad urban dramas playing out just beyond my eyeline. The only clue of what is there comes when a naval frigate emerges slowly from behind Penlee Point. As I return to the car, skipping down the rough steps from the chapel, the sweet smell of gorse and the earthy odour of bracken combine to make a rich, sickly scent that catches in my nostrils.

The city is still hidden at Cawsand. In neighbouring Kingsand retirees sit around tables outside the Devonport Inn, looking satisfied with their lot as they watch the water glitter on Cleave Beach and share news over noonday drinks. I continue around the peninsula's edge to Picklecombe Fort, a garrison first established around 1800 and then strengthened and extended under Palmerston's War Office. At the rear of the site a Tudor-Gothic-style building with towers and castellations once contained barracks and an officer's mess. The crescent-shaped battery in front has now been turned into apartments, with balconies, canopies and outdoor furniture softening its stern military bearing.

The road ends here. A footpath leads north through the grounds of the Mount Edgcumbe estate and on to Cremyll, where finally Plymouth reveals itself across the water. In the distance is the city's towering 1960s civic centre. Closer by a trio of blocks of high-rise flats are covered in scaffolding as their cladding is replaced. The Georgian grandeur of the Royal William Yard, the old naval victualling depot, sits in the foreground. The sudden appearance of this urban sprawl is at first disarming – it is hard to immediately process the contrast between bucolic, tree-lined parkland and the densely packed city opposite.

Mount Edgcumbe House, and the 865-acre demesne that surrounds it, are a fine indicator of the stature and wealth of the eponymous family that resided here, their position and power built up over 500 years. Richard Edgcumbe had to flee to Brittany after joining the rebellion against Richard III in 1483. He returned with Henry Tudor in 1485, and after fighting at Bosworth Field was rewarded with a knighthood and the posts of controller of the royal household and constable of Launceston Castle. In 1488 the King sent him to establish the monarch's authority in Ireland. Peter Edgcumbe succeeded his father aged twelve. In 1520 he was present at the Field of the Cloth of Gold, the summit in Calais that brought together Henry VIII and King François I for diplomatic discussions that played out against lavish displays of each ruler's great wealth.

His son, another Richard, also served in France, mustering a Cornish militia to relieve Calais after the town had been attacked and reconquered in 1558. But his greatest achievement was at home – the creation of Mount Edgcumbe. For 200 years the family house had been Cotehele, ten miles up the Tamar River. Richard realised that his deer park on the Rame Peninsula occupied a spectacular location, the perfect place to create something new and more obviously grand than the existing house. He was his own architect. His builder, Roger Palmer of North Buckland, was given strict instructions that he must follow 'always ... the devyse, advyse and plan' of Sir Richard. The mansion that took shape here in the late 1540s had a tall central hall with clerestory windows. Slender, round towers stood on each corner, as Pevsner noted: 'a feature found in French royal houses by this date but exceptional in England'.

It was a fine place to entertain. George Edgcumbe inherited a baronetcy, but was elevated to the rank of viscount after George III and Queen Charlotte came to stay in 1781. When they returned eight years later he was made an earl. In the 19th century Queen Victoria, Napoleon III and Sisi, Empress Elizabeth of Austria, were all guests at Mount Edgcumbe.

The house was completely destroyed by German incendiary bombs in the Second World War. Remarkably, at a time of great austerity and general aristocratic decline, Kenelm Edgcumbe, the sixth earl, managed to rebuild the house. He died in 1965, just after work had finished. As his only son had been killed at Dunkirk, the estate and the title of seventh earl passed to Edward Edgcumbe, a New Zealand farmer and distant cousin. In 1971 he sold the house and lands jointly to Cornwall County Council and Plymouth City Council, who maintain it today as a public park, wedding venue and tourist attraction.

* * *

The Edgcumbes may have considered themselves a great Cornish family, but until nearly halfway through the 19th century, Mount Edgcumbe was technically located in Devon. So too was the village of Kingsand, though adjacent Cawsand was in Cornwall, a sign on the wall of a cottage marking out where the boundary lay. This strange state of affairs was addressed by the 1844 Counties (Detached Parts) Act. The legislation, designed to tidy up exclaves and other boundary anomalies, saw Cornwall take control of all the Rame Peninsula.*

More than a century later Plymouth made an audacious attempt to get the land back – and much more besides. In the

---

* Werrington and North Petherwin had to wait more than a century before they were switched from Devon to Cornwall in 1966. (See Chapter 19.)

early 1970s local government was being shaken up with fresh boundaries drawn and new counties created. Plymouth Labour MP David Owen saw this as the opportunity to create a cross-border region that would be called Tamarside. It had been suggested that Plymouth should lose its status as a unitary authority, which gave it direct responsibility for its own affairs. Instead, it would be controlled from Exeter, barely a third its size and more than forty miles away. Owen countered with an alternative proposal that would both ensure Plymouth's continued independence, and extend its territory, giving it control of Devon towns including Tavistock and Ivybridge, and more controversially, the tranche of east Cornwall that lies along the River Tamar.

The politician incurred Cornish wrath the moment he announced in the House of Commons that he saw the river as a 'totally unrealistic boundary division'. He dug deeper, asking: 'Why cannot Saltash and Torpoint, which are, in effect, now part of Plymouth and many of whose families have been Plymothians and whose history has been increasingly linked with that of Plymouth, now join formally with Plymouth?' The suggested new county of Humberside provided him with proof of what could be done. There the new Humber Bridge would bring together the people of Hull, the East Riding of Yorkshire and the north of Lincolnshire. Surely, Owen suggested, the already-built Tamar crossing could be used to the same effect in the south-west.

Rural communities in South Devon and Dartmoor were alarmed at the idea of throwing in their lot with Plymouth; west of the Tamar the idea was received with horror. Many in Cornwall refused to even acknowledge what was being proposed. *The Times* reported that politicians in Truro had severed communications with Plymouth, the county council leader Alderman Kimberley Foster instructing his chief officers to ignore any verbal or political attempts to initiate talks.

South East Cornwall MP Robert Hicks suggested that the new county would inevitably be dominated by its urban population, something that 'could have adverse effects upon the character of the countryside located within any such authority'. An idea that Plymouth might build an airport on its newly acquired Cornish lands only strengthened the resolve of campaigners. The plans collapsed. On the morning of 1 April 1974 citizens of Bournemouth woke up in Dorset, rather than Hampshire, the population of Wigan became part of Greater Manchester, and Sedbergh moved from Yorkshire to Cumbria. But when the residents of Saltash, Torpoint and the Rame Peninsula leapt out of bed, their feet fell on what was still firmly Cornish land.

* * *

Saltash is Cornwall's first and last town. For travellers bound for Plymouth the station name board offers a gentle warning – time to gather up coats and bags, unplug phone chargers and throw away the cardboard coffee cup in preparation for arrival. Most London expresses don't bother to call here, but a Penzance-to-Cardiff stopping service gives me the opportunity to disembark and explore the town.

I wait for a second on the platform to watch the service depart. It is operated by that monarch of the diesel age, an Intercity 125, the train that British Rail built in the 1970s. The doors lock shut with a loud click, and the front engine emits a roar as it musters power to cross the Albert Bridge. But its high-speed abilities will not be tested here. Just beyond the platform the double track merges to form a single set of rails, and a speed-limit sign instructs a gentle pace – 15mph across Brunel's great Victorian bridge.

Saltash became a borough in the 12th century. Plymouth did not get the same status until 1439, the prompt for a once popular local rhyme: 'Saltash was a borough town when Plymouth was a fuzzy down.' I walk along Station Road past the church of St Nicolas and St Faith to the stuccoed Guildhall. Built around 1780, with the look of a grand Methodist chapel, underneath is a space that was once open to the street and housed a covered market. A turn into Lower Fore Street reveals a tantalising first glimpse of the concrete towers of the 1961 suspension bridge that runs parallel to Brunel's railway crossing. A sharp drop down to the river leads to where the ferry used to depart.

In 1811, as part of a tour of Devon and Cornwall, the artist J. M. W. Turner stopped here, painting the slipway and the river lapping the muddy sand of the Saltash waterfront. The critic John Ruskin described the resultant work as 'what the mind sees when it looks for poetry in humble actual life'. Packhorses await their burden, in the background a soldier in scarlet uniform chats with market traders, their goods spread on blankets on the ground. Boatmen wait for business. Two sloops with rudimentary sails are available to travellers wanting to cross the river, or they can take their chances on a smaller craft, its oars positioned ready for action. The last ferry ran on 23 October 1961, the new road bridge opened the next morning. A plaque marks the occasion – the day that Ferry Road was renamed Old Ferry Road.

Today the sun casts sharp shadows of the bridges onto the foreshore below. I have to screw up my eyes to properly see the underside of the road crossing – angular metal joints and beams, rivets the size of human heads, gantries, ladders and high-level access doors marked out in various tones of grey. A terrace of four houses, painted pink, blue, green and yellow, are squeezed into the tight gap between the two superstructures, homes that spend some of their day in man-made shade. Further along is a life-size statue of Brunel wearing his eight-inch stovepipe hat. The engineer stood at a little over 5ft tall, and used the headwear as a prop to ensure his presence was not missed. Brunel, along with dozens of sailors and soldiers, features in a vivid mural painted on the wall of the pub nearby, The Union, its name seeming to stand as a gentle rebuke to anyone who might dream of a more independent Cornwall.

It was pure luck that Brunel's bridge survived World War Two, when the heart of Plymouth was destroyed by German bombs. When war began its residents took pride in the key role their dockyard was playing in the conflict. HMS *Exeter*, built and based at Devonport, was one of the three ships that defeated the German cruiser *Admiral Graf Spee* on the River Plate in the first naval battle of the war. When she arrived home on 15 February 1940, hundreds lined the quayside to welcome her, including the First Lord of the Admiralty, Winston Churchill.

In early June the city became a transit centre for 80,000 French troops evacuated from Dunkirk, while the 1st Division of the Canadian Army passed through on its way to Brest. On 6

July, not two weeks after France's surrender, the first bombs fell on Plymouth, killing three people. There had been twenty-one raids by the end of October, setting oil stores ablaze, damaging hospitals and cutting electricity supplies. A particularly heavy bombardment over the nights of March 20th and 21st 1941 saw the destruction of Charles Church and the Guildhall, forcing ARP controllers working in former prison cells in its basement to abandon their posts. The French writer and journalist André Savignon was in Plymouth and described 'the almost physical impression of a city slipping away from under ones very feet'. He reported empty streets, the population hiding in whatever safe space they could find. 'Ashes, mud, dust,' he continued, 'this poignant acrid smell, this effluvia of death.'

By the end of the German campaign there had been a total of 59 raids, 1,172 civilians had been killed, 3,754 houses had been destroyed and more than 18,000 damaged. Eight cinemas, twenty-six schools, forty-one churches and a hundred pubs had been lost. The overall population had shrunk from 208,000 to 127,000. Plymouth was the most devastated city in England, and had to be made afresh.

Lord Astor, the New York-born newspaper proprietor Waldorf Astor, was the city's wartime Lord Mayor. He wasted no time. Lord Reith, Churchill's Minister of Works, had engaged the respected town planner Patrick Abercrombie to address London's post-Blitz recovery. Astor demanded Abercrombie's services too, instructing City Engineer James Paton Watson to collaborate with him. The two men started work at the height of the bombing campaign in autumn 1941. Their report, *The Plan for Plymouth*, was finished in September 1943, seven months before the last bombing raid. The devastation was so great that the old street plan could be forgotten, and replaced with a completely new layout, the influences for which included Walter Burley Griffin's Canberra, Ebenezer Howard's Welwyn Garden City and Edwin Lutyens' Delhi.

The new centre was to be built around a pair of grand boulevards. Armada Way would run north–south, in a direct line between the railway station and the Naval Memorial on the Hoe. Running east–west would be Royal Parade, with shops to the north and a civic and entertainment district to the south. Everything had its zone, including faith – in time new places of worship for Unitarians, Baptists and Catholics would be built around Notte Street. The Roman Catholic Church of Christ the King, with its soaring campanile, was the last building designed by Sir Giles Gilbert Scott, completed after his death in 1960.

The plan referred to the virtually undamaged Barbican area as 'historic Plymouth'; the area for 'industry' was to the west on a route that led to the civilian docks at Millbay. Abercrombie and Paton Watson's purview also included industrial areas, high-density housing, suburbs, ring roads and satellite towns, but it was in the centre that they left the greatest legacy. An insight into their work is provided in *The Way We Live*, a 1946 film by the pioneering documentary maker Jill Craigie. The footage it contains of a city in the immediate aftermath of war is shocking – a service takes place in the ruined shell of St Andrew's Church, hoardings protect bomb sites, Nissen huts provide temporary accommodation, traders' signs mark out where shops had stood before the onslaught.

Abercrombie and Paton Watson are given the chance to make their case for a new city that ends slum housing and 'gives everyone the chance of living a full life'. Realising the plan, they suggest, should be seen as a tribute to those Plymothians killed in action or in the bombing raids. Determined to create a closing scene that would stick in the mind of her audience, Craigie arranged for thousands of local youths to march through the city centre carrying banners demanding better housing, safer roads, social clubs, theatres and holiday hostels. Michael Foot, the young Labour politician, makes an appearance, filmed campaigning in Devonport, the parliamentary seat he won at the 1945 election. Central government, he argues, should help to fund a plan that could make Plymouth the most beautiful city in the world. Four years after he was first elected, Foot and Craigie married, remaining together until her death fifty years later.

There was no lack of ambition to what Abercrombie and Paton Watson proposed – looking at their scale models, maps and diagrams, it is striking how many of their ideas were realised. Shortly after St Andrew's Church was bombed a hand-painted sign saying 'Resurgam' was hung on the north door. The church did rise again, along with the bombed-out grey limestone Guildhall next door. Charles Church was left as a ruin, a memorial to civilians who had lost their lives. A determined advocate of the new, Abercrombie seemed happy to deem most of the surviving pre-war buildings as being surplus to requirements. Paton Watson and city architect Edgar Catchpole managed to save some of them, including the 1938 neo-Georgian *Western Morning News* office and the Regent and Royal cinemas. But Abercombie's hatred of Victoriana was well known – presumably he was not pleased that the Derry's Cross clock tower and the Wilts & Dorset bank survived – the latter now a public house. But these were rare exceptions; most of the other old structures were demolished.

The plan was put into action at speed, with demobbed servicemen quickly employed in the construction industry. In the decade after the war ended, Plymouth was rebuilt faster than anywhere else. In 1954 the *Architects' Journal* noted that one in twelve men in the city was employed in the building industry; in Coventry the figure was one in fifty. Forty per cent of destroyed business facilities had been restored; in the central area two-thirds of the required work was either done or in hand. Plymouth had built 46 new council homes for every 1,000 people, compared to 20 per 1,000 in Portsmouth.

New housing was essential, but the city fathers knew they also had to inject some glamour and colour into the austere post-war landscape. One of the first substantial buildings to be completed was a great retail landmark. Edward Dingle had opened his drapery business in 1880; when the war started the company was employing 500 staff, its multiple departments run out of different shops across the city centre. Thomas Tait, who had previously designed Selfridges in London, was engaged as architect for a new store which would bring all the Dingle interests together under one roof.

He built a shop that was a temple to modernism, clad in Portland stone, with generous plate-glass windows and marble floors. It opened eight months ahead of schedule in September 1951, with 35,000 square feet of sales space across four floors.

Despite rationing limiting what was available in its food hall, 40,000 shoppers visited on its launch day, Plymouth's first escalators one of the attractions.

* * *

My brothers were born over a seven-year period, starting with William in 1954. After producing four sons, I think my parents probably thought that the family was big enough. A decade later my mother discovered that she was pregnant again. That ten-year gap put me in an enviable position – enjoying all the benefits of older siblings and all of that extra love and attention that an only child often receives.

As I entered my teenage years, Christopher – closest to me in age – had graduated, returned home for a year to work in a local pub, and was about to embark on what would turn out to be a long and successful career with the United Nations. William – the oldest – was working in the City of London, living a metropolitan life that I aspired to and delighting me on his visits home when he would arrive smelling lightly of cologne and cigarette smoke and talk of politics, restaurants, theatre and opera. Andrew exuded the easy glamour of the handsome young army officer he was, making occasional appearances in his vintage sports car. Johnny was the one who was there all the time. He had done a short-service commission in the army, before returning to Cornwall to work in the fish business. Until I was fifteen, he lived at home with Dad and me. He played a vital role in my life at that time. He was the only one of us who never lost his temper, ready to intervene when rows between my father and me threatened to overheat. Johnny and I might not have been great at finding words to express our emotions, but his calm presence provided just the support needed as together we tried to come to terms with the death of our mother.

Johnny had a car – a second-hand Volvo – and generally seemed happy enough to ferry me around. Sometimes we would head off on adventures together, driving to Truro Station, and then taking the train for a day trip to Plymouth. Upon arrival we would invariably head for Dingles, a quarter-of-an-hour walk from the station, straight down Armada Way.

I would scurry ahead of him excitedly as we progressed through the brightly lit, sickly-sweet-scented perfume hall, passing implausibly made-up staff offering sample sprays and makeovers. We would take the four sets of escalators up to the café, where the day would be planned over a Danish pastry and a cappuccino, its foam heavily dressed with chocolate powder. My long-suffering brother would say little as I dragged him around the furniture and homeware floors, designing in my mind the look of the urban apartment where I wanted to live. Then there would be forty minutes or so coming and going from the changing rooms as I decided which shirt or pair of trousers to spend my birthday money on.

Dingles seemed to epitomise the rich potential of the city. My Blackwood grandparents, who had lived in Plymouth for a time, would reminisce about meals in the Dartmoor Restaurant, where shining cutlery and sparkling glassware was neatly laid on damask cloths, waitresses in black pinnies providing silver service. Pictures of the store in the sixties show cabinets filled with lavish delicacies in the food hall, comfortable chairs for customers to rest their feet as they inspected a vast selection of wools and fabrics, crowds watching fashion shows featuring evening wear in contemporary London styles. In the mid seventies part of one floor became a boat showroom, and superstar hairdresser Vidal Sassoon visited to demonstrate the latest cuts.

To this dreamy young teenager Plymouth had a sense of glamour distinctly lacking in Cornwall. People appeared smarter and more self-assured. The shops stood on broad boulevards rather than narrow high streets, and as you walked along there was a chance of seeing a local television star out for a lunchtime stroll. On one trip I persuaded Johnny that we should visit the viewing platform on the fourteenth floor of the Civic Centre – a confident example of municipal modernism, the tower seeming to float above the adjoining Council House. Riding the lift to the top was a novelty in itself; Cornwall did not do tall buildings. Nor, at that point, did we have a proper theatre. The Theatre Royal Plymouth opened in 1982, the last part of Abercrombie and Paton Watson's plan to be realised, its fly tower dominating the west end of Royal Parade. Here I saw Danny La Rue, Harry Worth, Terry Scott and Les Dawson in pantomime, came on school trips to see the Royal Shakespeare Company and the National Theatre, and revelled in lavish productions of *South Pacific*, *Brigadoon* and *Cabaret* that kick-started a love of musical theatre.

* * *

Though Plymouth was over the border, it felt a key part of my Cornish childhood, and it seems right it should be part of this journey of rediscovery. Then it was the only 'big city' I really knew. I return to it after decades in London, spells in Hong Kong and Manchester, and the privilege of a life that has included shorter trips for work and pleasure to dozens of other grand metropolises.

'Britain's Ocean City' is Plymouth's new slogan – writ large on signs at Plymouth Station. Abercrombie and Paton Watson envisaged a grand terminus – their drawings show buildings with open terraces and gabled roofs, built to a scale not far short of Mussolini's grand Milano Centrale. The budget allocated by British Railways did not fund their dreams – the platforms cower behind an undistinguished Victorian terrace and a multistorey car-park.

I walk through a subway below a roundabout to reach the start of Armada Way. Hastily built blocks of student accommodation and a nondescript hotel stand at the top, not the standard of architecture that the progenitors of the new Plymouth intended. The pleasingly stark stone-fronted Salvation Army Congress Hall, its name spelt out in well-spaced blue capitals, is the first building that indicates the simple elegance that they sought, but it is not until Royal Parade itself that the ambition of *The Plan for Plymouth* becomes clear.

Here the structures have a sense of confidence, open spaces enabling each building to be enjoyed as an independent entity. Despite post-war shortages, high-quality materials were used. An overall sense of stark neoclassical formality is tempered by fine detailing – carved stones showing a medieval market scene on one building, reliefs of exotic fruits and flowers on another.

338

In 2018 the *Herald*, Plymouth's evening newspaper, carried doom-laden headlines announcing Dingles was to close, leaving what it described as a 'yawning gap' in the city centre.* It is certainly a different place to what it was when I made teenage visits. Plymouth City Council have moved out of the Civic Centre tower which awaits conversion into high-rise apartments. The old Co-operative department store now houses a branch of Argos and a Premier Inn. Pearl Assurance House is a Poundland. An alarm rings from the abandoned Debenhams building but no one takes any notice. A pigeon is roosting on the second 'e' of the shop sign, its discharge staining the wall below.

But somehow Dingles still trades, though its glory days seem long past. The doors stand open, and once in I am greeted by a familiar blast of cloying, scented air. But there is no floorwalker to address my requirements and send me off in the right direction, and there are only a handful of customers in sight. The lighting is dim, racks of sport- and leisure-wear have replaced mannequins clad in contemporary styles.

I take the escalators to the top floor where roughly placed crowd-control barriers block the entrance to the Dingles Restaurant. Pushing between them, I walk through the lines of empty tables towards the picture windows that offer panoramic views

---

*The rise and fall of the regional newspaper industry is well reflected in the changing addresses of the *Herald* and *Western Morning News*. In 1993 they left their pre-war city-centre office on Frankfort Street for a new headquarters in Derriford. Northcliffe Newspapers commissioned the architect Sir Nicholas Grimshaw, who designed a vast glass edifice, nicknamed 'The Ship', with the newsroom in the prow and a boardroom cantilevered from a 22-metre tower designed to resemble a ship's bridge. In 2015 the building was saved from threat of demolition when it was awarded listed status. The newspapers are now owned by Reach [lc, and published from the third floor of an anonymous-looking office building on Millbay Road.

across the city. Unexpectedly a man emerges from the shadows – and asks if he can help me. I feel my cheeks flush red – once again I am an awkward thirteen-year-old up from Cornwall. I mumble something about looking for the gents. He points to an obvious and well-illuminated sign. When I emerge a few minutes later he is waiting by the barriers, but now his tone has softened. Apologising for the closure, he tells me the café might reopen soon. 'I imagined it had closed for good,' I tell him. 'It's like Plymouth,' he says, 'a phoenix from the ashes. We shall rise again.' I hope he is right.

CHAPTER 19

Mapping the Tamar

The Duke of Cornwall glows in the early-evening sun, its architecture more redolent of *fin de siècle* Paris than central Plymouth. I count over a hundred windows on the façade of the once grand hotel, from the tall bays that flood light into the public rooms on the ground floor to the dormers in the old servants' quarters four storeys up. The steep slate roof is punctured by high chimney stacks; a glazed tower shaped like a nautical light offers a 360-degree panorama of the city – a space exclusively available, according to the hotel's website, to the occupants of the grandest suite.

Inside there are fine wrought-iron and wood railings to help guests ascend a gently rising staircase, from which balconies lead off to long corridors of bedrooms. Attached to the wall is a butler's bell box that once alerted staff to calls from the writing room, ballroom, manager's sitting room and cocktail bar. The receptionist welcomes me warmly as I check in. The hotel may not be particularly well suited to the needs of either the modern business traveller or the reveller seeking a hen- or stag-night crash-pad, but its faded elegance suits me well.

The Duke of Cornwall opened in 1863 to cater for passengers using the liners that departed Plymouth bound for the East Coast of the United States. In the 1930s two transatlantic ships left the city daily, the popularity of the route due in part to the fact that the journey took a night less than sailings from Southampton or Liverpool. Millbay Station, then Plymouth's principal railway terminus, was just across the road from the hotel. A siding ran down to the docks so boat-train passengers could be deposited directly at the quayside.

Lloyds of London stopped listing the city as a transatlantic port in 1963, and today the site of the former railway depot is occupied by the 1990s metal-and-glass shed of Plymouth Pavilions, built as a leisure centre and concert arena, its once thriving ice-rink and swimming pool now abandoned. The only indication that this was a waypoint on the journey to the New World are two anonymous-looking granite posts that once held the station gates.

After a good night's sleep, and breakfast in a sparsely populated dining room, I set out on the final part of my journey – not over the seas, but up-river along the sixty-one miles of the Tamar, the border between Cornwall and the rest of England. This extraordinary waterway rises close to the Atlantic near Bude and flows into the Channel off Plymouth – if it ran for just a few more miles, Cornwall would be an island.

There are more than twenty road bridges on the river, some of them built in the 15th century and still in use today. Once there were five railway bridges. The most southerly crossings are by ferry, with two services plying the Hamoaze, the ancient, exotic-sounding name of the estuarine Tamar.

The Edgcumbe Bell takes eight minutes to carry foot passengers and cyclists between Cremyll and the Royal William Yard. The Royal Navy left the former victualling centre thirty years ago, and today its early 19th-century stores, mills, bakeries and offices have been repurposed as apartments, bars and restaurants. A little upstream, the first Tamar road crossing makes use of a chain-dragged car ferry to convey vehicles between Torpoint and

Devonport. While passengers from Cremyll might rejoice at the beauty of their short voyage, the Torpoint ferry provides more utilitarian passage. The vessel's high walls obscure any sight of the water, the few gaps there are blocked by advertising hoardings that bombard the weary commuter – fascias, gutters, cladding and conservatories from Boringdon Plastics; the Spice Aroma Indian Restaurant of Torpoint; personal and relationship media-tion from Plymouth Counselling.

I start my frontier journey by train, on the Tamar Valley railway line. I am one of a handful of passengers on the 8.22 from Plymouth to Gunnislake. We call at Devonport and then Dockyard, where there is a chance to survey three centuries of military architecture – assured Georgian elegance alongside the confident Victorian and Edwardian buildings of an imperial navy, and the battered prefabs that reflect the realities of late 20th-century military spending. The letters 'R.N.' are spelt out in blue seats arranged amid the otherwise red tiers of a football stand. On the other side of the tracks rows of tightly packed terraces bear names reflecting a firm naval embrace – Admiralty St, Fleet St, Victory St, Renown St, Ocean St.

Soon after, we break away from the main line and run down-hill to the banks of the Tamar, passing under Brunel's Royal Albert Bridge. The railway reached Plymouth in 1849. In order for it to continue into Cornwall, a 1,100ft span of river had to be crossed. The first plan was for a floating bridge, the idea of Captain William Moorsom, one of the chief engineers of the Cornwall Railway. Under parliamentary cross-examination, he airily brushed away concerns about the safety of his proposal, central to which was a one-in-ten gradient ramp, down which locomotives and carriages would freewheel onto a ferry. Brunel was one of those who gave evidence. Asked: 'Do you think there would be any danger in running your train through the boat into the Hamoaze?', Brunel gave but a brief response: 'I think, and decidedly.' Those words ended any hope for Moorsom's scheme, the way left open for Brunel's own dream of a bridge across the river.

At first Brunel proposed a wooden structure. It would have been the largest timber bridge in the world, with six 100ft spans and a central section stretching 250ft. But the Admiralty, who had control over the Hamoaze, demanded a bridge that would be wide and high enough to allow the largest naval ships to pass safely under. Brunel returned to his drawing board, and came up with an arrangement that used two 465ft spans, supported by a deep-water pier in the middle of the river and two further piers on the foreshore. Two arched tubular trusses would sail above the track, balanced by tension chains hanging on each side. Brunel was in no doubt as to the challenges of the project – initial tests revealed that the foundations for the central pier would have to sit on rock 80ft below the high-water level. Thick beds made of centuries of oyster shells would have to be smashed away before the surface rocks were reached. Brunel designed a special machine to enable the necessary excavations, a variation on a diving bell which accommodated skilled masons and labourers in a cylinder 35ft in diameter, with pumps to suck water out and blow air in.

Once the foundations of the piers were in place, the first truss was floated into position. A public holiday was declared in Saltash on 1 September 1857. Tens of thousands of people flocked to the edges of the river or lined the hills above to watch. Church bells rang, flags and bunting hung on every street, and it was reported that the town's 'houses of entertainment' had laid in 'enormous stores of edibles and drinkables'. Brunel had become a celebrity not only because of his brilliant engineering skills, but also because he understood the power of theatre. He insisted on complete silence during the delicate operation, which he supervised from a podium mounted in the centre of the truss. As one eyewitness wrote: 'not a voice was heard as by some mysterious agency, the tube and rail, borne on the pontoons, travelled to their resting place, and with such quietude as marked the building of Solomon's temple'.

By high water the truss was fixed in place, and a Royal Marine band struck up 'See the Conquering Hero Comes' from Handel's *Judas Maccabeus*. Over the next year the truss rose to full height as the masonry underneath it was completed, and the second tube was floated the following July. This time assistant engineer Robert Brereton supervised the works; Brunel was now confined to bed with fatal kidney disease. He was absent too on 2 May 1859 when Prince Albert opened the bridge, having travelled by a special train that left Windsor at 6 a.m. The mayor of Truro and other Cornish dignitaries missed the opening as well, after *Argo*, the locomotive hauling their train, broke down at Liskeard.

Brunel saw his completed bridge a few weeks later, when a loco-motive towed an open truck across, the engineer recumbent on a specially installed couch. This time there were no crowds or bands, the only noise that of the wind blowing through the spans of his masterpiece. Brunel died on 15 September 1859, aged only fifty-three. The directors of the Cornwall Railway paid tribute by spelling out his name and profession in huge letters on the portals at either end of the bridge.

The Gunnislake line runs along the Devon bank of the Tamar. A gap in the trackside greenery offers a glorious, split-second view of the underside of Brunel's bridge, and the adjacent suspension road bridge, opened to traffic in 1961. Two remarkable structures separated in age by a hundred years, a pair of heavyweight twins that reach out across the water and carry more than fifty trains and up to 50,000 vehicles every day.

Quickly the sprawl of the city is forgotten. While it runs through Plymouth this line is part of an urban transit system; in the countryside it becomes a sleepy railway outpost, a route that only survived the Beeching cuts due to the area's poor road provision. It is the only branch line on the national network that has a village, rather than a town or city as its terminus.

The two-carriage train rattles over the eight bowstring girders of the bridge at the head of the Tavy, the river which rises on Dartmoor, lends its name to the town of Tavistock, and then flows into the Tamar. Sight of the river is temporarily lost just before we reach the first rural stop, the Devon village of Bere Ferrers. Beyond is Bere Alston, once an important junction on the London and South Western Railway, where through trains departed for Waterloo. There is no track north of the station any more – here the train switches direction, the driver giving me a friendly nod as he walks past the carriage window on his way to reverse the train onwards.

The line passes through open farmland and then darts into a cutting blasted out of stony hillside, its banks lined with a crop of toxic foxgloves. For a moment we are embraced by thick woodland, the path of the track suggesting a long and winding drive that might eventually lead to a hidden country house. And then, with little warning, the river border is underneath us.

Can any village boast a grander approach than that offered by the viaduct that takes the train into Cornwall at Calstock? Its arches soar up to 120ft high. There are twelve in total, half spanning Devon farmland and floodplain. Three sit on the bed of the river itself and the remainder are tucked in between sharply raked terraces of yellow, pink and pale-blue houses. As the train slows, the side of the valley seems to rush up towards me, and I have that same feeling that comes in those last seconds before a plane touches land. The platform of Calstock Station offers a reassuring hug after our high-altitude railway crossing.

The viaduct carries a single track, and is gracefully delicate and thin. It feels a little heretical even to think it, but a bit of me wonders if this bridge is even more attractive than Brunel's. It is as grand as one of the great bridges of New York or Newcastle, yet its architect ensured that it complements rather than overwhelms its rural setting. This is a late flower of the golden age of British railway architecture, built in 1908 by a Cornishman, John Charles Lang, a public works contractor from Liskeard who chose to use precast concrete blocks, transporting them across the length of the site and gently lowering them into place from an aerial walkway.

Later I return to Calstock to walk along the river to Cotehele, the original house of the Edgcumbe family. They first lived here in 1353 and it remained in their ownership for nearly six centuries until 1947, when the sixth Earl of Mount Edgcumbe handed the property to the National Trust, who had accepted it in lieu of death duties. In the mid 1960s my Aunt Barbara, looking for a job after she returned from running a hospital in Kenya, became its administrator, living in a flat inside the house. What was her kitchen is now used as a store room where visitors can leave bags and coats while they explore. In the year before Covid, the house received 175,000 visitors. Barbara dealt with just 16,500 per annum, leaving her plenty of time to drive her Hillman Minx around the lanes of the estate, and walk her dog Tamu in the gardens.

As I wander towards Cotehele from Calstock, the impact of the viaduct is such that I keep stopping and looking back. I have to walk nearly half a mile before the dozen spans can be squeezed onto the screen of my iPhone. The high arches are neatly framed by the Cornish hills that roll away behind, while in the foreground black-and-white cattle sleepily graze the rich Devon pasture.

Back on the train the other passengers in my carriage have all disembarked, leaving me alone in my private railway saloon. Calstock Station feels high enough, but there are another 500ft to climb before we reach the end of the line. This is Cornwall's equivalent of an Indian hill railway; I can feel the steep gradient as the train strains its way forward, the wheel flanges grinding nosily along the track. The Waze app on my phone reports we are travelling at the stately speed of 17mph. Footpaths cross the track, with wooden gates and signs telling walkers to 'Stop, Look, Listen'. Several times we halt completely at open level crossings, the driver instructed to 'whistle before proceeding'. The order comes from the age of steam, today it is an air-horn that gives warning, but the source matters little this morning – there are no cars around to hear it. Finally, we come to a gentle stop just ahead of the buffers at Gunnislake, where three of us disembark. That does not mean the service is not popular – at least sixty people are waiting to board: families, couples and a school group heading for a day out in Plymouth.

Gunnislake railway station is in a hamlet called Drakewells; the village itself is a fifteen-minute walk along the busy A390 towards Tavistock. It is a steep drop down to the river – a sand-lined escape lane is provided for trucks to use, should their brakes fail. The Tamar has shrunk now, the water flowing gently, the surface reflecting the hanging foliage that masks the banks. The New Bridge was new around 1520. In 1809 it was widened to allow horses and carts to pass each other. Until the Tamar Bridge opened in 1961, this was the river's most southerly road crossing. It is not wide enough for modern cars to pass two abreast – drivers exiting Cornwall get priority, those seeking to leave Devon politely queueing until the bridge is clear. The arches are slightly pointed so as to create refuges for pedestrians. I take shelter in one, and oblivious of the passing traffic, admire the view up and down river.

There is an old tollhouse on the east side, and a sign that says: 'Welcome to Devon'. Across the water Cornwall offers something much more ornate – a crest featuring tin miner, fisherman, choughs and fifteen gold bezants, along with the bilingual greeting '*Kernow a'gas dynergh*, Welcome to Cornwall'.

Gunnislake has the feeling of a frontier town about it – never more so than in the winter of 2020 when Covid regulations briefly made Devon subject to Tier Two restrictions, forcing the closure of pubs – while Cornwall remained in pint-permitting Tier One. Amy Newland, landlady of the White Hart, told the *Devon Live* website of her worries after receiving calls from Plymouth drinkers enquiring about her opening hours; online there was heated talk of the villagers arming themselves with pitchforks to ensure the bridge was not breached.

I continue my journey from here by car. It is the week after midsummer and even though the school holidays have not yet started, Cornwall is busy. The nearest cheap place to stay is in Devon – a Travelodge on the A30 at Okehampton. I wake early and get coffee and a bacon roll from the roadside branch of Greggs – a breakfast 'Worth Waking Up For', according to the digital sign behind the server. Mizzle seems to have set in for the day, but my heart lifts as I spot a copse of tall trees on a high bluff above the road. All my adult life these hundred or so beeches have signalled that Cornwall is just a few bends of the road away – some people call them the 'nearly home trees'. Soon after they have been passed, the road drops down to Dunheved Bridge, which carries the four lanes of the A30 over the Tamar.

Leaving the dual carriageway at the Launceston exit, I drive to Polson Bridge, a 1930s structure in the place where a medieval crossing was once the main route into Cornwall. This is horse country – immaculately dressed eventers ride their well-groomed mounts around courses set up on the training pitches of Launceston Rugby Club, the tannoyed commentary drifting over the morning air. It is quieter by the river, where four solo anglers make great efforts to ignore each other as they fish under the bridge. It was here in 1643 that Parliamentary forces waited for the right moment to start the Battle of Launceston against the

Royalist Cornish army. Those loyal to the King were at prayer in St Mary Magdalene Church when news of the enemy presence reached them; they waited for the service to finish before leaving to launch a successful counter-attack.

I witness a different act of rebellion as I park at Higher New Bridge. Two men in an open truck glare at me as I edge past them. Minutes later they speed away, bits of masonry falling off the back of their vehicle, which is heavily loaded with rubble and building waste. This beautiful corner of the land is not immune to the ugly plague of fly-tipping. The 'PL15 crew' – Ben, Fiona, Erika and Tom – have scratched their names on the old council plaque informing visitors that the bridge was built c.1504. It served travellers for nearly five centuries before it was replaced. The new crossing, the sign says, was opened in 1986 by Christopher Beazley, Member of the European Parliament for Cornwall and Plymouth. Back then European support here was relatively limited; Brussels treated Cornwall and Devon as a single entity, so Devon's wealth masked Cornwall's post-industrial poverty. After much lobbying Cornwall was awarded Objective One status in 1999, recognition of its unique geography and heritage as well as its parlous economic position. We were soon receiving the highest level of EU structural funding, benefitting from over a billion euros of investment. But on referendum day in 2016, 56.5 per cent of Cornish people voted for Brexit.

* * *

According to the Old English manuscript the *Anglo-Saxon Chronicle*, King Æthelstan was crowned ruler of Mercia in September 925. A few weeks later, on the death of his half-brother Ælfweard, he added Wessex to his domains. It seems he was a man who demanded clarity, and wanted to know exactly where his lands began and ended. It was Æthelstan who established the River Wye as the border between England and Wales. Next, he and his council met in Exeter, where they found there was increasing animosity between its Anglo-Saxon residents and its population of émigré Cornish Celts or West Britons, as they were known. The King solved the problem by fortifying the city and sending the Cornish home, declaring that the River Tamar should mark the Cornish border.

The Victorian map that hung on the wall of the sitting room at St Martin clearly showed the line of the river frontier. But my eye was always drawn to one anomaly, an unexpected kink in the route just above Higher New Bridge, where it looked as if a Devonian fist was punching its way into Cornish territory. The borderline, marked in pale red, left the Tamar and followed the River Ottery north-west to Canworthy Water. Then it went north-east to Week St Mary and then south-east to Boyton. Just below Boyton Bridge the Tamar reasserted control, but this strange quirk meant that two Cornish parishes, Werrington and North Petherwin, were under Devonian control.

In the 11th century the manor at Werrington had become the property of the Abbot of Tavistock. As a consequence, the villages were moved out of the political and legal jurisdiction of the Cornish Hundred of Stratton, and into the Hundred of Black Torrington – part of Devon – where they remained until 1966.

The land had later passed to Sir Francis Drake, nephew of the famous admiral, who set out a 500-acre deer park. In 1668 the Royalist Parliamentarian William Morice retired here after eight years' loyal service as Charles II's Secretary of State, dedicating his time to his extensive and valuable library. After a century and a quarter the Morices sold to the dukes of Northumberland, who wanted the land for political purposes – owning Werrington meant they controlled representation of the area in the House of Commons. While they were generous benefactors to the community, their actual presence in Cornwall was limited to a few weeks each year as part of an annual grand progress through their estates.

They lost interest after the Great Reform Act, and in 1865 sold to Alexander Campbell, a Manchester cotton merchant who spent lavishly to ensure he was first returned and then re-elected as the local Member of Parliament. The *Launceston Weekly News* reported the tenantry being entertained by firework displays and lavish meals, one of which featured two bullocks roasted whole. On another occasion 550 people came for tea and 240 were given dinner. But the fun did not last long. His business did not recover from the cotton embargo of the American Civil War, and Campbell sold Werrington after just four years. Finally in 1882 it was bought by John Charles Williams, and has remained in the Williams family ever since.

The mining brothers James, Davey and Richard Williams

had come to Cornwall from Wales around 1650, settling first at Stithians. By 1715, James's grandson John was living at Burncoose. He was an ambitious entrepreneur determined to do well from the tin and copper boom. He became manager of Poldice Mine near St Day, where he modernised the production process by creating a network of drainage channels that allowed miners to reach rich seams deep underground without any risk of flooding.

The Williamses became one of Cornwall's richest families, with interests in politics, banking, quarrying and smelting. In 1854 Michael Williams purchased Caerhays Castle, moving the family power base from the industrial mining districts of the west to the altogether more bucolic Roseland peninsula.

Caerhays, gloriously picturesque and with a sublime view over the sea at Porthluney Bay, was the work of the Regency architect John Nash. Pevsner describes it as Nash's 'largest surviving essay in castellated Gothick, a breathtaking composition of square and round towers and battlemented walls'. The architect had been commissioned by John Bettesworth-Trevanion, a man once described as 'the very *arbiter elegantiarum* . . . a complete man of fashion in the best sense of the word'. Alas, his taste and ambition exceeded his financial reserves; while building Caerhays he ran out of cash, and had to flee to the Continent to escape his creditors, dying in Brussels in 1840.

John Charles Williams was a celebrated plantsman and filled the gardens Nash had laid out at Caerhays with rhododendrons, camellias and magnolias. At Werrington he built glasshouses to raise seeds and planted shrubs and trees collected by the globe-trotting horticultural explorers George Forrest and Ernest Wilson, some of whose expeditions to Asia he had sponsored.

In 1993 Michael Williams inherited Werrington, running the estate while also maintaining the family tradition of public service, as a Deputy Lord Lieutenant, and for twenty-five years vice-chairman and chairman of the Royal Cornwall Show. In 2020 he and his wife Sarah passed the main house on to their eldest son and moved to a nearby mill.

It sits just a few hundred yards from the intersection of the Ottery and Tamar Rivers, the trees that line both waterways clearly showing the path of the old and new boundaries. Accompanied by his dogs, Michael and I set off on a walk along the Ottery. Great Cornish mansions were often built on low ground, but Werrington sits proudly at the peak of a hill, facing south. The original abbot's house, remodelled by Drake in 1641, is hidden behind a stuccoed, symmetrical early 18th-century front range. Stables and the estate yard sit to the east. We walk past a fish pond set out by ancient monks, its water level kept permanently topped up by a leat that runs in from the river. An avenue of limes leads back to the house, thought to have been planted in the late 17th century to honour William III, their seasonally orange leaves a salute to his Netherlandish heritage.

'There was an old family story that the 11th-century boundary change was the result of a good lunch, after which ancient map makers got the Tamar and Ottery confused,' Michael tells me. 'It always irked my grandfather Alfred that it was listed in the Devon edition of Pevsner. He was MP for North Cornwall in the 1920s, and yet his residence was in the Tavistock constituency. He always regarded himself as a Cornishman and was delighted when the Boundary Commissioners decided to restore the Tamar's supremacy in 1966.' Ordnance Survey cartographers quickly replotted the alternate dots and dashes that mark out county borders on modern maps. 'It's always looked like a glaring error,' concludes Williams. 'It's just a shame it took nine hundred years to fix.'

* * *

There is an old metal sign on each side of Boyton Bridge, one in the name of the clerk of Devon County Council, the other signed by his opposite number in Truro. The wording is slightly different, but the message is the same – the bridge is not strong enough to carry the weight of a heavy locomotive. If you are driving one, stop right now and go no further without the express permission of the county surveyor. I stand on the hump of the bridge and look both ways. From here Cornwall seems to possess a tousled, slightly rackety charm, a contrast to Devon's smooth English sophistication. On the Devon side trees have been planted with consideration around the edges of a perfectly trimmed hayfield. There seems to have been no planning behind the Cornish woodland, and the river bank is decorated by a burnt-out oil drum and a rusting quad bike. Even Devon's road surface seems newer and smoother. Different lands unfolding at each end of the bridge.

There are no signs on the Victorian North Tamerton Bridge. The original medieval crossing was destroyed in great floods that afflicted Cornwall in July 1847. The Tamar was not the only swollen river – all but two of the bridges across the River Camel were washed away.

I drive on through Bridgerule. The Tamar runs through the middle of what was once a divided village. Like the Rame Peninsula, this was one of the places that caught the eye of the planners in 1844. Bridgerule was placed in its entirety into Devon; on its square of the map the county border line once again deviates from the path of the Tamar.

Closer now in width to a broad stream, the river gets a last chance to swell in size as it feeds in and out of two reservoirs. The Lower Tamar Lake was constructed in the 1820s to supply water to the Bude Canal. The original plans, given royal assent in 1774, envisaged a route that would link the Atlantic and the Channel, with a ship canal built from Bude to Calstock, from where the Tamar was navigable to the docks at Plymouth. The Napoleonic Wars put a halt to the scheme, and what was eventually built was rather simpler. Large ocean-going vessels could enter a canal basin through a (still working) sea lock built in 1819 next to Summerleaze beach in Bude. Lime-rich sand used to improve agricultural soil was the main trade. Cargoes would be carried inland on tub boats – small, wheeled barges towed in trains and eased up and down inclines by chains driven by underground waterwheels. The canal was the longest of its kind in England, running for thirty-five miles, with branches to Blagdon Moor Wharf in Holsworthy and Druxton Wharf near Launceston.

The canal lasted for most of the 19th century – but then the opening of railway lines to Holsworthy and Bude, and the availability of better-quality fertiliser, saw its business go into terminal decline. By the start of the 20th century the upper reaches were being used to supply drinking water to Bude, and the reservoir had become an angling lake. Company archives from 1904 report that the Reservoir Cottage and Garden were let to a Major Mann for five years at an annual rent of £12; the major also held a five-year lease on the fishing rights for which he paid £25 each year.

I wander through the woods below the reservoir, following the narrow canal. Shafts of sunlight shoot through the foliage above. A bright-blue peacock appears, and struts determinedly ahead of me, resisting all my attempts to pass. Eventually it disappears into the garden of a house by a road that leads to another river crossing. Here the full-service 'Welcome to Devon' sign sits on the east side of the bridge, right next to a cast-iron notice proclaiming 'Kernow'. That the signs are right next to each other seems to compromise the expected neutrality of a border bridge, a structure that should surely be a no-mans-land, a buffer zone between the two counties.

A dam built of slabs of grey concrete holds safe the 300 million gallons of water in the Upper Tamar Lake. The border passes through the middle, following the route the river took before it was corralled in the 1970s, when eighty acres of land were flooded in order to ensure a secure supply of water for the towns of north Cornwall.

It is less than two miles on to the final road bridge across the river, found on a lane between two farms – West Youlstone in Cornwall and East Youlstone in Devon. I turn right off the main road by the units housing the headquarters of Will Urquhart, bull semen provider – his business slogan 'Breeding top quality genetics in the south-west'. This bridge barely warrants its name, the slip of water it crosses is so weak and narrow. There is no welcome-to-Cornwall sign here, but there is a Devon one. Not that I spot it immediately; it's been turned to face the woods rather than the road. Climbing on the bank, I try to twist it back around, but whoever first rotated it is stronger than me and has managed to lock it in place. For a few seconds I stand legs akimbo, one foot in each county, then I hurl myself fully back into Cornwall.

My journey is near its end. I pull into a layby on the A39 – the Atlantic Highway – and look on the map for Woolley Barrows. Barrows are among the earliest surviving funerary monuments, mounds of earth, rubble or drystone, some dating back to the early and middle Neolithic periods. Over 500 barrows exist nationally, the one at Woolley considered the finest in Cornwall. Its location is what really interests me – on a ridge that overlooks the source of the Tamar. Once I am near, I cross-reference the barrows' position with the mapping app on my phone, the GPS dot suggesting that the river's source is adjacent to the lane I am walking along. But no sight or sound of water permeates the thick hedge.

A hundred yards further on, a padlocked metal gate stands across the entrance to a patch of managed pine forest. There is nothing to indicate that this is private land. I duck under and walk quickly through the waist-high grass towards the trees. The light fades and the temperature drops as soon as I pass under their cover. Ordered rows of ruler-straight conifers veer out of the gloom, the ground is springy underfoot – this is the sort of space occupied by the horror-film chases of bad dreams. I walk for five minutes or so, vault over several drainage channels, and finally see a ray of sunlight, made sharp by the dust I have stirred up. Ahead is an area open to the sky.

Thick moss covers the branches of fallen trees, a moorhen sings, some wild orchids add delicate colour. In the middle of the space a tiny water source bubbles up from the ground. It makes the softest of sounds, a noise that reminds me of a gently gurgling baby. I step onto the mud and watch the water well up behind the miniature dam made by my boots. For a moment I wonder if I have halted the flow of the mighty river, stopped these first drips that will grow into the broad channel that runs under the high bridges at Calstock and Saltash, passes the ships moored in the Naval Dockyard and gives a final nod to Mount Edgcumbe and the Rame Peninsula before pouring out into the sea. Here it seems so fragile, this tiny spring that marks the border between Cornwall and England, that demarcates the frontier of this proud, contrary, richly-storied place of more than half a million people, stretching south-west seventy miles to Land's End. I think of the miners, fishermen, cablers, sailors, builders, ministers, teachers, agricultural labourers and landed families who shaped these lands; the writers, artists, linguists and collectors of myth and legend who recorded its history; those who left to earn a living and the wealthy who arrived here and remade what lay around them. A land of long-set tradition that has seen radical, sometimes destructive, change – but my country, whatever my name is, and wherever I was born. My reverie comes to an abrupt end as water seeps into my boots, a forgotten tear in the leather leaving my right foot sodden. I step back and set the young River Tamar free to continue on its journey.

A NOTE ON SOURCES

Watching my Cornish library grow exponentially has been one of the joys of this project; the pleasure of tearing open a book dealer's brown envelope and poring over a dusty, stained or slightly foxed work is one never to be underestimated.

A far from exhaustive survey of books and papers I have consulted while writing *Trelawny's Cornwall* follows – may I first recommend five sources that I have returned to multiple times, and which would grace any Cornish library. Dr Philip Payton's *Cornwall – A History* (University of Exeter Press, 2017) is rich in information and the perfect primer, covering a staggering amount of ground in less than four hundred pages. The *West Briton* newspaper has been the chronicler of Cornish life for over two centuries. It is worth searching for a set of *Life in Cornwall*, a four-volume reader of the paper's news coverage in the 19th century (published in four volumes by Dyllansow Truran and D. Bradford Barton 1971–1997, ed. R. M. Barton). Though focused on Falmouth, Charles Fox's *On the Brink: The Story of G. C. Fox and Company: A Quaker Business in Cornwall through Eight Generations* is a good read that says much about Cornish history and provokes thought about the future (Zuleika, 2019). Grand families of miners, adventurers, explorers and eccentrics have helped shape this place; Crispin Gill provides a helpful guide in his *Great Cornish Families* (Cornwall Books, 1995). As soon as the border has been crossed, the revised edition of *The Buildings of England – Cornwall* by Peter Beacham and Nikolaus Pevsner (Yale University Press, 2017) should be removed from the car glove box and kept in the passenger's lap for easy reference.

1 Home

The woodland around the Helford River is described by Oliver Rackham in *The Ancient Woods of the Helford River* (Little Toller Books, 2019). Mark Stoyle's paper 'The Gear Rout: The Cornish Rising of 1648 and the Second Civil War' was published in *Albion: A Quarterly Journal Concerned with British Studies*, vol. 32, no. 1, The North American Conference on British Studies, 2000. Nuclear/civil emergency communications are the subject of a wonderfully of-its-time British Telecom information film accessed at https://bt.kuluvalley.com/view/dkPuTN7sMe6#/. Pevsner's travels are the subject of Susie Harries's *Nikolaus Pevsner: The Life* (Chatto & Windus, 2011).

2 Chapel

I was able to research the rise and fall of Cornish Methodism using the broad range of books, research papers and documents held in the Courtney Library and Archive at the Royal Institution of Cornwall at Truro. Papers I read included David P. Easton's 'Ceased to Meet' (2002) and Martin Webber's 'The Appeal of Methodism in West Cornwall' (1994). Other books referenced were Thomas Shaw's *History of Cornish Methodism* (D. Bradford Barton, Truro 1967), contributions by Ian Haile and Richard Jones to *Essays by Prominent Methodists* (Truran Books, 1988) and *The Letters of John Wesley Volume Four* (Epworth Press, 1931). *Twenty Years at St Hilary* by Bernard Walke (Methuen, 1935, republished by Truran, 2002) is a brilliantly readable memoir of an Anglo-Catholic priest in West Cornwall in the early 20th century. The St Keverne Local History Society showed me Adoniram Judson's *Letter on the subject of Ornamental Dress* (Wright and Albright, 1840). W. R. Ward is author of the entry on Billy Bray in the *Oxford Dictionary of National Biography* (subsequently *DNB*). Further information for this chapter was gleaned during the making of *The Disused Chapel on the Cornish Skyline*, a Radio 4 documentary which I presented in 2015, produced by Julian May. It is still available to listen to on BBC Sounds.

3 Born of the Sea

Terry Moyle's *Tamm Gwyns a'n Howldrevel (A Scat of Easterly Wind)* and Cyril Hart's *Cornish Oasis: Biographical Chronicle of the Fishing Village of Coverack, Cornwall* are two locally published social histories of Coverack and St Keverne Parish. The description of the Coverack flood by Bill Frisken comes from a report I contributed to *From Our Home Correspondent* (BBC Radio 4, 22nd October 2017). *Born of the Sea* can be rented or purchased online at amazon.co.uk. Information about Archie Rowe's appearance on *This Is Your Life* comes from the information-rich fansite https://www.bigredbook.info.

4 The Manacles

Cornish Shipwrecks – The South Coast by Richard Larn and Clive Carter (Pan Books, 1973) is a gripping read. *The Times* provided extensive reports of the official inquiry into the *Mohegan* disaster in 1898, and much coverage of other contemporary shipwrecks. Chris Holwill's *Mohegan – The Cornish Titanic* (Tothill Publications, 2013) is a comprehensive account of the ship and its sinking; I also read Terry Moyle's *The Mohegan 1898–1998* (Talbot, 1998). I first read about the fate of Maud Roudez/Roudebush in the *New York Times* (Oct 30th, 1998); the Metropolitan Opera Archive cites her subsequent performance dates. The Canon Diggen archive, and other accounts of Manacle shipwrecks can be read at the St Keverne Local History Society website www.st-keverne.com/history/home/index.php.

5/6 Helston & The Flora Dance

A good account of Henry Trengrouse's life is provided by Richard Larn and Bridget Larn's *Henry Trengrouse – The Cornish Inventor of the Rocket Life-Saving Apparatus* (Truran Books, 1996). I also read *DNB* articles on Henry Trengrouse (A. F. Pollard), Sir William Godolphin (J. P. D Cooper), Sidney Godolphin (Anne Duffin) and Davies Gilbert (Phillip Miller). My interest in the Angel Hotel was sparked by both memories of schoolboy visits and a short history of the building that appears on the Helston History website www.helstonhistory.co.uk/

helston-historical-buidings/angel-hotel-2/. Ronald Perry and Hazel Harradence's biography of Silvanus Trevail (Francis Boutle, 2008) is both well written and well illustrated. The CAST film on Helston Secondary Modern School can be viewed at www.cornishmemory.com/item/HGS_86. The events and history of May 8th are well covered by Jill Newton's *Flora Day* (Bossiney Books, 1978) and Ian Marshall *The Amazing Story of the Floral Dance* (Songs of Cornwall, 2003).

7 Falmouth Bay

Edmund Newell writes about John Henry Vivian and John Vivian in the *DNB*; Richard Hussey Vivian's life is described by R. H. Vetch (rev. James Lunt). Derek Carter's locally published *Memories of Meneage* contains good pictures and descriptions of life at Bosahan. A. S. Oates writes about Helford as a smuggling centre in *Around Helston in the Old Days* (Dyllansow Truran, 1983). Information on SOE activities in Cornwall comes from M. R. D. Foot's *SOE in France* (Routledge, 2004) and *Monopoli Blues* by Tim Clark and Nick Cook (Unbound, 2018). *Barclay Fox's Journal 1832–1854* is a joyous read (ed. R. L. Brett & Charles Fox, Cornwall Editions Ltd, 2008).

8 From Cornwall to the World

The late historian and Cornish nationalist Dr James Whetter provided a useful *History of Falmouth* (Dyllansow Truran, 1981). Tony Pawlyn offers a detailed history of the Packet Service in *Falmouth Packets 1689–1851* (Truran, 2003); Arthur Norway's *History of the Packet Service* is available to read via Project Gutenberg https://www.gutenberg.org/ebooks/59310. Alex M. Jacob writes about *The Jews of Falmouth – 1740–1860* in *Transactions*, the journal of the Jewish Historical Society of England, accessed at www.jstor.org/stable/29777894.

9 Under the Sea

The powers of St Leven are one of the gems recounted in Canon Gilbert Hunter Doble's *Saints of Cornwall*, a six-volume survey published by the Dean & Chapter of Truro Cathedral in 1960. The Porthcurno cable station's story is told in *Changing Places,* a short account by Steve Bladon, (PK Portcurno, 2016); the museum has usefully republished historical articles including *A Nerve Station of Empire* (from the *Syren and Shipping* magazine of 1911) and W. F. A. Bell's *Porthcurno in Wartime* (1945). Gerald Ash gave a talk on *The Rocking Stones of Cornwall* on the BBC printed in *The Listener* (Oct. 16th 1947). For this chapter I read the *DNB* article on Sir John Pender (Anita McConnell).

10 Through the Air

Michael Sagar-Fenton (with Stuart B. Smith) has written a study of *Serpentine* (Truran, 2005). The competitive relationship between Porthcurno and Poldhu is explored in *The Spies at Wireless Point: The Eastern Telegraph Co. and Marconi's Early Wireless Experiments in Cornwall at Poldhu and Bass Point* by John E. Packer (PK Porthcurno, 2005). Giorgio Dragoni wrote the *DNB* entry on Guglielmo Marconi; the Italian's passion for publicity meant I was able to draw on extensive contemporary newspaper coverage of his achievements. Arthur H. Norway's *Highways and Byways in Devon and Cornwall* is a charmingly dated account of the authors travels (Macmillan, 1904). Second-hand copies are easily available and the book is digitised on Google Books. John Moyle writes about modern Goonhilly and other matters in *Cornwall's Communications* (Twelveheads Press, 2015)

A picture of Barbara Hepworth's *Three Hemispheres* can be seen at https://hepworthwakefield.org/our-art-artists/collections/the-hepworth-family-gift/three-hemispheres/. TeleGeography's regularly updated Submarine Cable Map is a rabbit hole worth falling into: https://www.submarinecablemap.com/.

11 'If There Is a Hole Dug Anywhere on Earth, You're Sure to Find a Cornishman at the Bottom of It'

George Henwood's writings are drawn together in *Cornwall's Mines and Miners* (ed. Roger Burt, Bradford Barton, 1972). The life and times of the Basset are considered in Crispin Gill's *Great Cornish Families*, and also by Nicholas Kingsley on his fine website landedfamilies.blogspot.com. Roland Thorne writes about Francis Basset in the *DNB*. The dangerous life of Cornish miners is one of the subjects covered by Roger Burt and Sandra Kippen in their paper *Rational Choice and a Lifetime in Metal Mining: Employment Decisions by Nineteenth-Century Cornish Miners* published in the *International Review of Social History* Vol 46 (Cambridge University Press, 2001). Allen Buckley explores the difference between tutmen and tributers in the paper 'Solomon the Tributer: A Camborne mining tale of the 1920s' (*Royal Institution of Cornwall Journal*, 2012). The emigration figures from late-19th-century Cornwall come from Dudley Baines's paper 'Migration in a Mature Economy: Emigration and Internal Migration in England and Wales 1861–1900' (*Cambridge Studies in Population, Economy and Society in Past Time*, Cambridge University Press, 1985). *Pigot and Co's Directory of Cornwall* can be viewed in full via University of Leicester Special Collections: https://specialcollections.le.ac.uk/digital/collection/p16445coll4/id/98611. Davies Gilbert writes about Camborne in his *Parochial History of Cornwall* (J. B. Nichols and son, 1838; available on Google Books). Bruce Pennay tells of Josiah Thomas's life in the *Australian Dictionary of Biography Volume 12* https://adb.anu.edu.au/biography/thomas-josiah-8779. The Camborne men who fought in the First World War are the subject of *These Men Were Our Grandfathers* by Susan Roberts and Alison Pooley (Bridging Arts, 2019). My great-grandfather William Blackwood's obituary, by 'E.T.', appeared in the *British Medical Journal* of August 27th 1960. Ian Mallory writes about plummeting tin prices in 'Conduct Unbecoming: The Collapse of the International Tin Agreement', *American University International Law Review* 5, no. 3 (1990) https://digitalcommons.wcl.american.edu/cgi/viewcontent.cgi?article=1593&context=auilr.

12 Educating Cornwall

Joanna Mattingley and Graeme Kirkham review the plan of Glasney College in a section of a paper 'Excavations at Glasney College Penryn' (ed. Dick Cole, *Cornish Archaeology*, Vol 55, 2016). The decline of the Cornish language is explored in *Henry and Katherine Jenner : A*

Celebration of Cornwall's Culture, Language and Identity (ed. Derek R. Williams, Francis Boutle, 2004). Dean Evans's *Funding the Ladder: The Passmore Edward's Legacy* is a great read (Francis Boutle, 2011). I also read *DNB* entries on Henry Jenner (Peter W. Thomas), Robert Morton Nance (Brian Murdoch) and John Passmore Edwards (A. J. A. Morris).

13 Hireth

Sue Ellery-Hill has tirelessly ensured that the music of her mother, Brenda Wootton, remains alive. She is the author of a biography, *Brenda – For the Love of Cornwall* (2019) and runs the website brendawootton. org. Details of the history of the Flora Cinema come from Brian Horsey's *Ninety Years of Cinema in Cornwall* (2005); I am indebted to the cinema buildings researcher Ken Roe for further information. Mark Jenkin's films *Enys Men*, *Bronco's House* and *Bait* can be viewed on the BFI Player. Malcolm Arnold is the subject of two good biographies *Rogue Genius: The Life and Music of Britain's Most Misunderstood Composer*, by Anthony Meredith and Paul Harris (Thames Publishing, 2004) and *Philharmonic Concerto: The Life and Music of Malcolm Arnold* by Piers Burton Page (Lime Tree, 1994). I also read Philip Hunt's article on the Cornish National Music Archive https://cornishnationalmusicarchive. co.uk/content/malcolm-arnold-an-article-by-phillip-hunt/. Arnold made recordings of his *Cornish Dances* with the London Philharmonic Orchestra (Lyrita) and the City of Birmingham Symphony Orchestra (Warner Classics). Richard McGrady's paper 'Joseph Emidy: An African in Cornwall' was published in the *Musical Times*, vol. 127 (1986) www. jstor.org/stable/964272?origin=crossref.

14 Cathedral City

Mike O' Connor writes about 'Ann White, Cornish Vocal Star, Impresario and Mother' in the *Royal Institution of Cornwall Journal*, 2022. The *West Briton* gave extensive coverage to 19th-century events at the Truro Assembly Rooms; the history of the venue is covered in *Curtains – New Life for Old Theatres* (John Offord Publications, 1982). Ian Kelly writes about Samuel Foote in his sparkling biography *Mr*

Foote's Other Leg: Comedy, Tragedy and Murder in Georgian London (Picador, 2012). *The Trefoil* was the title of A. C. Benson's biography of his father Edward White Benson (John Murray, 1923). I have also read *DNB* articles on E. W. Benson (Mark D. Chapman), John Loughborough Pearson (Paul Waterhouse, rev. Anthony Quiney) and Richard Lander (Elizabeth Baigent), and articles in Grove Music online on Charles W. Hempel (Michael Kassler) and Angelica Catalani (Elizabeth Forbes). Eldred Evans's obituary was published in *The Times* (31st March 2023. Christopher Gray, former Director of Music at Truro Cathedral kindly shared his research on music there and the Truro history of Nine Lessons and Carols. H. Miles Brown has written a helpful introduction in *The Story of Truro Cathedral* (Tor Mark, 1991).

15 Three Poets, Four Churches.

Sabine Baring-Goulds Hawker's biography *The Bishop of Morwenstow* was published in 1876; it is available online at http://anglicanhistory. org/england/rshawker/vicar/index.html. Andrew Landale Drummond writes further about the priest in his essay 'Parson Hawker of Morwenstow' in the *Journal of the Historical Society of the Episcopal Church*, vol. 33, no. 2 (1964) www.jstor.org/stable/429730. Further insights can be found in C. E. Byles *The Life and Letters of R. S. Hawker* (John Lane/The Bodley Head, 1905). *The Listener* is a good source of Charles Causley's memoir-based journalism, including the articles 'So Slowly to Harbour' (17th March 1977) and 'In the Angle of the Waters' (22nd September 1977). The American critic Dana Gioia's piece on Causley, 'The Most Unfashionable Poet Alive' is published on his website https://danagioia.com/essays/reviews-and-authors-notes/the-most-unfashionable-poet-alive-charles-causley/. I also read *DNB* articles on Hawker (Piers Brendon) and Causley (John Mole). Bevis Hillier's Betjeman biographical trilogy contains much on the poet's Cornish days: *Young Betjeman*: *New Fame, New Love*; and *The Bonus of Laughter* (John Murray, 1988/2002/2004). I also quote from *The Betjeman Letters, Volume 1* edited by Candida Lycett Green (Methuen, 2006). I gleaned further information from Philip Payton's *John Betjeman and Cornwall – The Celebrated Cornish Nationalist* (University of Exeter Press, 2010).

16 Maria Asumpta

This chapter is largely drawn from conversations between Philip Chatfield and the author in 2022/2023. The detail of Betjemann Snr's double 'n' comes from Bevis Hillier's *Young Betjeman*, and news of the plundering of the *Maria Asumpta* wreck site was reported in *The Times* (June 1995).

17 The Slow Train – Three Cornish Branch Lines

Betjeman reflected on his favourite Cornish station in a BBC Radio talk printed in *The Listener* (March 29th 1940). Detailed accounts of Cornish branch lines are provided by Vic Mitchell and Keith Smith in *Branchlines to Falmouth, Helston and St Ives* (Middleton Press, 2001), Richard C. Long's *The St Ives Branch Line* (Pen & Sword Transport, 2022) and T. W. E. Roche's *The Withered Arm – Reminiscences of the Southern Lines West of Exeter* (Branch Line Handbooks and West Country Handbooks, 1967). Terry Gourvish wrote Sir David Serpell's *DNB* entry; I also refer to his *Daily Telegraph* obituary www.telegraph.co.uk/news/obituaries/2512056/Sir-David-Serpell.html. The fragmentary Helston Railway (helstonrailway.co.uk) and rather more complete Bodmin Railway (bodminrailway.co.uk) both make for amusing and satisfying day trips.

18 Plymouth Approaches – The Most Beautiful City in the World

Two books are essential for anyone wanting to learn more about Plymouth, its devastation in the Blitz and its post-war recovery. Crispin Gill's two-volume *Plymouth – A New History* (Vol. One *Ice Age to the Elizabethans*; Vol. Two *1603 to the Present Day*) was published by David & Charles (1966/1979). Jeremy Gould's *Plymouth – Vision of a Modern City* is filled with photos and contains diagrams and drawings of Abercrombie and Paton Watson's *Plan for Plymouth* (English Heritage, 2010). David Owen made clear his ambitions for Tamarside in a debate on the Local Government Bill on 16th November 1971 https://api.parliament.uk/historic-hansard/commons/1971/nov/16/local-government-bill.

369

I also refer to *DNB* entries on Sir Richard Edgcumbe c.1443–1489 (J. L. Kirby) and Sir Richard Edgcumbe 1499–1562 (Patricia Hyde). Jill Craigie's film *The Way We Live* is available on the BFI Player.

19 Mapping the Tamar

John Binding's *Brunel's Royal Albert Bridge* (Twelveheads Press, 1997) is an excellent introduction to the bridge and its engineer. I also read Hugh Howes *The Struggle for the Cornish Railway – Fated Decisions* (Twelveheads Press, 2012) and L. T. C. Rolt's *I. K. Brunel* (Penguin, 1990). Sam Hewitt's article, Branch Line Focus – Rails to Gunnislake, (*Railway Magazine*, May 2017) provided useful background. Tamar crossings are considered by Eric Kentley in his *Cornwall's Bridges and Viaducts* (Twelveheads Press, 2005). Past owners of the Werrington Estate are listed by Joan Rendell in *Werrington – A Parish Album* (Columbian Press, 1990).

ACKNOWLEDGEMENTS

My BBC colleagues Alan Davey, Richard Denison, Brian Jackson, Sam Jackson and Susan Kenyon allowed me to leave London and broadcast from Cornwall for extended periods of time while writing this book. Radio 3 is blessed with a team of fine production staff and studio managers who uncomplainingly embraced long-distance radio, and Jamie Blake, James Churchfield, Julie Scantlebury and Daphne Skinnard were among those who made me feel welcome at BBC Radio Cornwall in Truro.

In Cornwall and elsewhere many were generous in sharing information and time – special thanks go to Kensa Broadhurst (dedicated advocate of the Cornish language), Tim Bullamore, Professor Anne Carlisle, Jan Driver, Sue Ellery-Hill, Richard and Christine Graham-Vivian, Professor Emma Hunt, Ian Jones, The Rt Reverend Philip Mountstephen, Karen Richards (proud keeper of St Keverne's history), Father Jeff Risbridger and Gary Anderson, Susan Roberts, Nick Stokes, James and Sarah Williams, Michael and Sarah Williams, Rebecca Wills and Sir Ferrers Vyvyan Bt. Annabel Philips and David Thomas (Kresen Kernow) provided useful information for the radio documentary on Cornish Methodism which sowed the seeds for Chapter 2. Annette MacTavish, Joe Panes and Karen North at the Museum of Cornish Life in Helston, Alan Renton (PK Porthcurno), Katie Herbert (Penlee Gallery) and Katharine Carter (M&S Archive) all helped source photographs. Vesta Darnell, Terence

Trelawny-Gower and Carole Vivian kindly shared their research on the Trelawny family. Angela Broome, archivist at the Royal Institution of Cornwall, was ever helpful; her death in November 2023 was a major loss to Cornish studies.

Throughout the writing process I felt cherished by the many friends who took an interest in this project, and on occasion provided leads and ideas: Michael Arditti, Guy Black and Mark Bolland, Emma Bloxham, Julien Boast and Dr Andrew Shaw, Henrietta Bredin, Paul Bullock, Nicholas Chalmers, Philip Chatfield, Richard Coles, Liz Curnow, Dr Paul Edmondson. Ben and Rachel Elwes, Graham Fitkin and Ruth Wall, Paul Frankl, Patrick Gale and Aiden Hicks, John Gilhooly, Teresa Gleadowe, Julian Glover and Matthew Parris, Linda Grant, Christopher Gray, Selina Hastings, Thomas and Annabel Howells, Rebecca Johnson, Madeleine Kasket, Clare Latimer, Donald MacGregor and Robin Hellier, Julian May, Colin Midson and Fanny Johnstone, Kevin Moore, Paddy O'Connell, Paul Parsons, Russell Pascoe, Greg Powlesland and Katie Fontana, Rupert Powlesland, Sean Rafferty, Ann Roberts, Tim Sayer and Anne Marie Norton, Nicholas Serota, Zeb Soanes, Alan and Rebecca Treloar and Stanley Wells.

Alan Samson proposed and commissioned this book, and my agent Alex Armitage gave me the confidence to take the project forward. Weidenfeld & Nicolson is blessed to have a passionate and highly talented team. It was a pleasure to work with Elizabeth Allen, Natalie Dawkins, Simon Fox, Hennah Sandhu, Maddy Price and particularly Lucinda McNeile and my editor Ed Lake, whose marginalia, notes and encouraging epigrams helped me shape this book into what it has become.

This book was largely researched and written over a series of dark Cornish winters, when my dear sister-in-law Alison Trelawny provided accommodation, a cosy room in which to write and the company and unconditional love of her dogs Rocky and Belle. I would like to thank my brothers Andrew, Jonathan and Christopher, and my aunt Professor Gillian Cooper Driver. In periods of downtime Melinda Patton, Tatiana Kennedy and my niece Clementine Trelawny provided companionship and laughter, while Ian Rosenblatt and Emma Kane, Denis Staunton and Michael O'Sullivan provided wise counsel and long-distance support. Michael was one respected friend who read early drafts and generously offered thoughts and advice – along with Heather and the late Ivan Corbett, Charles Fox, Gavin Plumley and Alastair Tighe, Tony Scotland and Julian Berkeley and George Trelawny. I am very grateful for their support.

Kernow Bys Vyken!

ILLUSTRATION CREDITS

The pictures of a Methodist tea treat (Page 43), the 'Sly Reynard' satirical poster (Page 100), historic Flora Day Dancers (Page 113), the former Bosahan House (Page 121) and arches celebrating the arrival of the Helston Railway (Page 303) are reproduced by kind permission of the Museum of Cornish Life, Helston.

Eamonn Andrews and Archie Rowe on *This Is Your Life* (Page 78) – BBC Photo Archive

The photo of Marks and Spencer's staff in Falmouth (Page 150) is taken from the 'Sparks' staff magazine (Sept-Nov 1949) and reproduced by kind permission of the M & S Archive, Leeds.

The engraving of a ship laying a cable at Porthcurno (Page 161) is reproduced by kind permission of PK Porthcurno – Museum of Global Communications, Cornwall.

The cartoon of John Passmore Edwards (Page 224) by Carlo Pellegrini/ Look and Learn / Peter Jackson Collection / Bridgeman Images

Brenda Wootton (Page 230) by Jacques Loew/Photo12/Alamy Stock Photo

Malcolm Arnold (Page 243) PA Images/Alamy Stock Photo

Maria Assumpta (Page 296) Max Mudie/Alamy Stock Photo

The GWR poster 'See Your Own Country First' (Page 306) – Lordprice Collection/Alamy Stock Photo

The picture of staff gardening at Nancegollan Station (Page 309) is reproduced courtesy of The Penlee House Gallery and Museum, Penzance.

JMW Turner's 1811 painting 'Saltash with the Water Ferry, Cornwall' (Page 329) is reproduced through the Open Access scheme offered by the Metropolitan Museum of Art, New York.

All other images are © Petroc Trelawny, 2024.